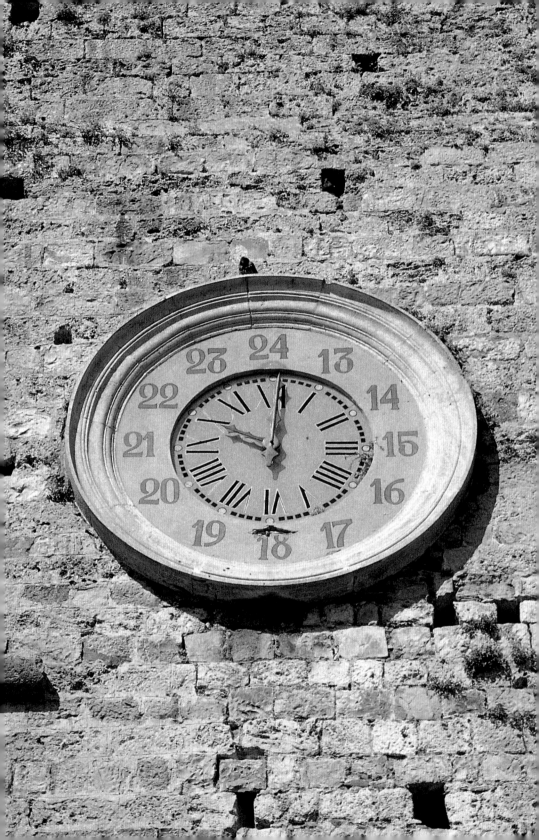

Created and Directed by Hans Höfer

INSIGHT
GUIDES

Tuscany

Edited by Rosemary Bailey
Principal photography by Albano Guatti
and Patrizia Giancotti
Editioral Director: Brian Bell

APA PUBLICATIONS

Tuscany

First Edition (5th Reprint)
© 1993 APA PUBLICATIONS (HK) LTD
All Rights Reserved
Printed in Singapore by Höfer Press Pte Ltd

Distributed in the United States by:	Distributed in Canada by:	Distributed in the UK & Ireland by:	Worldwide distribution enquiries:
Houghton Mifflin Company	**Thomas Allen & Son**	**GeoCenter International UK Ltd**	**Höfer Communications Pte Ltd**
222 Berkeley Street	390 Steelcase Road East	The Viables Center, Harrow Way	38 Joo Koon Road
Boston, Massachusetts 02116-3764	Markham, Ontario L3R 1G2	Basingstoke, Hampshire RG22 4BJ	Singapore 2262
ISBN: 0-395-66275-3	ISBN: 0-395-66275-3	ISBN: 9-62421-093-4	ISBN: 9-62421-093-4

ABOUT THIS BOOK

T he Stendhal syndrome is an affliction that crops up frequently in this book – it has affected visitors to Florence and Tuscany for centuries, and its peculiar symptoms of fainting and ecstasy at the sight of overwhelming beauty are hazards for anyone writing or editing a book on Tuscany.

Many of the following contributors were already victims and they bravely risked further attacks in the course of their research. Project editor **Rosemary Bailey** first succumbed to the beauties of Tuscany while visiting friends in their villa near Lucca. She was badly bitten by mosquitoes and had to forgo a planned trip to San Gimignano and its famous towers. "I was obliged to spend the entire day sitting on the terrace reading Mary McCarthy's *The Stones of Florence*, contemplating a sublime view of vines and cypresses, surrounded by the scent of wisteria. That made me realise what a perfectly arranged place Tuscany was."

Bailey is a freelance writer and editor, specialising in travel writing and literary profiles, and is a regular contributor to the London *Sunday Times* and *Elle* magazine, and has edited a guide to New York.

For this Insight Guide she explored the provinces of Pistoia and Massa-Carrara, describes the whimsical delights of Tuscan villas and gardens, and recommends a visit to one of the region's many health spas.

Lisa Gerard-Sharp wrote a substantial proportion of this book, and proved extremely knowledgeable about all things Tuscan, from Etruscan grave robbing to the finer points of expatriate living in Chiantishire. She investigates the essence of the Tuscan miracle, describes the importance of festivals in Tus-

can life, and analyses modern Tuscany. She has also provided an informed and witty guide to the provinces of Siena and Livorno. Her love of Italy developed from "an infatuation with Masaccio's paintings and a doomed affair with a haunted Sienese farmhouse." Although currently London-based as a writer and broadcaster editing travel books and launching a European magazine, she feels it is inevitable she will return to live in Italy where she previously taught English and edited programmes for RAI Television.

Tuscany was, of course, the birthplace of the Renaissance in art and architecture. Renaissance scholar **Russell Chamberlin** tackled the vital chapters on art and history, combining them with a detailed guide to Florence. "I first got hooked on the Italian Renaissance in Florence cathedral in the 1960s when I wondered why on earth the Florentines had dedicated an enormous mural portrait to a semi-bandit, the *condottiero* John Hawkwood. Tracking down the career of this mercenary soldier gave me the material for my first book – and I've never looked back, for we're still trying to unravel how and why the Renaissance came about." Chamberlin has written 27 books on European history and travel, and in 1988 was awarded a M.Univ (Master of the University) honorary degree by the University of Surrey in recognition of his work.

Architecture and travel writer **Paul Duncan** explored the provinces of Florence, Arezzo and Lucca for this book. He is especially good at spotting the perfect hidden fresco in a remote little church, which is what going to Tuscany is all about. He "specialises in discovering forgotten, unknown and ignored buildings and then writing about them." He has an MA in art and architectural history

Bailey   *Gerard-Sharp*   *Chamberlin*

from Edinburgh University, and writes for *The Architects' Journal*, *Country Life*, English *Vogue* and is a correspondent for *Casa Vogue* in Italy and Spain.

Wine is an essential aspect of Tuscany – and Chianti is still the most famous wine from the region. Wine writer **Maureen Ashley** explains why Chianti is no longer the only important Tuscan wine and she provides an invaluable guide to drinking and a succinct history of the wine industry. Italians happily serve wine to children and so she became an enthusiast at a tender age during childhood holidays in Italy. In 1984 she became one of the few women to qualify as a Master of Wine, and now specialises in writing about Italian wine.

Valentina Harris describes the simple pleasures of Tuscan food, and the history of olive oil. She has plenty of experience, having been brought up and educated in Rome and on her family's Tuscan homestead. She is an authority on Italian food, author of *Perfect Pasta* and *Regional Italian Cookery*. She still thinks of Tuscany as her real home, although she currently lives with her husband and two sons in a tiny Norfolk village.

Author **Barry Miles'** most recent book is a biography of American poet Allen Ginsberg. As well as a lifelong interest in art and literature, he has a passion for architecture and here he explores the Roman ruins of Tuscany and explains the importance of the Pisan Romanesque style of architecture and its spread through Tuscany and beyond.

Marco De Stefani and **Lorella Grossi** live and work in Bologna where Grossi is an industrial heritage historian with the Bologna museum and De Stefani works as an economist. They spend as much time as they can in their medieval property in a tiny village in Grosseto; their enthusiasm and intimate knowledge of Grosseto and the Maremma provide an excellent guide to a still little known region of Tuscany.

Susan Zucker, who also contributed to the article on Grosseto, worked in London as a fashion consultant and writer before moving to Rome. She and her family now live in the Grosseto region and Zucker supplies information on a wide range of tourist facilities and pursuits.

Yvonne Newman bravely took on the considerable task of compiling the vital Travel Tips section, gathering information on an exhaustive range of topics from all over Tuscany, and still found time to provide a detailed guide to the Pisa province. She worked in Italy with the British foreign office, followed by lecturing and freelance writing. She has contributed to a number of guidebooks, and specialises in providing detailed local information.

Finally, proper tribute should be paid to **Brian Bell**, Apa's London-based editorial director, whose support throughout has been invaluable. Whenever things got tough, he was always ready with a glass of wine (not necessarily Italian) and reassuring stories about even worse disasters.

There is more than enough information in this *Insight Guide to Tuscany* to send any visitor reeling with a heavy dose of Stendhal's syndrome, and you must excuse our writers if they occasionally get carried away by it all. None of them have gone quite as far as Sean O'Faolain, who describes the Italians as "a race that of all the races of the world best knows what it is to devour life not only to the last crumb and drop, but to the eating of the cups and plates as well."

Buon appetito!

Duncan   *Ashley*   *Harris*   *Newman*

CONTENTS

TRAVEL TIPS

THE TUSCAN MIRACLE

From the top of a village tower the Tuscan landscape lies below: the most civilised rural scene on earth. Yet driving through southern Tuscany at night there is little sense of civilisation, still less of domesticity—even farm animals are kept indoors.

In the distance, a succession of small lights trail across the black countryside: tenuous links with separate, inward-looking communities. The spaces in between are remote, uncivilised. The blackness and emptiness of the countryside go back to medieval times and beyond; the "Tuscan miracle" only illuminates the cities.

D.H. Lawrence described Tuscany as where "men had been at their intensest, most naked pitch, here at the end of the old world and the beginning of the new." To Florentines, Michelangelo's David is the symbol of the ancient republic and the epitome of their own character. David is not just a study in naked intensity, but an awkward new spirit, struggling to be born out of marble. Emilio Pucci, the aristocratic fashion designer, often visits David for inspiration: Michelangelo's grace of line inspires Pucci's designs in silk.

In giving birth to the Renaissance, Tuscany designed the modern world. In his painting, Giotto projected Tuscany into space. Brunelleschi crowned space with his Florentine dome, the greatest feat of Renaissance engineering.

In the Carmine frescoes, Masaccio peopled space with recognisably human figures. His newly-restored *Expulsion from Paradise* now reveals Adam and Eve in all their naked beauty. Gone is the medieval coyness about nudity; present is the palpable suffering of a couple who have lost everything. Even Michelangelo's version in Rome's Sistine Chapel does not plumb such tragic depths.

Florence's hospitals regularly have to revive tourists who have fainted with symptoms produced by over-exposure to

unaccustomed beauty. However the Tuscan miracle is not a frozen Renaissance portrait but a living procession of Tuscans at ease with their artistic setting and identity. Tuscans do have an innate aesthetic sense but the Tuscan tapestry is a rich weave compounded of many different threads. Literary Tuscany is a strand traced through Boccaccio and Petrarch. Dante's verses adorn many Florentine walls and Tuscan squares. Republican Tuscany is best glimpsed through its fortified town halls

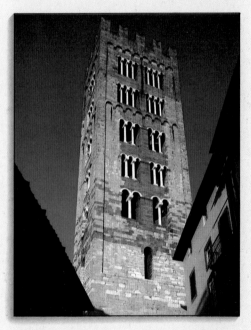

while humanist Tuscany is enshrined in poetry, sculpture and art, the fruits of patronage and craftsmanship.

Aristocratic Tuscany lingers in Medici palaces, villas and sculptured gardens, not to mention the ancestral homes of the Rucellai, Corsini and Frescobaldi. Bourgeois Tuscany parades along Florence's Via Tornabuoni, patronises the arts and restores family farms.

Peasant Tuscany traditionally takes a little of everything from the land: game, beans, chestnut flour, unsalted bread, olive oil, and, of course, the grapes needed to make Chianti and Brunello. Tuscan cuisine combines proportion and variety. Like the Tuscans

Preceding pages: bullfighters in the Campo, Siena; spiralling hysteria at the *Palio*; the Chianti harvest; quintessential Tuscany. Left, Contrada loyalty. Above, *Campanilismo*: bell-tower of San Frediano, Lucca.

themselves, it is of good peasant stock. Variety on a small scale is also the secret of Tuscany's townscapes: from medieval hilltop towns to Etruscan villages; from *fin de siècle* spa towns to sophisticated mountain resorts; from the splendour of a Renaissance cathedral to a stark Romanesque church.

Architecturally, the cities are microcosms of all periods. Etruscan Maremma fades to Romanesque Pisa; Gothic Siena to medieval San Gimignano; and Renaissance Florence to Grand Ducal Chianti.

The natural landscape is powerful, stretching from Carrara marble quarries to Maremma wilderness; from Livorno's rugged coastline to the mountainous

various greens of the growing crops appear an embroidered veil on a wilderness of bare geology".

With few exceptions, it is foreign poets who dwell on the cultivated tranquillity of corn, olives and vine. Tuscans are historically wary of space, preferring a safe, tribal existence in small towns to an alien, romantic notion of the countryside. Tuscan poets record the battles, the austerity, the protections of city life. *La campagna* was fit only for abbeys, monasteries, battles and exile.

Lorenzetti's *Citta sul mare*, the first known European landscape painting, depicts an elaborate walled city against an

Casentino. Much of the land appears tamed: the Chianti hills, the lush Mugello valley and "the Arno swirling past with its usual coffee-coloured foam." (Virginia Woolf).

Wooded Monte Amiata and the Sienese moon craters reveal another truth. Etruscans cultivated the land, Tuscans have tried to civilise it and foreigners romanticise it. A deep relationship with the land has always been present but it does not imply an ease with the land, still less a mastery. As Mary McCarthy wrote, "The peculiar beauty of the Tuscan landscape is the combination of husbandry with an awesome and elemental majesty and silence; the olives' silver and the

austere backdrop. *Good Government*, the Sienese masterpiece, is idealistic in its portrayal of a cheerful, busy countryside. The pillaging and looting in *Bad Government* look infinitely more convincing. So the "Tuscan miracle" is, surprisingly, urban.

Unlike English towns, most Tuscan towns have been paved since the early 13th century. There are pavements through which no grass has ever grown. Given an urban heritage going back over two and a half millennia, Tuscany, even by Italian standards, is highly civilised. Tuscans prefer living in large villages or small towns today, echoing the Etruscan ideal, which was confirmed by the rural perils of medieval Europe.

Etruscan cities were conceived of as entities, settlements carved out of the countryside, never mere urban sprawl. When the civilisation disappeared, its imprint remained for D.H. Lawrence to record. "Because a fool kills a nightingale with a stone, is he therefore greater than the nightingale? Not he! Rome fell, and the Roman phenomenon with it. Italy today is far more Etruscan in its bones than Roman, and always will be."

This triumphant elegy is borne out by modern and medieval "Etruscans". Tuscans mongering tribe. The ideal of *civiltà* in the form of urban identity extended from the largest City State to the smallest town. Each town was a small state with its own land, local government and traditions.

In claiming an urban identity, small places, technically villages, still feel like towns today and consider themselves as such. *Città* is a perception of status, not size. The concept of "town" has always cut across economic and social divisions within the town. Battles for independence have reinforced but not forged this cultural identity: it was always there.

The secret of Tuscan identity lies in each town's sense of completeness. Tuscan towns

feel no guilt in acquiring Etruscan treasures from local tombs. A family's ill-gotten Etruscan urns are treasured ancestral relics, valued above Roman coins. Etruscan settlements, not Roman grids, provided the framework for the Tuscan townscape and identity.

In medieval Lucca and Florence, fractious nobles were often obliged to spend part of the year in town in order to instill a sense of belonging to something bigger than a war-

Left, Cortona: Tuscans prefer a safe, tribal existence in small towns. Above, cultivated tranquillity of corn, olives and wine.

go against the current of modern homogeneity and internationalism; Florence is becoming more Florentine and Siena more Sienese; inside image is more important than reality. Despite trade, tourism and mass communications, Tuscan towns feel spiritually self-sufficient. The town opens inwards to its inhabitants; everybody shares in its traditions and is regenerated. In large cities this identity is maintained against great odds. Great passion is attached to local traditions: to a Sienese bank manager, his role as usher for his *contrada* in the *Palio* is more important than his career.

For a Tuscan, city life feels narrow, but it

is also invitingly deep. For an outsider, the exhilaration lies in the city's confident sense of self. Elisabeth Jennings wrote that in such a setting as Florence,

It is simple to be a stranger,
To have a mind that is wide
To permit the city to settle between our thoughts,
As between those hills, and flower and glow inside.

Tuscans are iconoclasts who have believed in and broken many gods: Greek and Roman idols, Etruscan human sacrifices, Epicureanism. In Savonarola, the "mad monk" who railed against human vanity and excess, Florence gnawed away at natural expression of identity. The power and disturbing truthfulness of the art is the mystery of the miracle.

The "Tuscan miracle" is more than the sum of its artistic parts. Even the notion of the "Tuscan artist" is a geographical expression, an outsider's label for Florentine, Pisan, Pistoian or Sienese artists. It is meaningless to compare Giotto's early Renaissance belltower in Florence with the Romanesque leaning tower of Pisa. While Pisan architecture practices sober restraint, Florentine is elegant experimentation.

As for art, Duccio's grave Madonnas embody medieval Sienese chivalry while the Macchiaioli Impressionists paint a coherent

Catholicism. *Campanilismo* (provincialism: literally, loyalty to one's own bell-tower), is a longer, deeper faith and guarantees a future to local saints.

The miracle is rooted in the Tuscans' sense of place, family and craftsmanship. Olive Hamilton, speaking of a Lucchese, said: "It does not surprise a Tuscan that a chemist in our small town has written a two-volume work on the region from early Etruscan times." In this sense, even more than in the strictly artistic sense, Tuscans are highly cultured.

Dante excluded, Tuscany is steeped in visual rather than literary traditions; art is the picture of 19th-century Livorno. Even within Renaissance art, diversity is the norm. Piero della Francesca's mystical frescoes in Arezzo echo Masaccio's naturalistic Florentine frescoes: yet the alternative approaches of mysticism and realism represent the yin and yang of Renaissance art.

In Tuscany, the gap between an artist and an artisan is smaller than elsewhere. To a picture restorer in Arezzo or to a weaver in Prato, the distinction is irrelevant. Adamo, chief wine taster with Contessa Contucci's firm, considers that after 30 years of drinking Vino Nobile he is both a master craftsman and an unsurpassed artist. Tuscan virtues do not include modesty.

Questi primitivi is a term often applied to foreigners, southerners and Sardinians, in increasing order of scorn. During the war, Bernard Berenson was rebuked by a Florentine manicurist whose support he wanted: *"O Signore, per noi tutti gli stranieri sono ugualmente odiosi"* ("Oh, Sir, for us all foreigners are equally hateful").

Prejudice aside, Tuscans are polite, expect politeness in return and often criticise another Tuscan for being *maleducato*. If in doubt, such blandishments as *"è un posto meraviglioso"* ("it's a wonderful place") can be used indiscriminately, even in Livorno's

mosquito-infested swamps, industrial Poggibonsi or in the aptly-named Scrufiano.

A direct appeal to local pride can lead to unexpected gifts: the chance to meet Signor Parenti's "unique" donkey, "the only one within Florence's city walls" or to visit an abbey normally closed to the public. Even to watch a wealthy hotelier's joy in her grave-robbed Etruscan jewellery—"Why not? I'm Etruscan."

Left, picking olives, as pictured by a 15th-century artist. Above, shepherd near Chiusi: peasant Tuscany takes a little of everything from the land.

"Fare bella figura" literally "looking good" or "making a good impression", stresses the importance of "face", a Tuscan's image in the community. Appearances are a touchstone of civilised behaviour. Indigenous Etruscan looks can be found in the streets of Chiusi or Volterra, "the full dark eyes, the pointed beard, long inquisitive nose and the Mona Lisa smile of a terracotta tomb figure" (H.V. Morton). Tuscan looks are the product of perfect genetic engineering: classic Medici; luminous Sienese; austere Masaccio; cheeky Sodoma. Tuscany's foreign invaders have also left Moorish, Spanish, German and Sardinian imprints.

If Tuscans have a collective urban identity, the "pure" Tuscan dialect has helped in giving disparate towns a regional identity and national status. Modern Italian is the Tuscan dialect. Florence and Siena rival each other in claims for linguistic "purity", thus proving that City State superiority is thriving, although the "purity" dissolves among country dialects.

Tuscans reveal themselves in their language. The Florentine proverb, *"Uomo senza roba è una pecora senza lana"* ("A man without clothes is like a sheep without wool/wealth") indicates the importance of appearance and medieval Tuscany's original source of wealth. Tuscan includes colourful oaths such as *"porca miseria"* ("holy pork") and *"per cortesia"*, an expression of great civility. An old saying confirms Tuscan wariness: "Keep away from sick doctors…dogs that don't bark, men that don't speak, people who go to mass twice a day…and quarrels with those who are bigger than you are."

Certain images of the Tuscan miracle remain. *Città sul mare*, the city as bastion against the darkness; and the *civiltà* that led a Tuscan Pope to construct a palace around a view, the first time the concept of a view entered European architecture. Two images of people interlock: the modern Tuscan holding her jewellery like a religious relic; and the ancient Etruscans, echoing through the centuries like the names of their own lost gods. While watching oxen slowly pulling a plough through olives and vines, Bernard Berenson recorded "a feeling that I was looking at what has been going on ever since civilisation began."

THE ETRUSCANS

Modern Tuscans are proud of their Etruscan heritage and they feel no shame about stealing their own heirlooms; sadly, the ransacking of newly discovered tombs is rife. One farmer recently pretended to be growing tomatoes under cover while furtively uncovering a magistrate's tomb! Most middle class Tuscans have at least one item and a few conceal collections worthy of a museum. Many a wealthy dinner party ends with a showing of Etruscan treasures. A gold brooch is readily available for the price of a small Fiat. Pots are caressed with love and jewellery is examined under a magnifying glass, its minute images of deities and animals admired and luxuriously enjoyed; an orgy of sensual indulgence the Etruscans would have loved.

As the freshest face in the ancient world, the Etruscans are often seen as a mythical people out of time. The Etruscans were "rediscovered" in the Romantic era and since then a "scholarly" Etruria and a "poetic" Etruria have been at variance. While Etruscologists have pieced together a picture of a complex urban civilisation with robust art forms, Tuscans see a myth shrouded in ritual sacrifice, an indecipherable language and delicate eroticism. Mystery aside, the colour and life of Etruscan art contrast with the cold marble perfectionism of the Greeks and Romans. This alone encourages Tuscans to speculate on racial continuity and to recognise themselves in the Etruscan rather than in the Roman civilisation.

Etruscan origins are hotly disputed. The Romantics and latter-day writers believed that the Etruscans sailed from Asia Minor. However, Dionysius, writing as the Etruscan civilisation neared its end, held that the Etruscans were natives with an indigenous culture too deeply engrained to be Oriental. Most modern scholars believe that the Etruscans migrated from Eastern Europe over the Alps and represent the flowering of the early Italic tribes. What is clear is that between 8 and 4 B.C. "Etruria Propria" flourished as a

confederation of 12 city-states in central Italy. Northern Etruria, roughly equivalent to modern Tuscany, included Arezzo, Chuisi, Cortona, Populonia, Vetulonia and Volterra.

Etruscan seafarers and merchants first settled on the coast and began smelting iron ore from Elba and importing Oriental ceramics, glass and silverware. Greek naval supremacy meant an opening to Hellenistic culture: ships sailed to Corinth with honey, gold and bronze figurines and returned to

Vetulonia and Populonia with perfume and painted wine jars. The inland cities such as Chuisi and Volterra thrived on hunting, farming and internal trade.

Over the next two centuries, the Etruscans allied themselves to the developing Roman power and by the first century B.C. all the Etruscan territory was annexed. Although Etruscan and Latin coexisted, Etruscan culture was crushed and the region transformed into quiet Roman provinces. The Etruscan cultural role degenerated into the provision of soothsayers, musicians, dancers and fighters for Rome.

The original confederation had a complex

Preceding pages: the elemental majesty of the Tuscan landscape. Left, Etruscan tomb painting. Above, Etruscan tombs at Populonia.

urban and social structure: each city was originally run by a king, later by local aristocrats and finally by a priestly oligarchy. The lords owned large landholdings or navies and were served by serfs and slaves. Whereas the serfs were rewarded with agricultural plots, the slaves danced and sang for their supper. With urbanisation, an independent class of artisans and merchants emerged, often of Greek or Phoenician extraction. The granting of the same Roman citizenship to the middle classes as to the aristocratic priests and magistrates was a blow to the Etruscan princely tradition.

Since there is no extant Etruscan literature, our knowledge of the living Etruscans

aristocratic Etruscans had considerable freedom, social status and economic influence. They are depicted attending banquets without their husbands, riding covered wagons to their landholdings and playing flutes or lyres at funerals. According to Theopompus, a Greek contemporary, "The women often strip off in the presence of men" and "do easily give in to anybody". Their offspring were all fed, "ignoring their paternity."

In art, the men are rarely still: they charge through games, boar-hunts, processions, journeys, dances, banquets and diving competitions. Even semi-recumbent on the sarcophagi, they look ready to fight the underworld single-handed. The "ordinary" Etrus-

is oddly dependent on a reading of their funerary art for clues. We know them as they would like to be known, these idealised aristocrats elevated by Greek myths. In looks, they are certainly the Lawrentian "long-nosed, sensitive-footed, subtly-smiling Etruscans."

The women were depicted as pale while the men were uniformly reddish brown, either tanned by the sun or ritually painted. Friezes of serene married couples, tender lovers, absorbed wrestlers, erotic dancers, or grieving warriors reflect the fullness of Etruscan life.

In contrast to Greek and Roman women,

can is only glimpsed in passing: a prized blonde courtesan flits past dancing slaves; a serf clutching a plough mourns his dead master, perhaps a prelude to his own sacrificial death.

The Etruscans were called founders of cities by the Romans, expert at building cities of the living as well as cities of the dead. The *Libri rituales* prescribed the rites involved in selecting a sacred city site. The cities followed the contours of the land and sited the necropolis below the city walls and the living city above. If cities of the dead predominate today it is by accident and not by morbid design. Carrara marble was unknown so public buildings, built of wood and clay, did not survive. As D.H. Lawrence said, the fragile wooden temples were,"as effervescent as flowers". The tumbledown remains of a rare stone temple in Fiesole only hint at the vitality of the original building, once enlivened by friezes of dancers and mythical animals.

From what remains of the cities, there was enough to impress Roman and Renaissance architects. Volterra's Porta all'Arco is a deep gateway inspired by Mesopotamian architecture: its three faceless stone heads, perhaps deities, add gravity and protection to the city. The huge dry stone walls at Saturnia, rebuilt to defend the city against Roman

their owners. Death reflected life: the poor were often buried in shallow graves or their ashes put in small urns; the rich were buried in chamber tombs and stone sarcophagi decorated with pottery. Tombs, in every shape and form, can be seen in the Etruscan necropoli: "temple" tombs at Saturnia; melon-shaped tombs at Cortona; Oriental "trench" tombs at Vetulonia. At Sovana, "pigeon hole" tombs are niches cut into the rock, while at Chiusi, a mysterious labyrinth reputedly conceals the sarcophagus of Lars Porsena, mythical King of the Etruscans. Chiusi also contains early "well" tombs, those in which the ashes were placed in a shallow dish, perhaps covered by the dead

incursions, are still standing. Pitigliano, a rough honeycomb hewn into the rocky tufa, is an Etruscan inland town with medieval finishing touches. Sovana also keeps the original town plan, complete with ancient sunken streets, *vie cave*, and a drainage system dug into the volcanic rock. Roselle neatly compartmentalises its sacred, industrial and residential areas.

But it is the tombs that remain as a cultural testimony to the power, wealth and beliefs of

Left, the Mistress of the Tomb: myth shrouded in ritual sacrifice. Above, the delicate eroticism of Tuscan dancers.

man's helmet, and placed in a small round grave. The tombs and mode of burial varied according to the local custom and period.

At the height of the Etruscan civilisation, large "chamber" tombs emerged, often containing frescoes. Although most of the tomb painting lies just outside modern Tuscany, some can still be seen in their natural setting at Chiusi. Painted by skilled craftsmen, the frescoes portray domestic scenes and outdoor pursuits as well as the sacred journey. In the shuttered tombs, a sense of the outside world is recreated through hunting scenes dotted with exotic birds and flowers.

The Etruscans were as vital in death as

they were in life but underneath the liveliness lay a deep fatalism, underscored by the hopelessness of predicting the unknown will of the gods. Locked into an unequal relationship, the Etruscans were bound to a treadmill of fear and appeasement. In keeping with primitive religions, natural forces were personified as gods of the sea, earth and rising sun. The Etruscans also reinvented Greek gods in their own image: Zeus, Hera and Athena were Tinia, Uni and Minerva. Oriental and Greek motifs coexisted: Egyptian sphynxes watched Etruscan winged demons pursue menacing Greek Furies. Despite Classical influence, religion was far removed from Greek rationalism.

passed into the realm of the afterworld rather than surviving in the tomb itself. Until then, Greek myths had bolstered Etruscan legends and beliefs. This revelation, derived from the Greeks' experience, transformed the afterlife into a shadowy, demonic world without hope or human joy. As scepticism flooded in, the age of religious innocence gave way to the age of experience and Etruscan religion began to die.

In Etruscan funerary art, men and women are depicted differently. The man is often shown wearing his chains of office over his bare chest. He may hold an egg, container of the soul, or clutch the *patera*, a circular dish arguably symbolising the continuity of life.

Divination, human and animal sacrifice were used to stave off divine retribution. The Books of the Dead prescribe rules for interpreting thunder and lightning, animal entrails, and the flight of birds. But the central vision was one of a painful leavetaking or "death journey" to the underworld, hounded by demons. From there, if the gods had been appeased by sacrifice, the dead had the potential to become divine. In this painful leavetaking, some see a lingering race memory of the original journey from the Orient or Eastern Europe.

But from 4 B.C. onwards, the Etruscans became convinced that the dead person

The bejewelled woman is surrounded by a mixture of feminine and sacred symbols: perfume boxes and earrings to beautify; a pomegranate or pine cone to symbolise sexuality and death; a mirror to reflect her physical and spiritual perfection. In effect, these were portraits commissioned to show to the gods the noble patrons at their best.

Etruscan art is essentially regional; Arezzo had a reputation for *Arretino*, fine red pottery and for its metalwork. The famous bronze *Chimera* remains a magical illusion: a goat's head springs from a lion's back and is seized by the lion's tail, suddenly transformed into a serpent's mouth. Chiusi boasts canopic urns, cinerary urns with an idealised effigy of the deceased on the lid, while Cortona's Giacometti-like bronze figurines represent Etruscan deities. Volterra runs the gamut of Etruscan demonology and Greek mythology. The "cinerary urns" are in fact small alabaster sarcophagi featuring sea monsters, beaked griffins and sirens in addition to Ulysses, Iphegenia and Oedipus.

The Etruscan language is as mysterious as the Etruscan origins. Although the alphabet is borrowed from Greek, the language, read from left to right, is part of no known language group and defies interpretation. Many claim to have found a key text equivalent to

the 18th century, the sounds of most letters, names and gods had been identified and simple texts translated. Today, the core grammatical and phonetic structure is known and, by deduction, most of the 10,000 shorter texts can be read accurately. These are mostly funerary inscriptions and religious dedications. The one known book, a priest's manual discovered wrapped around an Egyptian mummy, has now been partially deciphered.

The art critic John Ruskin saw an unbroken line of tradition from the tomb paintings of the Etruscans to Giotto and Fra Angelico. Certainly, the Etruscan influence on the Romans was considerable. Apart from intro-

the Rosetta Stone. In Marsiliano a writing tablet was found engraved with the Greek Euboic alphabet used as a model for Etruscan. The University of Perugia has created a database of 100,000 Etruscan words in an attempt to break the code.

Despite considerable progess, the unintelligibility of Etruscan is part of a glamorous myth. True, there are no external keys such as dictionaries or bilingual texts but even by

Left, fifth century Tomb of the Monkey, Chiusi. Javelin thrower with serving boy. Above, ruins of Etruscan city of Vetulonia.

ducing the purple toga, an abundance of gods and competent soothsayers to Rome, the Etruscans added a coherent set of religious, humanistic and regional values which outlived the Roman Empire. The Etruscans exerted a dynamic influence on Roman art before the original creativity was stifled by Classicism. Today, the Etruscan influence still emerges in modern art: Massimo Campigli's ochres and burnt browns are modelled on Etruscan landscapes, as are Paolo Busato's photographs. Tuscans still see the land as Etruria, untouched by the succession of imposed Roman and Catholic empires.

THE ROMAN LEGACY

The traveller leaves the airport at Pisa and pulls out into the traffic-clogged Via Aurelia, the main coast road between Rome and the north. A few feet below the trucks and buses, the honking drivers and exhaust clouds, lies the smooth stone slabs of the original Roman road, headed with military precision for the harbour of Pisae, which was once on the coast. Pisa is now five miles (eight km) inland, but the roads of Tuscany, as in so many other places, remain where the Romans put them.

Not all remaining roads are as busy. There is a surviving stretch of the Via Clodia, the Roman road from Rome to Saturnia; a straight march, a footpath between fields and overgrown hedgerows, leading from the baths at Terme di Saturnia up the steep hillside to Saturnia itself.

After a steady climb, the flat paving-stones make a U-turn then follow the sheer town walls, built by the Sienese in the 15th century but incorporating both Roman and Etruscan sections, until a long straight stretch sweeps the traveller through the Porto Romana, and into the town. There the road continues straight, past a few shops, until the worn flagstones disappear ignominiously beneath someone's garden wall.

Saturnia is a quiet little town, no more than a village, drowsing under the immense weight of its past. It was the Etruscan Aurinia, the main town of the Ager Caletranus, the intermediate zone between the great centres of northern and southern Etruria, which was under the control of Vulci just before the Roman conquest.

It came under Roman control as a *praefectura* in 280 B.C. and in 183 B.C. a Roman colony was founded there, attributed to the Sabatina tribe. The Romans re-named the town Saturnia after Jupiter's father. Surprisingly, there is very little to see: the Roman south gate, the end of the Via Clodia, is the most exciting thing there.

Roman towns in Tuscany were either built upon the foundations of Etruscan cities as part of a continuous development, as in Volterra, Vetulonia or Arezzo, or they were established as new Roman *colonia* on ruins of Etruscan towns, or as new settlements. In the second century A.D. Appian described the colonies in his *Bellum Civile*: "As the Romans subjugated the people of Italy successively, it was their habit to confiscate a portion of land and establish towns upon it, and to enrol colonists of their own in the towns already on it. They intended these for strongholds…either to hold the earlier in-

habitants in subjection or to repel enemy inroads."

Rome annexed Etruria in 351 B.C. and from the third until the second century B.C., as part of the massive road building programme which was to transform Italy, four great Roman roads were built across the territory: the Via Aurelia, which ran up the western seaboard to Pisae and the naval base at Genua in Liguria; the Via Clodia, which stopped at Saturnia; the Via Cassia, built in 154 B.C. to connect Rome with Florentia; and the Via Flaminia, built 220 B.C. to connect Rome to Umbria and the Adriatic.

It's hard to imagine the impact these giant

Left, *Primavera*: ancient Roman fresco anticipates the style of Botticelli. Above, mosaic floor Roselle, Grosseto.

IMPORTANT DATES

700-500 B.C.: Etruscan civilization; federation of states included Arezzo, Cortona, Chiusi, Fiesole, Populonia, Roselle, Vetulonia, Volterra.

480-290 B.C.: Romans in power; annexed Etruria and founded colonies at Ansedonia, Roselle, Volterra, Luni and Lucca.

A.D. 200-600: Invasions by Lombards, Goths, Franks.

A.D. 306: Constantinople becomes capital of Roman Empire; Byzantium period.

A.D. 476: Downfall of Rome.

1000-1300: German emperors conquer Italy; constant warring between Guelfs (supporters of the Papacy) and Ghibellines (supporters of the Holy Roman Empire).

1118: Consecration of Pisa cathedral.

1125: Florence begins its expansion with the takeover of Fiesole.

1265-1321: Dante Alighieri. The *Divine Comedy* is begun in 1314.

1266-1337: Giotto di Bondone. In 1334 Giotto begins Florentine campanile.

1289: Battle of Campaldino, last battle between citizen soldiers.

1302: Giovanni Pisano begins pulpit in Pisa cathedral.

1304-1374: Francesco Petrarch; his studies spark the resurgence of interest in antiquity.

1348: Black death strikes Florence, killing a third of the population.

1313-1375: Giovanni Boccaccio: his famous collection of tales, *The Decameron,* is set against the background of the plague.

1377-1466: Brunelleschi. In 1436 Brunelleschi's dome for the cathedral in Florence is completed.

1384: Arezzo is conquered by Florence.

1386-1466: Donatello; sculptor famous for the active poses of his revolutionary *Judith and Holofernes* and *David*.

1390: John Hawkwood, condottiero, becomes Captain General of Florence; inter-city wars fought by mercenaries.

1401-1428: Masaccio: develops use of perspective in art.

1406: Pisa defeated and becomes part of Florentine state.

1420: Papacy returns to Rome from Avignon.

1434-1464: Cosimo de' Medici rules Florence

1452: Alberti publishes his *Ten Books on Architecture*.

1452-1519: Leonardo da Vinci.

1469-1527: Machiavelli. *The Prince* was written in 1513.

1469-92: Lorenzo de' Medici ruler of Florence

1475-1564: Michelangelo Buonarotti.

1498: "Mad monk" Savonarola is burnt at the stake in the Piazza Signoria for heresy.

1527: Sack of Rome.

1555: Florence defeats Siena and incorporates its rival into the Florentine state.

1558: Cellini's *Autobiography*.

1564-1642: Galileo. Discovers principles of dynamics.

1743: Death of Gian Gastone, the last Medici; Tuscany falls to House of Lorraine.

1796: Napoleon's first Italian campaign.

1815: Grand Duchy absorbed into Austrian Empire.

1848: War of Independence.

1858-1924: Giacomo Puccini.

1859: Unification of Italy, initiated by Cavour.

1861: Proclamation of the Kingdom of Italy with Turin as capital.

1865-1870: Florence briefly capital of Italy.

1870: Rome becomes capital of Italy.

1915: Italy enters World War I on the side of the Allies.

1922: Mussolini comes to power.

1940: Pact with Germany and Japan. Italy joins World War II against Britain and France.

1943: Fall of the Fascists.

1946: Italy becomes a Republic.

1957: Treaty of Rome; Italy founder member of EEC.

1966: Massive flooding in Italy: the Arno overflows in Florence and many works of art are damaged or destroyed.

1985: Great frost destroys between 50 and 75 percent of the olive trees.

1987: Sorpasso; the "overtaking". The Italian economy outstrips its British and French competitors.

engineering projects must have had on the local inhabitants as surveyors and workmen spanned rivers with elegant stone bridges, built drains to prevent their new roads from flooding and, where necessary, cut through the hills themselves.

Etruscan roads were all designed to connect the interior with the coast, whereas Roman roads all led to Rome, thus the axis was turned 90 degrees, from east-west to north-south. The new Roman roads purposely avoided the great Etruscan cities which slowly fell into decline, whereas the new Roman cities such as Pistoriae (Pistoia), originally a small fortified town on the via Cassia, grew in importance.

New colonies were founded at Ansedonia, Fiesole, Roselle, Volterra, Luni and Lucca. The cultural identity of the Etruscans was gradually absorbed into that of the Romans, a process which accelerated in 91 B.C. when Roman citizenship was extended to the Etruscans. The Romans learned many things from the Etruscans—principally the Tuscan arch which they developed as a central structural element in their buildings, relegating the classical columns of ancient Greece to a

Left, Petrarch: to his contemporaries a living representative of antiquity. Above, excavated Roman city at Roselle, Grosseto.

more decorative role.

Using the arch, Roman architects and engineers built their extraordinary aqueducts and bridges. It was from the Etruscan kings that the Roman monarchy, and later the Republican magistrates, took their symbol of power: the *fasces*, an axe, surrounded by a bundle of rods, an eloquent symbol of the right to execute or scourge. (Sculpture depicting the *fasces* dating from 500 B.C. has been found at the Etruscan city of Vatluna, the Roman Vetulonia.)

The most complete remains in Tuscany are at Fiesole, Roselle and Cosa; the best villas are near the coast, at Elba, near Porto Santo Stefano and particularly the Isola di Giannutri, near Grosseto, where the magnificent ruins of a villa with a number of intact slender columns overlooks the Mediterranean. Most Tuscan cities have something to show, though sometimes a little detective work is required.

Ansedonia, the Roman Cosa, was founded as a Roman colony in 273 B.C. on the hilltop site of an earlier settlement, probably the Etruscan port of Vulci. The Roman city has been excavated and the site contains a main street, remains of a forum, a walled acropolis and, dominating the city on a southern hill, the ruined capitolium—a tripartite sanctuary for the triad of Jupiter, Juno and Minerva from which there are wonderful views out over the sea.

The city's 1.5 km of wall are virtually intact, as are many of its 18 guard towers, including the entrance at Porta Romana. The site is overgrown and many of the ruins are covered in brambles, giving it a melancholy atmosphere. Saplings are sprouting in the forum, returning the dead city to the earth. The lack of signposts and labels makes it easier to imagine the townspeople going about their daily routine.

Below the promontory is the silted up Roman port, and nearby, the Tagliata Etrusca (Etruscan Cut), which is not Etruscan at all but a drainage canal cut by the Romans to connect the port with the lake of Burano, to stop the lake and the harbour from silting up. The cleft in the rocks, the so-called Bagno della Regina (the Queen's bath), is not, as is sometimes claimed, a rock sanctuary, but part of the Roman drainage works.

Fiesole possibly dating from the eighth century B.C., is an Etruscan settlement overlooking the valleys of the Arno and the Mugnone and has a superb view of what is now Florence. As Faesulae, it was a Roman military colony from 80 B.C. and later became the capital of Roman Etruria. The Piazza Mino de Fiesole is on the site of the Roman forum.

The archaeological site is set on a hillside near the Duomo. There is a remarkably well preserved 3,000-seat Roman amphitheatre dating from 80 B.C., which is still used for performances. Nearby are Roman baths and on the other side, the ruins of a Roman temple both from the first century B.C. and a third-century B.C. Etruscan temple, set against the Etruscan city walls.

Detective work is necessary in Florence, the Roman Florentia; the Roman gridiron street plan is clearly visible in maps, with the Piazza della Repubblica following the outline of the old *castrum*. The perimeter of the amphitheatre, outside the city walls to the southwest, is still described by the little streets surrounding the Piazza S. Croce: the Via Torta, Via Bentaccord and the north side of the Piazza Peruzzi.

In Lucca, the original street plan is also still evident. Luca, as the Romans named it, began as a military colony in 178 B.C. (the last of the Roman colonies). The 10,000-seat amphitheatre was originally to the north of the Roman city, outside the walls. In time, it was largely dismantled, and most of its remains are below street level.

However, in the Middle Ages, houses were built using the remaining walls, thus fossilising its outline and four main entrances. Fragments of its outside arcading are still visible from the surrounding lanes, incorporated in the outer walls of the houses. In the 19th century, the houses filling the centre were cleared away to create the Piazza dei Mercato.

Luni, called Luna by the Romans, was founded in 177 B.C. and was the springboard for the conquest of the Ligurian tribes in 15 B.C.. It was originally settled by 2,000 colonists, each of whom received 3.8 acres (1.6 hectares) of land. Originally on the coast, Luni became prosperous shipping white Carrara marble from its fine harbour. The Roman city, its forum, houses, and amphitheatre have been excavated and it is an important site for archaeologists.

Another extensive excavated site is at Roselle, the Roman Rusellae. The Etruscan city was taken by Rome early in the third century B.C.. It was originally an island, dominating the waters of the gulf. The ruins are very complete, with a nearly intact circuit of Romano-Etruscan walls, a Roman forum, paved street, basilicas, villas, amphitheatre and baths.

Volterra was the Etruscan city state of Velathri. It became the important Roman municipality of Volterrae in the fourth century B.C. but was on the wrong side during the civil war and fell to Sulla in 80 B.C.. The Arco Etrusca has a Roman arched vault on massive Etruscan bases with three Etruscan heads incorporated into the arch.

The ruins of the first-century B.C. Roman amphitheatre are situated outside the city walls to the west of the Porta Fiorentina. They are best seen by looking down on them from the city walls.

By creating the roads and major cities of Tuscany, the Romans left a permanent imprint on the landscape. A millennium later, the ruins of their great bridges, amphitheatres and city walls were the inspiration for the next great blossoming of Italian culture; Tuscany's coming of age, the Renaissance.

Above, remaining city walls at Cosa, Grosseto. Right, head of statue at Villa Garzoni, Pistoia.

GOOD AND BAD GOVERNMENT

"The City stands in the centre of the State like a guardian and a master. Towns surround her, just as the moon is surrounded by stars. The Florentine State might be compared to a round shield, with a series of rings surrounding a central knob. The central knob is the City itself, dominated by the Palazzo Vecchio, a mighty castle, the centre of the whole shield. The rings around it are formed first by the walls and suburbs, then by a belt of country houses, and finally by a distant circle of towns. Between the towns are castles and towers reaching the sky."

This was how a Florentine writer, Leonardo Bruni, described his city at the beginning of the 15th century. It was then at the height of its power, with many other cities and towns subject to it. Bruni's pride and love are obvious: his city is as beautiful as the moon and as strong as a shield. What he does not say is that all the other towns and cities in the State are held down by brute force. But Bruni probably thought that hardly worth mentioning: after all, that was what all other Italian cities were striving to achieve.

Power bases: Between the ending of the Roman Empire, in the 4th century A.D. and the beginning of the foreign invasions in the 16th century, after which all Italy became subject to foreign powers, the story of Italy is a catalogue of conflict between its cities, each of which was a sovereign state. Gradually, the larger absorbed the smaller. In the far south, Naples dominated the area from Rome to Sicily. In and around Rome, the Popes built up a power base. In the North, the great city of Milan swallowed up all its neighbours on the Lombard plain. And in Tuscany, a three-way battle was conducted between Florence, Pisa and Siena.

In the early stages the battles between the city-states were conducted by the citizens themselves, all able-bodied men between the ages of 15 and 50 sallying forth beyond their city's walls to fight the men of the neighbouring city. Even such a great poet and scholar as Dante took his part in these conflicts, fighting in the last battle between

Left, Florentine nobles. Above, Lorenzetti's *Bad Government*.

citizen-soldiers which took place at Campaldino in 1289 when Florence finally crushed Arezzo. The blood-letting in that battle was so great that thereafter the cities began to fight out their differences with mercenaries, the *condottieri*.

Throughout the 14th century the *condottieri* held the balance of power. Commanding well-disciplined, well-armed companies numbering thousands of men, they sold their services to the highest bidder. The city which could afford them—and could control

them—dominated its neighbours. The extraordinary honour accorded these mercenaries is showed by the fact that, in Siena, Lorenzetti's great fresco in the Town Hall, *Good and Bad Government*, is dominated by a condottiero. In Florence, the Englishman John Hawkwood, who commanded the White Company, has a place of honour in the cathedral.

These wars between the cities were conducted, in theory, in the name of "Guelf" or "Ghibelline" partisanship. The Guelfs supported the Papacy in its long battle against the Emperor. Italian politics had become so confused that the "Holy Roman Emperor" was invariably a foreigner and, usually, a German. But the Ghibellines believed, while recognising that the Emperor was merely a figure-head, that only with some kind of imperial control could peace return to Italy.

That at least was the theory. In practice, "Guelf" and "Ghibelline" were little more than battle slogans. When one party defeated its rivals in a city it would immediately fragment; in Florence, for example, when the Guelf party triumphed it promptly split into Black Guelfs and White Guelfs. Dante was one of those who, though a Guelf, was a "Black" and so was forced into exile when the "Whites" came to power.

Outside Tuscany, most of the city-states had fallen under the dominion of a single ruler: the Signor. The Tuscan republics maintained their independence far longer but eventually even Florence fell to a single ruler when the Medici transformed themselves into dukes.

While the Medici were still only private citizens, Florence was intent on subduing its two greatest rivals in Tuscany. It was inevitable that Florence should come into conflict with Pisa, because Pisa controlled the mouth of the Arno, Florence's lifeline. The Pisans made common cause with the great Ghibelline city of Milan, but Pisa was too close to Florence to fight off its powerful rival and in 1406 Pisa became part of the Florentine State.

Siena was at first more successful in resisting the Florentine embrace—but only by surrendering totally to Milan. Eventually, however, it too was absorbed into the Florentine State which had, under the Medici, become the Grand Duchy of Tuscany. This, in turn, came to an end with the death of the last Medici in 1743. There then followed the long tussle known as the Tuscan Succession at the end of which the Grand Duchy was absorbed into the Austrian Empire in 1815.

During the 1830s nationalist feeling began to grow and the *Risorgimento* movement was born, leading to revolution in 1848 and, finally, unification of Italy. From 1865-1870 Florence had a brief moment of glory as capital of a newly united Italy.

Right, Giorgío Vasari *Foundation of Florence* **1563-65 Ceiling of Salone dei Cinquecento, Palazzo Vecchio.**

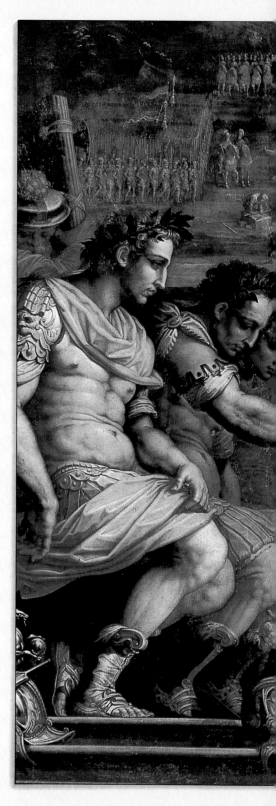

THE RENAISSANCE

One of the great myths of history provides a kind of Hollywood scenario for the "birth of the Renaissance," linking it to the fall of the Greek city of Constantinople in 1453, when scholars were supposed to have escaped, clutching their precious Greek manuscripts, to Italy. There, these manuscripts became a kind of magical seed, taking root, growing and bearing fruit almost immediately as "The Renaissance".

Of course, this is nonsense; like any other human phenomenon, the Renaissance had roots deep in history. Today, we know quite a lot about *how* the Renaissance happened. We still don't know *why* it occurred at that particular time and, above all, in that particular place.

Contemporaries were equally puzzled. Writing in the 1430s, the scholar Lorenzo Valla said: "I do not know why the arts most closely approximating to the liberal arts had been in so long and deep decline and almost died out, nor why they have come to be aroused and come to life in this age."

Valla might also have added: "Why did it happen in Florence?" It was, of course, the political fragmentation of Italy which created the Renaissance, each little city-state contributing something unique to the whole. But, the process certainly started in Florence, and the city dominated the cultural scene until the early 16th century.

The best book on Renaissance statecraft is by the Florentine writer, Machiavelli, and the best book on commerce by the Florentine Pegolotti. Art history owes everything to the Florentine Vasari, and the whole course of art was changed by the Florentines Giotto, Botticelli, Michelangelo and Leonardo da Vinci, to mention the most obvious.

Again and again over the centuries, attempts have been made to analyse the causes of the Florentine flowering, with reasons ranging from the poverty of the soil to the quality of the light. But it is no more possible to "explain" this than any other mystery of the human spirit.

Left, Sandro Botticelli: *St Augustine in His Study* c.1480, Church of the Ognissanti, Florence. Above, grain merchants in Florence.

The very word "renaissance" is a Florentine invention. In his book *Lives of the Most Excellent Architects, Painters and Sculptors*, first published in 1550, Giorgio Vasari, first of the art historians, remarks that the reader, "will now be able to recognise more easily the progress of [art's] rebirth (*il progresso della sua rinascita*)."

But what, exactly, did Vasari mean by *rinascita*? What was being "reborn"? Vasari was referring to a rebirth of the art and architecture of classical times; that is, before

Emperor Constantine transferred the seat of Empire to Constantinople at the beginning of the 4th century A.D., causing Byzantium to become the centre of art and culture. A distinctive architecture, based on Roman models, using bricks and featuring domes and cupolas, was developed. Byzantine artists covered the interiors with mosaics, a Roman decorative form which they developed into a sumptuous art form; the thousands of glazed stone fragments catching the light in a way no fresco ever could giving the images a shimmering, glittering presence in the semi-darkness—the "golden gloom" of Byzantium. The best examples in Italy are in

Ravenna, made in the 5th and 6th centuries, but the style prevailed in the 11th century in St Marks, Venice, and even in the 13th century in the magnificent Baptistry in Florence. It was the stiff formalised work of the Byzantine artists that Vasari, who dismissed them as "a certain residue of Greeks," was attacking, and which was completely overthrown by the new naturalism of the Renaissance artists.

Architects drew and measured the ruins of the Roman cities, rediscovering their building techniques and their rules of proportion: the "classical orders." Vitruvius' *Ten Books on Architecture*, the only surviving manual from classical times, was studied anew and became the basis, in the 15th century, for Alberti's treatise of the same name.

Painting, which of all the arts, is preeminently *the* art of the Renaissance, owed little to antiquity, though the great originality shown in the visual arts may be due partly to the fact that no Roman examples survived to be used as models. Renaissance artists broke new ground discovering perspective and observing the natural world which surrounded them. Nature meant little to the Greeks and the Romans, whereas one of the characteristics of the Renaissance artist was his ability to go back to first base. The 14th-century Florentine artist Cennino Cennini gave good advice to his fellow artists. "If you wish to draw mountains well, so that they appear natural," he wrote, "procure some large stones, rocky, not polished, and draw from these." The idea of a handful of stones standing in for the Alps or the Appenines might seem ludicrous, but it was a pointer to the new road the artist was taking, the road to reality in nature.

The classical world provided the inspiration for the artist to rise above the narrow medieval world, with its emphasis on theological studies. But, once started, he went his own way. What was reborn was an artistic sensibility but a re-cycled past.

Changing times: Art historians divide the great period of transition into three subperiods, using the logical Italian terms Trecento, (1300s) *Quattrocento* (1400s) and *Cinquecento* (1500s) instead of our rather confusing 14th, 15th and 16th centuries.

Right, Leonardo da Vinci. *Adoration of the Magi* **1481, Uffizi.**

THE TRECENTO
THE ARTISTS' WORKSHOPS

Until the Quattrocento, the term "artist" had no particular significance, being virtually interchangeable with "artisan" or "craftsman". All were members of guilds, or *arti*: There was an *arte* for the shoemaker, no more and no less valid than the *arte* for the goldsmith, itself a subdivision of the immensely powerful Silk Guild.

The guilds extended their control, as a matter of course, over the decorative as well as the useful arts. Sculptors and architects were enrolled, logically enough with the masons, and painters formed a sub-division of the apothecaries on the general principle that they had to have some acquaintance with chemistry to prepare their colours.

Far from resenting the obligation to join associations, painters and sculptors formed their own groups, or *compagnie*, created both within and across the boundaries of the larger guilds. The reasons were both social and technical. Socially, members could help each other, the group as a whole sharing both profits and losses. Technically, an increasing amount of work was done in co-operation, either on a kind of conveyor-belt system (two or three men might be engaged at successive stages in the shaping of a pillar, from rough hewing to final carving, or working side by side.)

The growing popularity of the process known as *buon fresco* demanded such an approach. It had been introduced about a century earlier, and time had shown that it was the most permanent of all forms of mural art since the colouring became an intrinsic part of the plaster itself. (Michelangelo was to use the technique in the greatest of all works carried out using the process, the Sistine Chapel in Rome).

The wall was first roughly plastered, and on this the master would make a rough outline drawing in charcoal. Over this outline was laid a layer of fine, smooth plaster, the *intonaco*. The outlines of the full-scale cartoon, as the original drawing was known, were punched through with a series of pin-

Left, Giotto, *Madonna and Child*, c.1320-30. Above, *Madonna enthroned*, c.1280-85; detail by Cimabue, who discovered Giotto.

holes (often speedily done with a small spiked wheel known as a roulette.) Charcoal was then rubbed through the holes, leaving the outline on the wet plaster as a series of dots. This technique is called "pouncing." For backgrounds, or when the master himself was doing the painting, the work was done from memory, with the original cartoon placed nearby. Only so much plaster was laid as could be covered in one day's work and, provided there was room, any number of men could work side by side from the top of

the wall downward. It was a system which placed a premium on the skill of the individual at absorbing the style of the master—the man who had created the cartoon—so that, no matter how large the mural, the treatment was homogeneous.

In addition to these large, set tasks, the *bottega* (or workshop) would produce a variety of smaller articles for sale, either on speculation or on commission, ranging from painted scabbards and armorial bearings to holy pictures and statues. There was widespread demand for religious art which provided the bread and butter for hundreds of small *botteghe*. A peasant may have scraped together a few lire for a picture; a parish priest might have a large sum at his disposal and commission a mural or even an altar piece: or a merchant who had made his fortune might be anxious to propitiate fate.

The potential client had little interest in the identity of the craftsmen producing his order. But, if expensive colours were used (gold, silver, or blue made from the semi-precious lapis-lazuli), then the fact was clearly stated in the contract, along with the date of delivery of the finished piece. Commissioned work was almost invariably done on these written contracts which, in addition, usually specified how many figures were to appear in the finished painting, their activities and attributes. Religious paintings touched on the delicate area of religious orthodoxy and the wise craftsman ensured that his client stated exactly what he wanted.

A typical patron was Francesco Datini, the wool merchant of the little town of Prato, ten miles from Florence, whose story is told in Iris Origo's book *The Merchant of Prato*. After he had made his fortune, both social and religious pressure prevailed upon him to decorate his house with religious paintings. He was a superstitious rather than a religious man, indifferent to any form of aesthetics, and he went about the business of commissioning holy pictures with the same dour eye for a bargain which made his fortune in wool.

In 1375 he was ordering from a *bottega* in Florence "a panel of Our Lady on a background of fine gold and a pedestal with ornament and leaves, handsome and the wood well carved, making a fine show with some figures by the best painter, with many figures. Let there be in the centre Our Lord on the Cross or Our Lady—whomsoever you find, I care not so that the figures be handsome and large, and the best and finest you can purvey and the cost no more that 5½ or 6½ florins."

Members of a *bottega* usually contracted for three years, renewing or disbanding their company but always either reforming it or joining another. The practice began to die out at the beginning of the Quattrocento under new pressures—in particular, the dominance by a number of great painters who could afford to regard members of the

Right, workshop of Giorgio Vasari, 1567-72. Fresco in Palazzo Vecchio.

52

bottega virtually as their employees, and by the emergence of grand patrons such as the Medici.

The vast majority of the workers in these art shops are virtually anonymous. They were conscientious and skilled, rather than brilliant, but they formed the sub-soil from which the genius of the Quattrocento could flourish. The actual working pattern of the *bottega*, whereby a group of lesser men would paint the main body of a picture, leaving it to the identified master to put the finishing touches to it, would continue on into the so-called High Renaissance of the Cinquecento, making it difficult and at times impossible for the most skilled art critic to

tion—joy, grief, anger. Contemporaries might be uncertain about why this great change occurred but there was a universal chorus of agreement as to who started it: Giotto di Bondone according to Vasari, "restored art to the better path followed in modern times."

Born in Florence around the year 1267, tradition has it that Giotto was a shepherd boy until discovered by the great traditional artist, Cimabue, for whom the boy drew a perfect circle by freehand. Despite this supposedly rural experience, even in Giotto's work nature is formalised and in the background. It is the humans who occupy the foreground, vibrantly alive.

say that such a painting is, beyond a doubt the work of a particular famous artist.

First impressions: Any Italian art gallery arranged on a chronological basis will provide a dramatic shock for the visitor. The first section of the gallery will be endless stiff paintings of the Madonna and Child, or martyred saints. Eventually, the most religious visitor will tire of the monotony, drift on—and encounter a radical change.

Instead of a half-length painting of the Madonna clutching a large, fat naked Child, or a statuesque representation of a saint liberally covered in gold, the eye encounters real human beings, displaying real emo-

In Florence, Giotto's main work is in the Franciscan church of Santa Croce. His work (and, of course, that of the *bottega* that assisted him) covers the walls of the two chapels to the right of the choir. In a series of vivid vignettes they tell the story of the Finding of the True Cross, and the Life of Saint Francis.

Giotto died in 1337 and nearly a century would pass before his work was taken up by others. But, when the seed finally sprouted, it brought forth astonishing fruit.

Above, Florentine woodcut of banking scene, 1490. Right, portrait of Cosimo de' Medici, by Jacopo Pontormo.

THE MEDICI

The Medici were the most outstanding art patrons in European history because they combined a genuine aesthetic sense which enabled them to detect new trends in culture, together with great commercial acumen and ruthless political skill. Although the Medici were associated with Florence for over 400 years, from the mid-14th to mid-18th centuries, attention is always focussed on two, father and grandson, in the 15th century. Cosimo de' Medici, who died in 1464, has been rather overshadowed by his glamorous grandson, Lorenzo the Magnificent, but it was Cosimo who brought about the fusion of business sense and aesthetic appreciation which made the Medici so significant.

The family owed its fortune to banking. When the founder of the bank, Giovanni de' Medici, died in 1429, he left his son Cosimo the immense fortune of 180,000 gold florins. (Incalculable today but running into millions of pounds). He also left him an appreciation of the new learning because Giovanni himself had been a patron of the arts. In many ways they were the world's first capitalists, financing many of the European wars. The florin, named after the city, only went out of use in Great Britain when the currency was decimalized in 1971.

Cosimo kept very careful control of the family business while he jockeyed his way into political power. His famous grandson, Lorenzo the Magnificent, was frank as to the reasons why the Medici sought power: "It ill fares in Florence with any who possesses wealth without any share of the government." Both as political boss and as banker, Cosimo was the unofficial ruler of Florence by the time of his death at the age of seventy-four in 1464.

He poured out vast sums in subsidising the arts. His grandson once rather ruefully calculated that Cosimo spent at least 600,000 florins in such patronage (a sum which should be compared with the Medici bank tax-bill of 600 florins in its heaviest year). In 1444 Cosimo built the first Renaissance palace for his family, typically commissioning the restrained Michelozzo in-

stead of the more flamboyant Brunelleschi, and it is here that the Renaissance can be said to have come of age.

In the courtyard of the Medici palace were placed the statues of *David* and *Judith* that Cosimo's friend and protégé, Donatello (1386-1466) had been commissioned to create. The *David* (now in the Bargello Museum) was the first bronze work "in the round" to be seen in Europe for a thousand years.

Cosimo's son reigned briefly, and was succeeded by Lorenzo the Magnificent in 1469. The subject of countless legends, his extraordinary character was an astonishing mixture of moods and talents. One day he would be drinking with rowdy companions in rough taverns: the next he would be deep in philosophic arguments with brilliant scholars.

He was an ugly man, dark-skinned, heavy featured with a harsh, high-pitched voice. But he was so charming that people forgot his physical appearance and spoke of him as an attractive man. He was not good at business and his prodigal support of the arts put the bank under a severe financial strain.

The names of the artists he encouraged form a roll-call of the early Renaissance: Botticelli shared his childhood home; Leonardo da Vinci owed him his appointment to the Milanese court; he gave the 15-year-old Michelangelo a home in his palace. He was also a consummate statesman, holding Florence's place in the lethal cross-currents of Italian politics.

The early Medici were passionate republicans but, corrupted by power, the dynasty drifted towards despotism. Two of the family became Popes: Leo X (who tangled with Martin Luther) and Clement VII, who resigned during the disastrous Sack of Rome of 1527. The family ruled as Grand Dukes of Tuscany until 1743.

The modern city of Florence owes the Medici one incalculable debt. The last Medici, Princess Anna Maria Luisa left the entire Medici art collection to the State of Tuscany on her death in 1743, with the single proviso that it must all stay in Florence. The priceless collection forms the backbone of Florence's three main galleries, the Uffizi, the Pitti and the Bargello.

THE QUATTROCENTO
THE ARTIST EMERGES

Florence was pre-eminent but not unique among Tuscan cities in the arts. Pisa was particularly noted for its work in sculpture, both in stone and bronze. In 1330, the Florentines actually commissioned the Pisan Andrea Pisano to design and cast the first of the great bronze doors for their beloved Baptistry. Even before this in the 1240s, Nicola Pisano and his son Giovanni were creating the great carved pulpits which were to sculpture what Giotto was to painting.

In Siena, Duccio di Buoninsegna, working around 1315, brought the stiff Byzantine art so criticised by Vasari to something near humanity. His pupil Simone Martini was deeply influenced by Giovanni Pisano, but also drew on French Gothic for the great *Maesta* in Siena's City Hall. In that same beautiful building, Pietro Lorenzetti created the immense fresco *Good and Bad Government* between 1337 and 1379 which, in an allegory, provides a vivid illustration of the Tuscan countryside and the city of Siena of the period.

The Florentine dynamo: Brilliant though they were these artists were an end-product, the development of an existing trend. It is an undeniable fact of history that the great break-through took place in Florence, a moment so important that it can be dated to within a few years. Florence retained its dominance in art for barely a life-span because it exported so much of its native talent, ensuring the spread of Renaissance values and, with it, its own relative eclipse. But until the 1470s Florence was a kind of dynamo, providing light and energy for the entire peninsula.

In 1453 the scholar and polymath Leon Battista Alberti returned from many years exile and marvelled at the changes that had been wrought in his home. The dedication in his book *Treatise on Painting* is a tribute both to those who were making the change and the spell which Florence cast over its children. Movingly he describes how he

came back to his city "beloved above all for its beauty" and singled out a small band of artists for especial praise—"you, Filippo (Brunelleschi); our dear friend Donatello and the sculptor Nanni (Ghiberti) and Massacio," all producing work, he declared, worthy of comparison with any of the masters of antiquity.

The process began about the turn of the century when the Florentine *Signoria*, or government, decided to refurbish the ceremonial centre of Florence—the group con-

sisting of the Cathedral, the Campanile begun by Giotto in 1334 and finished after his death but to his design in 1359, and the octagonal Baptistry.

This little black and white building had a special place in Florentine affections and when, in 1401, it was decided to offer a thanksgiving for the city's escape from plague, the Baptistry was chosen to benefit. The wealthy Wool Guild announced that they would finance the design and casting of a second set of bronze doors for the Baptistry that would be even grander than those of Pisano's. The design was thrown open to competition.

Left, Brunelleschi's dome. Above, Masaccio, *San Giovenale Triptych*, 1422 detail, Madonna and Child; Uffizi.

Out of the many entrants, seven were chosen to live at public expense while each executed a panel on the same subject: the sacrifice of Isaac. Two of the entrants, the 23-year-old Brunelleschi, later credited as the creator of the "Renaissance style" in architecture, and the 20-year-old Lorenzo Ghiberti, produced a work which caused considerable difficulty to the judges. Both the panels exist today, one as part of the series in the door, the other in the Bargello Museum. Comparing the two, posterity finds it impossible to say which is "better". The *Syndics,* at a loss to choose, came up with a compromise, suggesting that the artists should share the work. Brunelleschi declined and took himself off to Rome, while Ghiberti began work on the doors, completing them 22 years later.

He was offered the commission to produce a second pair: these took him 27 years. During the almost half-century that he spent at work on the project, it is possible to see in his contracts the changing status of the artist. In the first contract he is treated essentially as an artisan, expected to put in a full day's work "like any journeyman". In the later contracts, he is treated far more as a free agent, permitted to undertake other commissions. Ghiberti, too, made explicit the change by boldly including his own self-portrait among the sculptures of the door.

Learning from the ancients: Meanwhile, in Rome with his friend Donatello, Brunelleschi was finding out just how the ancients had built their enormous structures. He was engaged in an entirely new approach to the past, examining originals rather than copies of copies. One of his discoveries—or possibly, inventions—was the *ulivella.* Intrigued and puzzled by the existence of regular-shaped holes in the huge stone blocks of the ancient buildings, he assumed that they had been made to allow the block to be gripped by some device, and designed a kind of grappling iron to fit. Whether or not the Romans had actually used such a device, it was extremely useful—a neat demonstration of the practical benefits to be gained by studying the past.

Brunelleschi returned to Florence at about the time that the *Syndics* of the Wool Guild, who also had the responsibility for the Cathedral, were puzzling over the problem of completing it. Arnolfo di Cambio had begun

it over a century before, in 1296, and it had been completed, all except for the dome, by 1369. Nobody knew how to bridge this immense gap which, for half a century, had been covered by a temporary roof.

In 1417 a special meeting was called to debate the problem and consider suggestions. One suggestion was to make an immense pile of earth and build over it. Mockingly, somebody suggested putting silver coins in the earth, which would speed its subsequent removal. Brunelleschi then put forward his own solution. He too was mocked for it because it dispensed with the wooden centering, over which architects traditionally built their arches and vaults, supporting their weight until the key stone was in place. But, in desperation, the *Syndics* offered him the job, and Brunelleschi accepted. He solved the problem by building a dome that was pointed in section, supported by ribs with the lightest possible in-filling between them. He built two shells, an outer skin and an inner one, the first known use of the double shell dome, and one of the ways in which the crushing weight of the dome, which had always prevented its construction, was considerably reduced. The work took 16 years, and was completed on 31 August 1436. This was the first Renaissance dome in Italy, the largest unsupported dome in Europe, bigger than the Pantheon in Rome which Brunelleschi had studied, bigger even than the great dome which Michelangelo raised a century later over St Peter's in Rome.

It was Brunelleschi's successor, the scholar Alberti, who first applied the classical orders to domestic architecture and created what we now think of as the Renaissance palace. Whereas Brunelleschi introduced the columns, pediments and cornices he copied from Roman ruins into his churches, there were no surviving examples of Roman domestic architecture for the 15th-century Florentines to copy. When Rucellai, a wealthy Florentine merchant, asked Alberti to design a palace for him, Alberti took as a model the Coliseum in Rome and applied its tiers of arches to the facade of a three-storey palace. Though it was the only palace he built, and though Brunelleschi's design for the Medici palace never got beyond the model stage, these two architects determined a type of building, the results of which can be seen today, from the City of London to New York; a system of proportion and an elegance of line which is still in use.

Brunelleschi's other major breakthrough was his use of perspective. Alberti described its effect to a generation for whom it appeared almost a magical technique. "I describe a rectangle of whatever size I wish which I imagine to be an open window through which I view whatever is to be depicted there." Donatello (1386-1466) eagerly used the technique in his bas-relief of *Salome offering John's head to Herod*. The observer is looking at a banquet where the diners are recoiling away in horror from the offering. Beyond the banqueting rooms a

His great painting of the *Trinity* is an intellectual exercise in the use of perspective that is also infused with religious awe. Beneath a classical arch stands the immense figure of God the Father, half supporting a cross on which there is an equally immense figure of Christ; below them are saints and donors.

The massive figures stand out of the background and appear to loom over the observer. As a young man, Michelangelo used to stand before these calm and solid evocations of spiritual truth, copying them again and again to fix the style in his mind. Eventually, therefore, some essence of this experimental period of the Renaissance found

succession of two more rooms giving a remarkable and, for contemporaries, almost eerie sense of depth.

A new perspective: Like the difference between Giotto's emotionally active figures and their static, formal predecessors, perspective gave a new vista to civilisation. Its most dramatic form was that employed by the young Masaccio in the Church of the Carmine. Born in 1401 and dead by 1428, Masaccio, in his brief life, took up where Giotto left off and added to it the mysterious, potent ingredient of perspective.

Above, Ghirlandaio's *Birth of the Baptist*.

its way into the Sistine Chapel, that shrine of the High Renaissance dominated by Michelangelo's work.

The classical arch in Masaccio's painting is a pointer to a curious development which took place during the Quattrocento—the clothing of Biblical figures in totally anachronistic form, either in classical Roman attire or in contemporary Florentine dress.

The frescoes which Domenico Ghirlandaio (1449-94) painted in the Sasseti Chapel in the church of S. Trinita supposedly concern the prophecies of Christ's birth and the location is supposed to be Augustan Rome. But it is an Augustan Rome which bears a remarkably close resemblance to 15th-century Florence and the people standing round waiting for the awesome news are all citizens of Florence wearing their normal clothes. Lorenzo de' Medici is there, and his mother the stately Lucrezia Tornabuoni, his children, friends and political colleagues—all easily identified.

In this odd approach to the past, ancient Hebrews, Egyptians or Romans appeared in costume that would not have seemed out of place in contemporary life. Apollo is usually depicted as a young dandy, Jesus Christ in the robes of a 15th-century scholar. In Verrocchio's *Tobias and the Angel* neither would have attracted much attention (except

for the Angel's wings) if they had been seen walking down the Via Tornabuoni.

Andrea del Castagno's *Last Supper* takes this theme to extremes. Supposedly working-class Jews sharing a frugal meal in a humble Eastern inn appear as upper-class Romans debating some interesting scholarly point while waiting for their banquet.

Mythological elements: The painters of the early Renaissance were preoccupied with technique. Their subject matter remained largely unchanged; religion was still the most important concern. But in the second half of the Quattrocento a new, exciting and somewhat disturbing element began to appear; the mythological and the allegorical.

The supreme practitioner in this field was Sandro Botticelli, who worked with Leonardo da Vinci in Verrocchio's workshop but developed in a totally different direction. His most famous painting, perhaps *the* most famous painting of the early Renaissance and certainly the most mysterious, is the *Primavera*, and it is worth considering at some length.

Nine supernatural creatures are placed in an exquisite natural setting. Behind and above them are the trees of an orange grove. Their feet float just above a flower-spangled meadow. On the left, a young man is aiming at, or pointing at, something. Next to him a group of beautiful, grave-faced women are performing a solemn ritual dance. On the right is the only figure who seems to be aware of the observer: a stunningly beautiful woman with a provocative half-smile. (Who was she? That young woman appears again and again in Botticelli's paintings.) Beside her what appears to be an act of violence adds a discordant note: a bluish-green figure is leaning out of the trees and clutching at a startled girl.

In the background, but dominating the whole, is the most enigmatic figure of all; a pale-faced woman whose expression has been variously described as frowning, smiling, gay, melancholy; whose stance has also been described in conflicting ways as dancing; as that of a consumptive; as pregnant; as blessing. The figure itself has been firmly identified as representing Venus and just as firmly identified as the Virgin Mary.

What Botticelli was trying to do was to restate classical mythology in Christian terms while remaining true to the original—and true to his own quirky self. He later came into contact with the gloomy, savage friar Savonarola, who turned Florence into a Puritan reformatory in the 1490s. The Florentines eventually turned against Savonarola but the experience deeply influenced Botticelli. Almost overnight, he ceased his joyous mythological paintings, concentrating on orthodox religious subjects. Even here, though, one can trace the face of the beautiful young woman whose identity has tantalised generations of art historians.

Above, 15th-century Florence. Right, Masaccio, *Trinity,* c. 1425.

Ioan. Stradanus inuent

THE CINQUECENTO
THE HIGH RENAISSANCE

When, in the 1840s, a group of high-minded British painters decided that art had gone too far down the path of a mannered, self-conscious, academic nature and had lost its freshness and moral seriousness and must return to an earlier, more innocent period, they sought the point in time when art seemed to have changed for the worst.

They decided that it took place some time during the career of Raphael, who died in the full vigour of his powers at the early age of 37 in 1520. They elected to return to that form of art practised before the time of Raphael and it is therefore as Pre-Raphaelites that Burne-Jones, William Morris and the rest entered art history.

Even to the untutored eye, there is a profound difference between the work produced before and after the 1520s in Tuscany and elsewhere, most noticeably in Florence. Partly this was the result of an immense political crisis. Italy had become a battleground invaded again and again by warring foreigners. In 1527, a savage army composed partly of mercenaries, sacked Rome and held the Pope to ransom. Italy was never to recover from that experience which was the curtain-raiser for a period of foreign domination which would not end until the 1800s.

The glory goes elsewhere: Shortly after the Sack of Rome, the Medici Pope Clement VII clamped down on his native city of Florence, ending republicanism and preparing the way for the first dukedom. Meanwhile, in the world of art, the glory was departing from Florence as the impetus of the Renaissance shifted to Rome and Venice. From the mid-century onwards, Florentine artists tended to be court artists, dancing attendance on the Medici dukes. Among them was Giorgio Vasari.

Until recently, Vasari's work as an artist was dismissed almost as contemptuously as his work as art historian was received enthusiastically. There has, however, been something of a swing in his favour. Admittedly, he

will never be classed in the first rank but posterity owes him a debt of thanks, both as architect and as painter. Not only did he build the Uffizi for Duke Cosimo I, but in his paintings in the great Salone dei Cinquecento, the parliamentary chamber of the Palazzo Vecchio, he created outstanding contemporary representations of the city and its surrounding countryside.

The genius of Leonardo: The glory might be departing from Florence, but the sunset was stupendous. It could scarcely be otherwise

with two such giants as Michelangelo and Leonardo da Vinci still working in the city. Leonardo, born in 1452, trained in the *bottega* of Verrocchio, thus carrying the medieval systems on into the new era. One of Vasari's anecdotes claims that Verrocchio, on seeing his young apprentice's work laid down his brush and never painted again. Inherently unlikely though the incident is, the anecdote shows that Leonardo was recognised as being almost a freakish genius in his own lifetime.

An illustration of his restless, endlessly enquiring mind is shown by that incident on 28 December 1478 when, passing the Bar-

Preceding pages: cycle of olive oil production, 16th century. Left, Florence in the 15th century. Above, Michelangelo, **The Holy Family.**

gello, he noticed a body hanging from a window—one of the Pazzi conspirators. Taking out the notebook he always carried, he sketched the corpse, then meticulously noted in his mirror-writing: "Small cap tan coloured: doublet of black satin, black-lined jerkin, blue coat lined with black and white stripes of velvet. Bernardo di Bandino Baroncelli. Black hose". No indication whatsoever of human emotion, either pity or satisfaction.

Leonardo left Florence for Milan at the age of 30, shortly after that incident. He came back again in 1502 when he was commissioned by the *Signoria* to create the great mural, the *Battle of Anghiari* in the Council Chamber, returned to Milan in 1506 then finally crossed the Alps and became court painter to François I of France. His contribution to the history of ideas is incalculable but his physical contribution to Tuscan art history is relatively small. Typically, both the *Battle of Anghiari* and the *Adoration of the Kings* in the Uffizi are unfinished. And his two most famous paintings, the *Mona Lisa* (a portrait of a virtuous but not otherwise distinguished Florentine housewife) and the *Virgin of the Rocks* are in Paris and London respectively.

Michelangelo Buonarotti is very different. His greatest creation, too, is outside Florence—the Sistine Chapel frescoes—but he did leave an enduring imprint upon his native city, in the form of the walls that gird it and the sculptures that grace it.

The next generation: Michelangelo was nearly a generation younger than Leonardo, born in 1475 when the Renaissance was approaching its apogee. His father was a poor but proud country gentleman who thoroughly disapproved of the idea of his son becoming an artisan or artist; in his mind there was no clear distinction. Michelangelo, too, was apt to be a little touchy on the subject. Although he served his apprenticeship in a *bottega*, that of Ghirlandaio, he later rejected the idea that he touted for trade, "I was never a painter or a sculptor like those who set up shop for the purpose."

One of Vasari's anecdotes describes how the young Michelangelo, then around 13 years old, made a drawing of the various

tools in the workshop. His master, Ghirlandaio, was so impressed when he saw the drawings that, very generously, he drew Lorenzo de' Medici's attention to the talented boy and so Michelangelo entered the princely Medici household, eating at the same table and studying with the same scholars as Lorenzo's own children.

During one of the bitter quarrels which punctuated the lives of Florentine artists, a bigger youth called Torrigiani (who, later, was to design the superb funeral monument of Henry VII in London's Westminister Abbey) broke his nose with a mallet. Michelangelo bore that disfigurement for the rest of his life.

He was just 18 when Lorenzo de' Medici died in 1492. Florence was plunged into chaos because Lorenzo's son, Piero, was extravagant and unpopular and, after two years, the Florentines chased him out of the city. Michelangelo's relationship with the Medici made Florence a dangerous place for him and he took the road to Rome.

There he undertook not only the work by which he is best remembered, but also worked on a task which, though he laboured at it for 40 years, was never finished. This was the great tomb for his patron and taskmaster, Pope Julius II. The unfinished statues for this tomb, the famous *Slaves*, are now

Left, Michelangelo, *David.* **Above,** *Saint Ambrose,* **by Ghirlandaio.**

in Florence's Accademia gallery. In them it is possible to see, five centuries later, the sculptor's technique.

The actual roughing out of the figures was done, as in a *bottega*, by apprentices, the master himself giving the finishing touches. It is profoundly moving to see in some of them, the shallow depressions surrounding the figure made by the rounded head of chisel which seems actually to be "freeing" the figure as though it already existed and was simply encased in the stone.

Florence has many statues by Michelangelo; even though they are often unfinished they always reveal the chisel strokes of a master. They include, the famous *David*,

and the statues of *Dawn*, *Evening*, *Day* and *Night* in the Medici chapel.

Universal man: In the Casa Buonarotti in the Via Ghibellina are displayed some of the sculptor's working drawings as well as a few of his earliest works. It was as a sculptor that Michelangelo Buonarotti saw himself, rather touchingly signing his letters "Michelangelo sculptore". But he, too, is entitled to that proud style of "universal man" accorded to such as Leonardo. Apart from painting, he was also an engineer of very considerable skill and a poet of sensitivity and insight.

Michelangelo was just 25 when Benvenuto Cellini was born in 1500. Cellini admired his great fellow-citizen so much that, when Torrigiani invited him to go to England, he turned down the offer, claiming he could not associate with a man who had so disfigured his hero. Or so he said in his remarkable autobiography, and it is probably true enough for, despite his many and manifest faults, Benvenuto Cellini had a warmly emotional nature.

Like so many of the artists of his time, he was skilled in a number of crafts—he was improbably enough, a gunner. He played a role in the tragic Sack of Rome which, in effect, brought the Renaissance to an end, acting as gunner in defence of the Vatican when, he assured his readers, the Pope promised him absolution "for all the murders that I should commit."

In Florence, his most famous work is that beautiful but curiously heartless statue of *Perseus slaying the Gorgon* in the Loggia dei Lanzi. But it is indicative both of him and of the phase into which the art of the Renaissance was moving, that his best known work was the elaborate golden salt-cellar which he made for François I of France.

The road to Rome: Raphael, the gentle, handsome young man who, remarkably, had no enemies (though Michelangelo made the occasional remark about him) was not a Tuscan. He was born in Umbria in 1483, and received his basic training in the workshop of Perugino, working on frescoes in Perugia. In 1500, however, at the impressionable age of 17, he came to Florence where he drank at the very source itself, absorbing in particular the works of Leonardo da Vinci and Michelangelo.

He left Florence some time in 1508, attracted to Rome like so many other artists, by the fiery Pope Julius II who was planning a tremendous series of architectural embellishments to the Vatican. There Raphael easily proved himself. He painted the series of rooms known as the Stanze della Segnaturi and, under the Medici Pope Leo X, was placed in charge of archaeological excavations in Rome itself. Thus, the last true artist of the Renaissance introduced into the mother city of Europe that passionate search for the past which triggered off the Renaissance nearly two centuries earlier.

Above, portrait of Benvenuto Cellini. Right, Raphael, *Agnolo Doni*.

RENAISSANCE LITERATURE

Dante placed the action of his great epic *The Divine Comedy* at Easter, 1300. Machiavelli died in 1527, just before the Florentine Republic came to an end. These two dates provide useful boundaries for a brief survey of the literature of the Renaissance. In a crowded field, three towering figures provide some orientation. Dante, Petrarch and Machiavelli follow each other chronologically and, because each caused, as well as recorded, great changes, it is possible to plot the course of the Renaissance through them.

Dante made the bold decision to write his epic in Italian, the language of the marketplace and the tavern, instead of the dead language, Latin. The Latin works upon which Petrarch prided himself have long been forgotten, and it is his lively letters, so modern in their description of everyday life and people, which are prized today. And poor Machiavelli—the dogged, disappointed, courageous Florentine bureaucrat whose name was to enter most European languages as a synonym for all that was deceitful and devious, as though he were responsible for what he described, laid down the blueprint for modern politics.

Cast into exile: Born in 1265, Dante was an exact contemporary of Giotto, whose work he admired for its originality. But where Giotto sensibly kept out of politics, Dante involved himself wholeheartedly and was exiled for his pains during one of Florence's perennial upheavals. He never returned to Florence, eventually dying in Ravenna in 1321. Today, Florence annually sends a gift of oil to light the lamps on his tomb on the anniversary of his death.

The Divine Comedy, dealing with the great mysteries of religion, had a profound effect on Italian thought. Everybody today knows at least one line, in translation, from the inscription over the gate to Hell:

Per me ci va nella cittá dolente
Per me ci va nell' eterno dolore
Per me ci va fra la perduta gente
Lasciate ogni speranza voi ch'entrate

Preceding pages: Giorgio Vasari, *Assault on Pisa*. Left, Dante by Andrea del Castagno. Above, Boccaccio by Andrea del Castagno.

(Through me is the way into the city of sorrow
Through me is the way to eternal sadness
Through me is the way among the lost people
Abandon all hope you who enter)

Today historians ransack the *Comedy* to identify historic figures (most of them in Hell where Dante tended to consign his enemies). It is a vivid story with a meticulous chronology and philosophers and theologians still debate its significance.

Francesco Petrarch, though a Florentine, was born in Arezzo, where his parents had been exiled during the same feuds that caused Dante's expulsion. He actually met Dante, and was a lifetime disciple, but his own interests lay in the classical past. Petrarch was one of the first to hunt down and discover the lost classical literature without which the Renaissance—the "rebirth"—could not even have begun. He travelled widely, had an enormous circle of friends and kept contact with them through his letters.

It was as much through these letters, as through any formal work, that the "new learning" was disseminated. But Petrarch also shared, with his English contemporary Chaucer, the dawning awareness that the humble and the humdrum were just as legitimate literary subjects as the noble and the extraordinary. In poetry, he devised the sonnet form which took his name—Petrarchan—and which was to have a great influence on the poets of Elizabethan England.

Niccolò Machiavelli was born, in 1469, nearly a century after Petrarch's death. Viewed from almost any angle, his life looks like a failure. As a career diplomat, rising to be Secretary of the Republic, he never wielded real authority. As a convinced re-

publican, he was obliged to spend his later years currying favour with the now openly despotic Medici.

His personal appearance and habits were totally at variance with the personality that comes across in his political writings. There he is ice-cold, logical, in total command. In real life he was shabby, lecherous, adulterous. Something of that dual character comes across in his portraits: his expression is almost hangdog, furtive, yet with an inner, self-mocking integrity.

He was, despite all appearances, an idealist. His notorious book *The Prince* was only one of a large output, which includes a de-

lightful comedy, *Mandragola*, still staged today. Altogether, there are few writers who have been so misjudged as this republican who wrote the classic textbook on the practice of tyranny.

One great class of Italian literature of which there are virtually no equivalents in other countries are the urban chronicles. Almost every city had some devoted citizen carefully recording history as it happened, some achieving the status of true literature. In Florence the outstanding chroniclers were the Villani brothers, writing in the first half of the 14th century. In Siena, at about the same time, Donato di Neri and his son were compiling the *Cronaca Senese* while in Pisa Giovanni Sarcambi not only made a lively literary record but also illustrated it with exquisite little line drawings that bring the times to life.

Although innovations in literature were less spectacular than in art and architecture, there are a number of outstanding "firsts". Francesco Guicciardini wrote the first true History of Italy and Giovanni Boccaccio (1313-75) produced Europe's first novel. *The Decameron* is a bawdy jolly collection of tales told by ten young aristocrats who retreat from the 1458 plague in Florence to a country house and while away the time telling erotic stories and poems, and poking fun at the wily ways of the clergy.

The Decameron opens with a detailed and grisly description of the plague which has become a classic in its own right; many of the stories themselves were so vulgar they were often toned down considerably in translation. All demonstrate Boccaccio's well-honed skills as a story-teller.

Finally there were the truly Renaissance figures who expressed themselves in all the arts, including literature. There is Michelangelo's poetry, and Benvenuto Cellini's swash-buckling *Autobiography*. Cellini, a brilliant sculptor, part-time soldier and, by his own account, murderer was also a superb writer. He wrote a heart-stopping account of the problem of casting the exquisite *Perseus* which stands now in the Loggia dei Lanzi. Cellini records that, at a crucial moment, he ran out of metal and had to throw in the family pewter to complete the statue!

Above, Boccaccio and Petrarch, 15th-century French manuscript. Right, Niccolo Machiavelli.

FOREIGN WRITERS IN TUSCANY

"A man who has not been to Italy is always conscious of inferiority," said Dr Johnson. But many English writers had already beaten Dr Johnson to Florence. In 1737, Sir Horace Mann, Minister to the Grand Ducal Court, announced: "If I could afford it, I really would take a villa near Florence but I am afraid of it becoming a cheesecake house for all the English."

A century later, *Inglese* was a generic term for all foreigners. A hotel porter would say: "Some *Inglesi* have arrived but I don't yet know whether they are Russian or German." Given the hordes of foreign writers in Tuscany, the manager might have welcomed Dickens, Dostoyevsky or Heine.

Shelley pronounced Tuscany a "paradise of exiles" tempted by art, adventure and escape from persecution. But the exiles' motives were as varied as their prose styles. Henry James preferred real Tuscans to "one's detested fellow-pilgrims", while Leigh Hunt expressed the accepted Romantic view. "Florence has more convenience for us, more books, more fine art, more illustrious memories, and a great concourse of Englishmen". A healthy climate, picturesque peasants, cheap villas and an abundance of servants decided the issue.

In the 18th century, travellers tended to be leisured aristocrats or eccentric dilettantes. Tobias Smollett, the misanthropic writer, found nothing to admire in Tuscany. Reflecting the prejudices of his class, he did not appreciate the entrepreneurial nature of the Tuscan aristocracy, finding it undignified for "a noble to sell a pound of figs or to take money for a glass of sour wine."

He abhorred the Tuscan practice of *cicisbei* (18th-century "toy boys") and generally considered the Tuscans immoral and treacherous. Little of Tuscany finds its way into his picaresque novels, while his *Travels Through France And Italy* are unmitigated gloom. The irascible Smollett died unrepentant thanks to a surfeit of cold baths, goat's milk and opiates.

The Romantic poets brought a much-

Left, John Ruskin, "a bishop of aesthetic taste."
Above, 19th-century Florence.

needed enthusiasm to Tuscany. But even the Romantics thought of material comforts: the exiled Byron travelled "lightly" with seven servants, five carriages and additional furniture carts. Once in Florence, the patrician republican identified with Dante's exile, later alluded to in *Childe Harold's Pilgrimage*. Byron threw himself into Renaissance art and was "dazzled, drunk with Beauty" in Santa Croce.

With equal passion, he condemned the Medici Chapels as "fine frippery in great

slabs of various expensive stones, to commemorate fifty nobles and forgotten carcasses". His novelettish affair with Contessa Teresa Guiccoli gave him an exceptional entrée into Tuscan provincial society and enabled him to boast that he had not "Florenced and Romed and Galleried and Conversationed" but had "been amongst all classes, from the *conte* to the *contadino*."

His friend Shelley devoured Pisan landscapes and Livornese seascapes but had little interest in the natives. As his wife Mary said after his death, "We lived in utter solitude". *Ode To The West Wind* was inspired by the floating leaves and autumnal chill in

Florence's Cascine Park:

Drive my dead thoughts over the universe
Like withered leaves to question a new
birth.

To A Skylark was composed after a dramatic storm near the Shelley's house in Livorno. In Bagni Di Lucca, Shelley washed away his remaining Northern European inhibitions. "My custom is to undress and sit on the rocks, read Herodutus until the perspiration has subsided, and then to leap from the edge of the rock into the fountain." When Shelley drowned near La Spezia, Byron and Leigh Hunt cremated him on the beach with offerings of wine, oil and frankincense.

Tuscany soon became a pilgrimage for the later Romantic poets such as Tennyson and Wordsworth. "Emotion recollected in tranquillity" was the keynote: neither poet particularly enjoyed Tuscany at the time, yet both later idealised their experiences, as in Tennyson's execrable verse:

"O love, what hours were thine and mine,
In lands of palm and southern pine."

Although officially a diplomat in Florence, Stendhal spent most of his time absorbing Renaissance frescoes and planning his novel, *Le Rouge et le Noir*. As with Byron, the Santa Croce Effect sent Stendhal reeling: once outside, "I walked in constant fear of falling to the ground." This aesthetic sickness, now known as the Stendhal Syndrome, struck the future art critic John Ruskin. In Giotto's Campanile, the "panorama of snow and marble" filled him with "wild, sickening yearning—the desire of the moth for the star."

Unfortunately, the literary effect of sublime beauty often brought this human moth's prose to the ground with a thud. As he matured, Ruskin's critical judgement matched his passion until he became, in Harold Acton's words, "a bishop of aesthetic taste" for his generation and beyond. Towards the end of his life, Ruskin's taste became more melancholic and quirky. He declared that "the dead are Italy's real inhabitants" in a vain bid to keep the modern world away from his Tuscan museum.

Top: Lord Byron, Robert Browning, Elizabeth Barrett Browning. Middle: Samuel Johnson, Percy Bysshe Shelley, Mary Wollstonecraft Shelley. Bottom: Henry James by John Singer Sargent, D.H. Lawrence, Virginia Woolf.

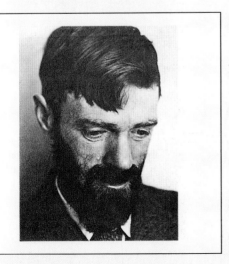

Henry James felt that Ruskin's discordant and dictatorial views prevented a visitor from appreciating the joy of Tuscan art in a changing Florence. "*Be artistic yourselves!* is the very natural reply the young Italy has at hand for English critics and censors." James was one of the few foreign writers able to see through Tuscany's literary and artistic veil. His *Portrait of Places* gives an opinionated but sensitive portrait of the region in the 1870s. "Beautiful works of art *[are]* the mere stock in trade of an impecunious but thrifty people."

If Tuscany only appears indirectly in his novels, it is because James transformed his experiences into real literature; he did not

feet, and there's a terrible deal of singing".

The most romantic mid-Victorian couple were undoubtedly the poets Elizabeth Barrett Browning and Robert Browning. Robert brought his wife to their Florentine palazzo because of her poor health. There he cunningly used local Chianti to wean Elizabeth off her long addiction to laudanum. According to Virginia Woolf, Elizabeth "tossed off a tumbler and slept the sounder."

Elizabeth attributed her improved health to the spiritual powers of the Tuscan climate. Her husband's lively erudition was stirred by Tuscan architecture, Mannerist painting and botany.

Elizabeth tolerated her husband's mild

want to be identified with the dilettante scribblers of "Little Tuscany". In *The Aspern Papers*, James included the Shelley Circle, in disguise, of course.

George Eliot also subtly transformed her Tuscan experience. Although her novel *Romola*, set in Renaissance Florence, is an unsuccessful pastiche, *Middlemarch* has a key Tuscan episode in which the puritanical "English" character battles with the life-giving "Italian" character. Dostoyevsky, exiled in a delightful spot beside the Pitti Palace, found little Tuscan inspiration for *The Idiot*. He complained that "the population of Florence spends the whole night on its

liberalism, but she herself was a fervent believer in Italian Unification. In essence, Browning loved the Florence of the past and Elizabeth loved the Florence of the future. Apart from their relationship, work and the house, neither lived much in the present nor had a burning desire to meet the natives. Both were inspired by a mythologised Florence, "When Galileo stood at night to take the vision of the stars." Their 15th-century palazzo, redecorated in Victorian style, is still a haunt of visiting writers.

This century brought E.M. Forster, with his ironic analysis of the resident English community at play. Forster's *Room With A*

View is justly famous for its portrayal of the heroine's encounter with alien culture and passions. Lost in Santa Croce without a *Baedeker*, Lucy panics and mistakes a Machiavelli monument for a saint. But gradually "the pernicious charm of Italy worked on her, and, instead of acquiring information, she began to be happy."

In her *Diaries*, Virginia Woolf looked at the Tuscan people with a cool appraising eye: "They seem stunted, dried up; like the grasshopper and with the manners of impoverished gentle people; sad, wise, tolerant, humorous." Along with many other writers on Tuscany, she sees her own image reflected in the landscape, "infinite emptiness,

reckon here men for a moment were themselves, as a plant in flower is for the moment completely itself. Then it goes off. As Florence has gone off."

World War II prevented further literary flowering, but in *War In Val D'Orcia*, Iris Origo, an Anglo-Florentine, painted a dramatic picture of the Tuscan battlefield. As a young woman, Origo was part of Lawrence's artistic circle but her instinctive understanding of the Tuscans set her apart.

Soon after the war, Dylan Thomas visited Tuscany for the first time and was entranced: "The pine hills are endless, the cypresses at the hilltop tell one all about the length of death, the woods are deep as love and full of

loneliness, silence..."

D.H. Lawrence, living in his "grave old Tuscan villa" in Scandicci, thought he was communing with the original Etruscans rather than with his farmer neighbours. "The curious, fine-nosed Tuscan face, with the half-sardonic, amber cold eyes. Their curious individuality with their clothes worn so easy and so reckless." Lawrence's philosophy dominated the landscape. In *Aaron's Rod*, his most Tuscan novel, he wrote: "I

Left, Adolfo Tommasi, *Villa di Belvedere a Crespina*. Above, Torre del Largo: "Emotion recollected in tranquillity."

goats." He led a hedonistic life, vegetating in the sun and devouring asparagus and strawberries, and wine at only 20 lire a glass which induced constant alcoholic stupor; "drinking chianti in our marble shanty, sick of vini and contadini and bambini."

Tuscany continues to befuddle the minds of visiting writers. While inspiring the writer's life, Tuscany often has a disturbing or numbing effect on literary output. The portrayal of Tuscany in contemporary foreign novels often lacks credibility. Although Tuscans are no longer portrayed as peasants or forces of nature, there is still "no foundation in natives" in literary Chiantishire.

Since the glories of Rome and the Renaissance, Italy has written little history. The head of Italy's Bureau of Statistics likens modern Italian history to a muddle, "a happy ant-heap where everyone is running about and no one is in control."

The alternative is the "strong man" view of recent history, as expressed in the Florentine saying, "whose bread and cheese I eat, to his tune I dance." But, while Rome danced to martial music, Tuscany sometimes starved or burned.

Tuscany has been buffeted rather than enriched by its recent past. Well-kept war memorials in shabby towns attest to the loss of two generations, one abroad and one at home. Look at Asciano, a village dwarfed by its Carabinieri stronghold, built by Mussolini and still used to maintain order. Visit Montisi, where for the price of a drink, locals will describe the German bombing of the village tower, a story complete with sound effects, gestures and genuine sorrow. Ask Florentines why the medieval houses on the south side of the Arno are lost forever.

Bold flourish: The welding of Tuscans into Italians started promisingly enough but the end result is still only to be seen abroad or at international football matches. Piazza della Repubblica, built in 1865 to celebrate Florence's brief spell as Italian capital, remains a bold flourish of nationhood. But when the capital of the new nation was transferred to Rome, Tuscan allegiance remained in Tuscany.

Unification, under the leadership of Cavour, a French-speaking Piedmontese, was seen as a foreign threat to the *de facto* sovereignty of Florence and the smaller city states. Defenders of the *Risorgimento*, the Movement for Italian Unification, appealed to nascent patriotism. Critics of Unification cited Dante's pleas to Tuscan liberty before both sides settled down to the serious business of subverting the power of the new rulers.

Preceding pages: leafy Roman road. Left, *Fare bella figura*; young bloods pose in front of Arezzo cathedral. Above, Siena *Palio*.

Unification represented a missed chance for Italy. By failing to help shape a national identity, Tuscans also fell victim to a "strong man's" clearer vision. Even before World War I, Mussolini was making inflammatory speeches while a weak parliament practised the art of "timely resignation", a ploy used ever since to stage-manage a new coalition.

Although the pre-war Tuscan economy thrived under weak government, it was no match for growing social pressures and a deepening gulf between society and state.

With or without policies, one of the last liberal governments blundered into World War I.

Italy's unpopular late entry cost Tuscan lives and support. The pyrrhic victory was exacerbated by a political power vacuum, economic problems and a revolutionary working class. Benito Mussolini, from neighbouring Emilia, wasted no opportunity in proclaiming, "Governing Italy is not only impossible, it is useless", before proceeding to govern it impossibly but fairly usefully for 20 years.

By 1922, the corporate state was literally under construction. The economic benefits lasted until 1929 but the aesthetic effects linger on in functionally "improved" cities all over Tuscany. Florence Station, from which trains presumably ran on time, was the first Functionalist station in Italy. At the outbreak of World War II, most Tuscans were cautiously neutral. Mussolini, despite having signed the Pact of Steel with Germany, did not enter the war until late 1940, after the fall of France. By 1943 the North was under German control but the Allies were progressing northwards from Sicily. Allied bombing, German entrenchment and an emerging Tuscan Resistance transformed Tuscany into a battleground.

Anti-Fascist cells had been secretly set up by the Communists and Catholics in key towns under German and neo-Fascist control. Florence was split: while it was the intellectual centre of the Resistance it also harboured strong Fascist sympathisers.

Even after the city was captured by the Allies, individual Fascists held out, firing from the rooftops at the citizens below. Surprising loyalties emerged: while the Director of the British Institute was a known Fascist sympathiser, the German Consul risked his life to protect Florentines who had been denounced. After the Liberation he was granted the Freedom of the City.

Florence was liberated in August 1943 but Mussolini and the German forces survived the winter behind the so-called "Gothic Line" in the Appenines.

Apart from Florence, the partisans were very active in the Monte Amiata area; also in the Val d'Orcia where Iris Origo, an Englishwoman married to an Italian Marchese, sheltered many refugees and prisoners of war in her villa, La Foce. "In the last few days," she wrote, "I have seen Radicofani and Cortignano destroyed, the countryside and farms studded with shell holes, girls raped, and human beings and cattle killed. Otherwise the events of the last week have had little effect upon either side; it is the civilians who have suffered."

Nor were the Allies blameless. The modernity of Grosseto, Livorno and Pisa owes much to Allied bombing in 1943.

The British War Office reports naturally exonerate the Allies: "No damage of any significance is attributable to Allied action *(in Florence)*." The Allies issued their troops with booklets listing historic buildings to be protected but baulked at Florence: "The whole city of Florence must rank as a work of art of the first importance." According to one report, "The great monuments, nearly all of which lie north of the river, escaped practically undamaged because, though the enemy held the northern bank against an advance, our troops deliberately refrained from firing upon them."

Feats of Allied bravery included the penetration of enemy lines via the Pitti Palace-Uffizi passageway, a secret route used by the Medici in similar crises. Florence nevertheless lost bridges, entire streets, libraries, churches, palazzi, paintings, and Tuscan lives.

But in contrast to the "mutilated victory" of 1919, it could be said that Italy had lost the war but won the peace. Massimo Salvadore, a supporter of the partisans in Florence, saw the war as character building: "Without it the Italians would surely have sunk into a morass of low politics and intrigues." That was still to come.

The political scene: Tuscans often compare their political system to the Leaning Tower of Pisa, an object of curiosity precisely because it defies appearances and does not fall down. The belltower is also an apt symbol of *Campanilismo*, the attachment to one's region.

In the 1950s, Senator Fanfani, four times Prime Minister, had the clout to cause a bulge in the Florence-Rome motorway. In wanting to bring the motorway nearer Arezzo, his home town, Fanfani showed himself a true Tuscan.

True Tuscans are provincial, conservative and independent. Still, Christian Democracy at national level and Communism at regional level is a curious recipe for success. Not that a Tuscan Communist fits an easy stereotype. She may wear Ferragamo, own a hotel and a BMW but she goes to work on a *motorino*. Except for local history, she is not well-read and prefers music and art anyway. Although Catholic and conservative, she votes Social-

ual liberty. Apart from family and local roots, the couple share nothing except political disaffection.

The 1987 vote for "Cicciolina", bare-breasted porn star and Rome member of parliament, was a protest vote against all politicians. Almost 50 post-war governments have come and gone. However, most faces remain the same, older but no wiser. Giulio Andreotti, known for obvious reasons as *Il Volpe* ("the fox"), has proved his cunning in 28 administrations.

Senior party leaders tend to die in office, whether by fair means or foul. Governments suffer from predictability, not instability; from opportunism, not lack of opportunity.

ist in national elections and would be afraid to see the Communists in government.

Her cousin may run his own company and have a Filipino maid but he socialises with his workers rather than with other managers. Although he does not declare all his profits, he is scrupulous about implementing guidelines on reduced working hours. He attaches more value to "personal culture" than to politics. He flirts with the radicals because of their commitment to referenda and individ-

So what's new, apart from "Cicciolina"? The "ungovernability" of Italy is not new. The 1946 Italian Constitution provides for a parliament elected under proportional representation. Italy's unique ungovernability does not lie in its flawed institutions but in its flawed administrations and administrators. Parliament is a cosy fiction, better known for its fish restaurant than for the quality or frequency of its debates. When the "beach season" begins, all roads lead out of Rome.

As far as Italians are concerned, politicians might just as well remain on the beach all year. Tuscans share the Italian belief that "government governs best that governs

Left, Convent schoolgirls. Right, 19th-century Florence.

least." In this sense, Italians have the government they deserve.

The ideal Italian solution has been likened to an orchestra in which every party could play separately or collectively as required. Indeed, Florence is run efficiently along similar lines by the former head of the Paris Opera House.

Partitocrazia, the party system, has supplanted democracy. The long arm of the party stretches from government to public corporations, industry, banking, the judiciary and the media. Even RAI Television is split according to the "64311" party formula: six slices of the media cake to the Christian Democrats; four to the Communists; three to

DC rests on its laurels as the only official opposition to Fascism and has seen itself as the only governing party ever since. At the outset of the Cold War, it excluded the Communists from power and despite a brief flirtation with power-sharing before Moro's death, it no longer knows what to do with its power except keep it.

There are allegations of past ballot-rigging and corruption, including involvement in the 1981 Vatican banking and masonic scandals. The DC retorts that the electorate wants the Communists in the provinces but the DC in government.

Real change is rare and dangerous in Italian politics. When Moro was kidnapped and

the Socialists; three to minor parties. But the reality of party power is genuinely subversive: the fostering of an "old boy network" based on *clientelismo*, political patronage and *raccomandazione*, advancement through preferment. In return for political support, an important "client" may expect a seat on the board of a state company; a lesser "client" can expect a lucrative building contract. Every "client" expects preferment and easy access to the "boss". These clients are an MP's real constituents; their preferred policies are his hidden agenda.

In national politics the Christian Democrats (DC) have always counted most. The

murdered in 1978, his body was dumped halfway between the Christian Democrat and Communist headquarters. This was a cruel joke to ridicule the "historic compromise", the DC attempt to involve the Communists in government. Although Moro's death is attributed to the Red Brigades, the message is that politicians tamper with political balance at their peril.

The dynamic Socialist Party (PSI), reborn under Craxi, presents itself as a new alternative. It is also victim of the old joke, "It doesn't know what it wants but it wants it right away." The Communist Party, (PC), often called "a Trojan horse in a bourgeois citadel", is at least clear that its one aim since 1944 has been to govern. After leading the Resistance, the PC was rewarded by early participation in coalitions and by exclusion from power until 1970.

Given the level of national opposition both to the PC and to devolution, the Party has had to evolve an aggressively pro-regionalist stance. The reward is the "red belt" across central Italy run by PC coalitions since the first regional elections in 1970.

Red Tuscany is the central strand between Emilia Romagna's model economy and rural Umbria. The "red" regions tend to be the the most efficient and least corrupt in Italy. If the Communists are untainted, cynics attrib-

As an alienated electorate, Tuscans retreat into regionalism when faced with a central government which is out of touch with their concerns. Historically, Tuscans see leaders, even faceless ones, as a threat to liberty—often with good reason. When Lorenzo de' Medici was on his deathbed, Savnarola reputedly said, "Lastly you must restore liberty to the people of Florence"—whereupon Lorenzo looked scornful and died soon after.

Tuscans still balance their love of liberty against fears of political instability. The odd solution is in keeping with their innate conservatism and desire for regional independence. In the end, provincialism rides roughshod over national politics.

ute this to lack of opportunity rather than to inherent purity. But until the PC plays an important role in national government, the argument for "absolute powerlessness corrupts absolutely" remains unproven.

The Tuscan left believes in a broad but increasingly secular church. Civic culture, regional pride and fierce individualism form the real faith. The power of the Left is as much a reflection of regional hostility to Roman centralisation as an espousal of Communist or Socialist principles.

Left, Pitigliano street scene; the narrowness and depth of urban life. Above, Carabinieri at play.

Communist Festa dell'Unita celebrations are held all over Tuscany in the summer. The Party tone is set by sombre banners of Berlinguer and Che Guevara but is soon offset by the party mood. As elegantly dressed locals eat *bistecca alla fiorentina* and down Galestro, the talk is of holiday homes, the accountant's bill and local gossip.

Even in "red belt" Tuscany, the region's most popular newspaper is the right-wing but regional *La Nazione*, not the left-wing but national *La Repubblica*. How could a Roman product compete with a Florentine/Sienese masterpiece?

Economic realities: Tuscany and Florence

are doing well but could do better. The Mayor of Florence, Massimo Bogianckino, put it more bluntly: "We have lost the battle with Rome and Milan and we are far less productive than Prato *[the booming textile town west of Florence]*. Florentines are intelligent and honest but while they talk, others produce."

The quality of life in historic town centres is excellent and Tuscans are not prepared to jeopardise it for a little more heavy industry. Topography also helps preserve the past: hill-top towns cannot expand so development is restricted to the plains or, in Florence's case, to its future satellite city.

In recent times, the Italian economy has moved slowly but finished fast. Tuscany followed this pattern with a late Industrial Revolution in the 1880s and a slow post-war recovery in the "long boom" of 1958-63. High labour costs in the 1960s and energy costs in the 1970s slowed down progress. Strikes, housing crises and outbreaks of terrorism did the rest.

But in 1987 came the much-publicised *Sorpasso*, or "overtaking", when the Italian economy outstripped its British and French rivals. Tuscany's contribution to Italy's jump was to slip smoothly from a rural to an industrialised society.

Luckily Tuscany's traditional industries show no signs of going out of fashion. Prato is living proof that the cloth trade was not just a 12th-century fad. Although its textile industry was fully mechanised in 1850, it still feels like a closed shop run by rich Guelf merchants. It is a highly skilled industry which remains a collection of family businesses. Florentine design genius emerges naturally in the styling of Ferragamo, Gucci and Pucci. Nor did the great Renaissance families all die out. Strozzi is still an important name in Florentine banking and business circles, as is Frescobaldi in the wine trade and Antinori in wine and food. Many popular medieval industries are still minor classics: Nannini's spicy panforte comes complete with its 15th-century recipe. The traditional craft industries are also thriving: Volterra's chess sets; intricate Florentine gold jewellery; simple terracotta vases; della Robbia style ceramics; glassware at Empoli.

These privately run industries cater to all tastes: generally tourists prefer the old and Tuscans the new. In Carrara, the marble

cutters are proud to tell you that Michelangelo selected marble from quarries that now produce a nice line in bathroom suites.

Such small and medium-sized firms are in the most dynamic section of the Tuscan economy: the private sector. Despite the pervasive influence of such giants as Fiat's Agnelli and Montedison's Gardini, the new managerial class consists of *padroncini*, "little bosses", drawn from the traditionally independent and affluent *borghesia*. It is strong in manufacture, the crafts, the retail trade and tourism.

Tuscans have a civilised approach to tourism because they take leisure seriously. Given the vast "black economy", such *pa-*

droncini are probably running a hotel by day and a restaurant by night.

The public sector has a high profile but low prestige in Tuscany. Most heavy industry is state-owned and run by *enti*, public authorities. IRI, the Institute for Industrial Recovery and ENI, the state energy company, run the region without either energy or industry. IRI, founded in 1933 by Mussolini to protect endangered or unwieldy industries, is a Christian Democrat stronghold. It is also the largest service and investment company in Europe.

Cynics say that IRI is not state-owned but that the state is IRI-owned. It runs banks, telecommunications, RAI TV, shipbuilding at Livorno and iron and steel works at Piombino. There have been iron settlements on the Tuscan coast for 3,000 years. Etruscans transported iron ore from Elba, the island they named 'Ilva' or 'iron,' and smelted it on the mainland. Piombino's iron and steel plant is now the second largest in Italy. Although by 1983 Italy's steel capacity rivalled Japan, in recent years the EEC has imposed reductions.

ENI, founded in 1953, is another politically shackled conglomerate, a Socialist citadel. This oil and chemicals giant runs power stations in the Val d'Arno area. ENEL, the state electricity corporation, is a

key Tuscan employer. Since Chernobyl, however, Tuscans' enthusiasm for nuclear power has waned and and in a 1987 referendum Italians voted overwhelmingly for a freeze on planned stations. Since then, ENEL's profit base has looked less secure and the head of ENEL has had to address Green Party meetings and eat plenty of lettuce in public.

The only signs of nuclear proliferation are those announcing Nuclear-Free Zones. But ENEL's geothermal experiments at Lardarello, near Volterra, provoke no worries. In this, the biggest experimental site in Italy, heat from Monte Amiata's extinct volcano is being tapped commercially. The severity of Volterra's mountain ridge and the strong smell of sulphur make it a dramatic but barren location.

It is easy to see Tuscan agriculture as a victim rather than a beneficiary of economic growth: a mass exodus from the land occurred between 1951-71. Although large-scale wheat and cattle farming have drawn many farmers back to the fertile Val d'Arno and Val di Chiana, traditional Tuscan farming is labour-intensive and relatively unmechanised.

But 35 years of industrial development have not erased three millennia of rural settlement. The Romans perfected the mix of grain and tree crops and this *coltura promiscua* is still characteristic of modern Tuscan farmscapes. The olive groves at Lucca date back to Roman times and Elban wine was linked to Etruscan bacchic rites.

Contrary to popular belief, most wine-growing is small-scale, grown on terraced slopes unsuitable for other crops. Although Chianti is the wine best known abroad, it is less valued by Tuscans than sweet Vin Santo, rich Brunello, amber Vernaccia or the sandalwood fragrance of Vino Nobile.

For this continuity of land use, Tuscans have much to thank their medieval *Mezzadria* or sharecropping system which brought security of tenure to the peasants. New *Mezzadria* contracts were officially banned in 1978 but the old patron-client relationship continues to exert a pull.

The "exodus from the land" is giving way to the "flight from the city" as urban Tuscans appreciate the attractions of old farmhouses in upland settings. Part-time farming, property inheritance, gentrification and the dramatic increase in second-home ownership are also winning a new population.

Likewise, the Government has re-thought its 1980s metropolitan slant and is now promoting the countryside, medium-sized towns and the revival of the *centro storico* or historic town centre. The region's harmonious blend of craft, service and manufacturing industries makes Tuscany a model economy. Its cultural heritage and natural beauties also make it a highly desirable tourist destination.

Left, the Tuscan nose. Above, portrait of Lorenzo de' Medici, a classic Medici profile.

CHIANTISHIRE

The doyen of Anglo-Florentine society, Sir Harold Acton, calls his adopted home, "a sunny place for shady people". The name "Chiantishire" is redolent of the dullness and domesticity of the English provinces. Not by chance is Tuscany twinned with Kent, the Garden of England and the guardian of Englishness.

Chiantishire is an archipelago of foreign islands. In the Chianti hills German shepherdesses tend errant sheep; bucolic Swiss cheesemakers produce pecorino cheese; French winemakers have abandoned Beaujolais for Brunello, while Ireland's Guinness family drink their estate wine instead of beer. Meanwhile the English literary set paces rural lanes and olive groves. Somehow the novelist Muriel Spark fails to encounter Peter Porter reciting his poetry, Miriam Margolyes rehearsing her latest part, Germaine Greer analysing the socio-sexual scene or John Mortimer pulling them all into a Chiantishire novel.

Everyone out of the mainstream feels at home in Chiantishire. All residents have in common is a firm avoidance of their native land and an antipathy towards their fellow countrymen. Art lovers are there to follow the Ghirlandaio trail while their offspring are enrolled on Renaissance "painting by numbers" courses in Florence. Art historians are there to remind Tuscans that, despite Michelangelo's useful contribution, Ruskin, Burckhardt and Berenson invented the Renaissance, and with it Tuscan tourism.

Academics on sabbatical enjoy a mental convalescence from real life. Literati scribble in the belief that beauty and art are contagious. Hedonists abandon a long British winter for drunken November lunches on the terrace. Scholarly eccentrics finish off theses about the help given by English Florentines to Mussolini's Blackshirts, topics inappropriate to Communist Tuscany. Foodies are simply there to add Tuscan antipasti to their repertoire.

Each major town has its own foreign fanclub mimicking Tuscan City State rivalry. It usually takes 10 years for an incomer to become an Anglo-Florentine, but this "citizenship" can take a month if one is famous, rich, beautiful or related to Harold Acton. Every year up to 10,000 British and 15,000 Americans try to complete the transformation in Florence alone. While Florence and Siena have captured the intellectual high ground, real Chiantishire blooms best in the countryside. The location is inevitably one of Tuscany's 200,000 isolated farms, often bought from a smart *contadino* who has left a hand-to-mouth existence for a luxury town house. Iris Origo, the Anglo-Tuscan writer, noted the transformation of the farm's stone

fireplace and marble floors into a chintz sitting room with framed prints, library books and "a fragrance of home-made scones and freshly-made tea. But no Italian can warm the tea-pot properly, my dear."

For the incomer, there are three golden rules: to eulogise the countryside, to be self-sufficient and to interact well with the natives. Enter the typical Chiantishire family with their light skin, straw hats, dark glasses, blazers and white linen trousers. When they arrive, their farmhouse, set at the end of a rough dirt track, is furnished with rustic minimalism. After unpacking the stocks of Irish linen, Lipton's tea, Colman's mustard, paint-brushes and mosquito-repellent, they admire the converted stables and go to sleep on the stone benches, formerly ox stalls. A night of discomfort effects a change of heart.

The first week is spent waxing lyrical about the chiaroscuro quality of Tuscan light, the silvery olive groves, the Matteo di Giovanni fresco in the local church, the clarity of the water. The only problem is that the Medicean well runs dry whenever the lavatory chain is pulled. Chopping wood with a rusty axe is not easy but they persevere…

The third week is spent in bed recovering from a mystery virus caught from bacteria in the well water. Gianni's rough *rosso dei Cacciaconti* provides much relief. The lights keep flickering if the refrigerator and the grill are on simultaneously. The washing machine fails in sympathy. A freak summer storm transforms the dirt track into a mud bath and, on the way to the *alimentari* shop

Preceding pages: the Chianti hills. Left, making *vin santo*; "There's no point in Italy when it's not being picturesque." Above, mental convalescence from real life. Giovanni Fattori, *Valerio Biondi at Castiglioncello.*

via the communal wash house, the car gets bogged down. Cold and hungry, they despairingly eat unripe olives and burn damp olive branches. As time passes, language is less of a problem: they now pick up some *acqua* and Earl Grey in the *supermercato*, but return home to find local hunters threatening the baby for getting in their line of fire.

After a year, they have the social system worked out: they buy overpriced wine from the impoverished local marchese, and individual carrot tops and mouldy funghi from the peasants. An understanding with the shopkeepers allows them to be cheated often but never by large amounts: in return, Anita will take phone messages, Gianni will hold the mail, Marco will no longer let the car tyres down, and the hunters will stop taking pot shots at the baby. In exchange for regular supplies of Johnny Walker whisky, the carabinieri will curtail their dawn raids in search of drugs or irregularities in the family's residence permits.

They now speak Italian in private but revert to loud English in front of the *contadini*. Quintessentially English, the wife reminds her husband to "put the *scarico* out for the dustmen, dear." Deep down, she knows there are no dustmen and that her husband will dump it over the nearest hill like all the other villagers. The local stream is usually full of indestructible blue plastic bags.Life is full of unexpected joys: the family is invited to join the locals in the olive harvest and to feast on *bruschetti* drenched in freshly-pressed olive oil. In the butcher's, the *macellaio* now laughs at her pathetic jokes: "A bird in the hand is worth two in the bush," she says as she takes a sparrow instead of the quail she had tried to buy.

The gulf between the residents and their visitors grows. They are quietly triumphant when English guests accuse them of "going native". Visitors are aghast at relying on faulty electricity, polluted well water and crafty shopkeepers. One quotes a character in a John Mortimer book, *Summer's Lease*, who proclaims: "There's no point in Italy when it's not being picturesque." But the English, like Michelangelo, accept the agony with the ecstasy.

WINE WARS

The wicker-covered Chianti flask called, as it happens, a *fiasco*, is rarer these days in Italian restaurants than red-and-white check tablecloths. This emblem of the early days of Tuscan vine culture has been superseded by an elegant square-shouldered bottle, reflecting the upgrading in quality of one of Italy's best-known wines.

If you order wine in a bar or restaurant in Tuscany, you will almost certainly be served the local *vino da tavola* (table wine) in an unlabelled jug or bottle. It is always drinkable and often very good. Now however, Tuscany is much more conscious of its standing as a producer of higher quality DOC (*Denominazione di Origine Controllata*) wines and increasingly you will find a sophisticated list of superior Tuscan vintages.

Nevertheless Tuscany *is* still Chianti. Of this there is little doubt—to the chagrin of producers of the region's other fine wines. But Chianti passed through a stormy period in the late 1970s and 1980s which caused many to despair of its ever being able to live up to the image that had been created for it. The problems stemmed from the laudable, and at first successful, attempts to control standards of wine production in this extensive area.

Winning formula: The heart of the Chianti district stretches in a large oval between Florence and Siena and there are branches extending west towards Lucca and Pisa, south to Montalcino, southeast to Montepulciano, east to Arezzo and past Pontassieve, and north past Pistoia. The heartland is called Chianti Classico, and it is over this territory that concern for quality has longest been evident.

The first move was in the mid-18th century when Barone Bettino Ricasoli, who later became the second Prime Minister of united Italy, laid down the formula for making the wine. It involved a blend of four grape varieties in specified proportions, two of which were white.

It also reaffirmed the traditional practice of *governo*, which involves keeping some grapes back during the harvest and leaving them to dry gently so that, when the main body of the wine has finished its fermentation, the reserved grapes can be added to the vat. This provokes a second fermentation, said to make the wine softer and rounder, but which mainly makes it livelier and ready to drink sooner.

The control of Chianti went a stage further in 1924 when a consortium, the Consorzio Chianti Classico, was founded to control production. The Consorzio confirmed the Ricasoli blend and added stipulations on minimum alcohol, minimum ageing and so on. Membership of the Consorzio was voluntary but it offered producers advice and promised efforts to stamp out the burgeoning amount of wine from outside the region calling itself "chianti". So most producers joined.

To signify that a bottle was "Consorzio-approved", a special sticker was placed round its neck. These stickers carried the symbol of the Consorzio, a black rooster (*gallo nero*), and the name Gallo Nero soon became synonymous with Chianti Classico.

Soon afterwards the satellite Chianti zones—Montalbano, Colline Pisane, Colli Senesi, Colli Aretini, Rufina and Colli Fiorentini—banded together to form their own consorzio, called Chianti Putto, with its symbol a *putto* or cherub.

Once it became part of the European Community, Italy had to develop a country-wide wine law. In line with EC regulations "quality" wines were designated *Denominazione di Origine Controllata* (DOC), which distinguished them from their "lesser" brethren, called just *vino da tavola*. In Chianti the law more or less followed what the Consorzi had already specified. By the 1970s, Chianti producers were hemmed in by tradition, national law and Consorzio rules, to making wines in one specific way.

The problem was that this approach did not produce the quality or style of wine they wanted. The best quality grape of Tuscany is Sangiovese, but producers were restricted to using between 50 and 80 percent of it; white grapes and *governo* make for a light wine for early drinking, but they wanted a fuller wine that would age well.

The solution was approached in typical Italian fashion. There were those who perpetuated the image of quality while lowering standards, cutting corners and engaging in a sales war that resulted in the price of Chianti dropping so low that its production was either fraudulent or loss-making.

There were others who decided to ignore the law and made high-quality Chianti as they believed it should be made, with whatever grapes they reckoned worthwhile. There were those who made much less Chianti and put their efforts into producing fine

One great give-away was always the emergence of a white wine. Tuscany is predominantly a red wine zone and new whites nearly always signified the producer was finding a profitable use for all those white grapes he was no longer putting into his Chianti.

Salvation came in 1984 when Chianti joined the élite that was entitled to call its wines DOCG, the G standing for *e garantita*. The change gave the chance for the revamp of the regulations that was so needed and it was willingly, if argumentatively, embraced.

Since 1984 Chianti has been improving beyond recognition. It was, though, too late

wine untrammelled by legal constraints; they gave each a *nome di fantasia* and sold it as *vino da tavola* but at a suitably high price. There were also just a few who soldiered on trying to make the best Chianti they could within the law.

Finding out what exactly each producer was doing required more than a little detective work. All swore their Chianti was both excellent and legal. To discover what they really did required interpreting the glint in their eyes as they spoke, and probably deferring the investigation until they felt more confident of their interrogator—perhaps over lunch.

to prevent firm establishment of a plethora of individually named, costly *vini da tavola*, dubbed "supertuscans". The wine list of any restaurant in central Tuscany will certainly include Chianti. It will probably also contain one or more names like Coltassala, Flaccianello, Mormoreto, Tavernelle, Tignanello, Le Pergole Torte—the list is endless.

These are often wines made solely with Sangiovese, or Sangioveto, a superior clone. Sometimes they are a blend of Sangiovese and Cabernet Sauvignon, the French grape which gives excellent results in Tuscany. They are occasionally made solely with Cabernet. The only way to divine their constituents is to scan the back label (which may not reveal all) or to ask.

To add a little spice to the quest for good drinking, a single name on a wine list will not necessarily signify a "supertuscan". Numerous estates have a particular vineyard whose wine, when kept separate, is always better than the rest. Each is labelled with its vineyard name as well as its official designation: Chianti or Chianti Classico. Tuscans are expected to know that Montesodi, for example, is a particular *cru* (single vineyard wine) of Chianti Rufina from the Frescobaldi estate. So the one word is often all that is put on the list. In shops, where the label can be scanned, life is easier.

rated by great celebrations, but this is rarely the case. The vintage is a nerve-racking period and nail biting is seen more often than singing and dancing. In late September and October the weather can be erratic and a rainy squall can turn perfectly ripe concentrated bunches into a dilute, rotting mass.

Even when the harvest is successfully completed, there is little time to relax. A year's livelihood and several years' reputation is tied up in the large vats of bubbling grape juice and they require constant attention and monitoring. Producers with rings round their eyes are far more likely to have been up all night attending to their wine than carousing.

The general, but not infallible, rule of thumb is that Classico is better than non-Classico. A good non-Classico producer can always outclass an average Classico estate. On the better, more matured, wines the label will state *Riserva*, which indicates the wine has been aged at least three years, mainly in oak. For easy drinking, lively Chianti non-*Riserva*, informally called *normale*, comes into its own.

One would have thought that the harvest of a wine of such renown would be commemo-

A regional celebration is impossible as the vintage, which can last three weeks or so, starts and finishes at different times in different zones. Then there are the Vin Santo grapes to guard.

Vin Santo ("holy wine") is a dessert wine made all over Tuscany from white Trebbiano and Malvasia grapes. Once picked, they are dried slowly, weather permitting, either hanging, or on straw mats, or in shallow stacked crates. Six weeks to four months later, raisin-like, they are pressed and the small amount of concentrated, sweet juice that results is put into small barrels. There it slowly ferments and matures, untouched, for

Left, the traditional Chianti *fiasco*. Above, more Chianti.

several years. Most Vin Santo is sweet, some dry. Nearly all is rare, expensive and often a real treat. It is often served at the end of a meal with *biscotti sechi*, hard almond biscuits to be dunked in the sweet golden wine.

Fierce debate: Red wine in Tuscany is still inextricably linked with Chianti, but it shouldn't be. It really ought to be linked with the Sangiovese grape. Chianti, well diffused though it is, is not Tuscany's only red wine; Sangiovese is far and away the predominant grape of the entire region, despite occasional outcrops of Cabernet Sauvignon. There are several clones of the grape planted: Sangioveto, Sangiovese Grosso, Sangiovese Piccolo, Prugnolo, Brunello and so on. A fierce

debate rages constantly about which are superior and which are similar.

Brunello is found around the town of Montalcino, well south of Siena. The wine, Brunello di Montalcino, is without doubt one of Italy's best, though it has a short history, dating back to 1870. It was the result of a firm conviction of Ferrucio Biondi-Santi, then only 20 years old, who put his beliefs into action, and his descendants have kept the name Biondi-Santi in the forefront of the wine's reputation. Lack of tradition can be a disadvantage—but there are advantages too. One of Brunello di Montalcino's prescribed characteristics is a long minimum

ageing period (four years, three and a half of them in oak).

This was felt by some to be too long for all but the grandest wines, which then need to mature longer in the bottle. So a younger wine, Rosso di Montalcino, was swiftly created in the same style. The two co-exist comfortably and the risk of discontented producers "bending" the law has been avoided. Chianti's traditions could never have accommodated such flexibility.

The Prugnolo clone of Sangiovese predominates further east and produces Vino Nobile di Montepulciano around the town of the same name. Vino Nobile may be best described as a half way house between Brunello di Montalcino and Chianti Classico. Like both these wines it has been decreed DOCG, giving Tuscany three of the first five wines in Italy so elevated.

Whites in Tuscany take very much second place. They are light, simple and pleasant but generally, despite continual improvements, could not be described as "great". Most are based on Trebbiano and Malvasia grapes and are named after the locality of their origin; many (like Galestro) have resulted from the need to use the white grapes no longer needed for Chianti production.

The main exception is the dry, elegant, but quite full-bodied Vernaccia di San Gimignano. Of which Michelangelo apparently said: "It kisses, licks, bites, thrusts and stings." The grape name Vernaccia crops up in a few parts of Italy but each bears no relation to the others: Vernaccia seems to imply no more than a "local" grape.

The other exception is very much the great fashion of the 1980s: the French variety Chardonnay. More and more producers have turned over one or more plots to the grape, many invested in small, new oak barrels from France, called *barriques*, to mature the wines, and whoops of delight could be heard all over Tuscany as the results started appearing.

Traditionalists who believe that all good things in Tuscany should be Tuscan in origin either had to let the excitement pass them by—unthinkable—or else retire to the libraries to try to prove that Chardonnay was planted in Tuscany long ago after all.

Above, wine festival to sample the new vintage. Right, freshly picked green olives.

LIQUID GOLD

Tuscany's olive oil has long been famous for its quality and excellent flavour and texture. The humid, temperate climate of the Tuscan hills is especially suitable for growing olives and the silvery gnarled branches of the trees, hung with white nets before harvest, are as characteristic a sight as vines or cypresses.

The oil produced is so good that *bruschetta*, a quintessential Tuscan dish, consists simply of a slice of bread, toasted, rubbed with garlic and trickled with thick green olive oil of the best possible quality. Tuscans are passionate about olive oil; they believe it is the most important cooking ingredient, its flavour and strength fundamentally affecting the final dish.

They are immensely proud of their oil, too; wherever you go locals will claim that *their* olive oil is the very best available. It is possible to become quite a connoisseur; there is a restaurant in Grosseto, *Enoteca Ombrone*, which has a cellar of olive oils, stocking over 40 varieties, and you can sample and compare them all at the table.

Olive's are grown all over Italy. As a general rule, the flavour of the oil becomes heavier and stronger further south. In the north it is at its lightest and most delicate. Oils such as those available in the Lake Garda area are completely different to Sicilian oils. Even within the boundaries of Tuscany itself, the oils can vary enormously in sweetness, fruitiness, flavour and colour from deep green to light gold. An olive oil from Siena or Florence may appear quite different from the produce of Lucca or Grosseto.

In Tuscany the olive harvest begins in November or December and the olives are picked and processed during the following weeks. Some olives are picked while green, but usually they have turned almost black before they are picked for oil. Olives should always be picked by hand if possible. To make sure that not a single one is lost, the ground underneath the gnarled trees is covered in fine nets so that the olives fall down into them and can be gathered up more easily.

The technique of picking olives is not unlike

milking a cow. The end of each small branch is held firmly in one hand while the other hand pulls downwards and strips off olives, leaves and twigs to let them fall on to the ground. It is a long and laborious task, but the machine has yet to be invented which can accomplish the job quite as effectively as the human hand.

Where feelings surrounding the final product run so passionately, nobody really complains about this. There is an immense feeling of pride and love connected to the pressing of olive oil; it is, after all, the one food element which comes closest to maternal milk for its composition of fats and vitamins.

After the olives are picked, they are taken to a local mill where they are pressed, traditionally by stone, nowadays more commonly using steel rollers. The initial "cold pressing" produces the very best and most expensive oils; thereafter the mash is pressed using heat which produces a much greater yield but inferior oil. The quality of olive oil is measured by its acid content; the finest being Extra Virgin with an acid level no higher than one percent, followed by *Soprafino*, *Fino* and Virgin olive oil.

Olive oil, like wine, is alive, with different characteristics depending on the year it is made and the area where the olives are grown. It goes rancid fairly quickly and should therefore be used within a year of its pressing. Also, it absorbs smells and flavours very easily, which means it must be stored with some care—and away from anything strong smelling or tasting such as garlic or onions.

Tuscan cooks use olive oil all the time, brushed on to meat for grilling and roasting, raw to dress salads or pour over warm vegetables or potatoes, trickled into soups and stews before serving, and for deep frying sweet cakes and fritters. The quality of oil chosen depends on what it is used for; richer oils are more suitable when the flavour is likely to dominate the dish.

A few excellent oils worth seeking out are Extra Vergine di Scansano, Extra Vergine di Macchiascandona, Extra Vergine di Montalcino, Extra Vergine di Seggiano cru Querciole, Extra Vergine del Chianti, Extra Vergine di San Gimignano cru Montenidoli, and Extra Vergine Badia a Coltibuono.

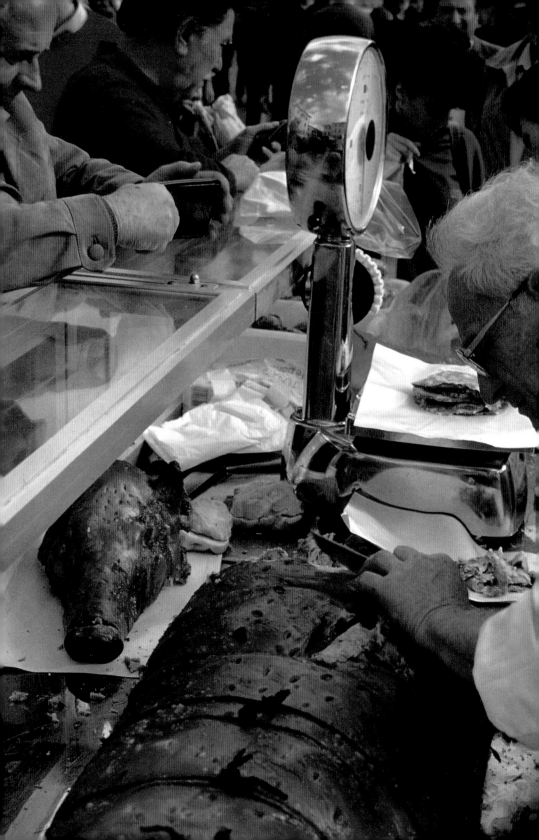

A TASTE OF TUSCANY

What is immediately striking about Tuscan food is that, no matter what you are eating or where you are eating it, it is always very rustic, very simple, designed to nourish the soul and the spirit as much as the body.

Tuscan cooking is never elaborate or excessive; there are no fussy decorations, complicated reductions of sauces or subtly blended flavours. But there is a basic, honest simplicity about their dishes which have made them popular for centuries the world over.

Tuscany produces its own inimitable versions of Italian staples: pasta dishes with gamey sauces of hare, wild boar, even porcupine; *polenta* with fresh *funghi*; rabbit or roast baby goat. But along with a particular attitude to food, Tuscany also has many dishes and delicacies unique to the region.

Hearty stews: Tuscans are known as *Toscani Mangiafagiolii*—bean eaters, because the versatile pulse is used so much in local specialities—adding a velvety smooth texture as only well-cooked beans can. Rich thick soups and hearty bean stews are served in rustic terracotta pots, often enhanced with a trickle of thick green olive oil added at the table.

Tuscan cooks favour cooking methods that can be carried out on a large scale and preferably out of doors—the spit or grill over an open wood fire is something you will come across in courtyards behind chic Florentine restaurants or in the garden of countryside *trattorie*. Fresh herbs like sage, rosemary and basil, are used, as they grow, in abundance.

The most important Tuscan meat dish is the excellent *bistecca alla Fiorentina*, a vast tender, juicy and succulent beef steak—preferably from beef stock raised in Val di Chiana. It is brushed with one drop of the purest virgin olive oil and grilled over the glowing embers of a scented wood fire of chestnuts or vine branches, then seasoned with salt and pepper before serving. In good Florentine, and Tuscan restaurants in general, you will

be permitted to see the meat raw before you order.

Another famous Tuscan meat dish is *arista alla Fiorentina*, consisting of a pork loin which is pierced all over and the holes filled with chopped rosemary and ground pepper. The origin of this dish goes back to the 15th century. At the Ecumenical Council of 1430 in Florence, the Greek Bishops were served this dish at a banquet and pronounced it *"aristos"* which in Greek means very good. The name stuck and it has become a feature

of Tuscan cuisine ever since. It is a particularly useful dish to cook because it keeps very well for several days and is even better cold that hot.

Local ham includes wild boar and there's a salami flavoured with fennel called *finocchione*. As well as the ubiquitous beans, soups include *acquacotta*, a vegetable soup with an egg added before serving, and *pappa al pomodoro*, a thick soup of bread and tomatoes.

The coastal province of Livorno produces the delicious *cacciucco*, an immense seafood and fish soup claimed to be the original *bouillabaisse*. The story goes that the soup

Preceding pages: Tuscan cooks. Left, slicing *porchetta* in Greve di Chianti. Above, *cinghiale* (wild boar), hams and salami.

originated in the port after a tremendous storm that left a widowed fisherman's wife desperately trying to feed her many children.

The children were sent from house to house, begging for something to eat. As the fishermen had nothing else to give, the children came home with handfuls of mussels, a few shrimps, half a fish and some fish heads. The clever mother put them all in a pot, added herbs and tomatoes from her garden and created the glorious *cacciucco*. While *zuppa di pesce* can be eaten all over Italy, *cacciucco* can be eaten only in Livorno and surrounding areas.

During the Renaissance, food had its place among the arts along with painting, sculp-

decades thanks to the Arabs who brought it over from North Africa.

When she left Florence to marry Francis I of France, she took many of her recipes and ideas with her. There are many Italians who claim that it was largely through her efforts that the French learnt to cook at all! To this day, the origin of rich hare stew, called *lepre in dolce e forte*, with candied lemon, lime and orange peel, cocoa, rosemary, garlic, vegetables and red wine, is contested by both Italian and French cooks. It is still called *dolce forte* in French.

The cheeses available in this region are plentiful and varied. There is a delightful overspill of cheeses from neighbouring

ture, poetry and music. Many extraordinary dishes were created around that time; menus at Florentine Renaissance banquets abounded with dishes such as pasta cooked in rose water and flavoured with sugar, incredible candied fruit and almond confectionery, the famous *lepre in dolce e forte* and many more.

Frozen delights: Caterina de' Medici was responsible for much of the renewed interest in the creation of original dishes. A keen gourmet, she encouraged her cooks to experiment and was responsible for the introduction of ice-cream to the northern regions from Sicily, where it had been eaten for

Emilia Romagna including, of course, the King of Cheeses, *parmigiano Reggiano*. It is used extensively to complement Tuscany's marvellous pasta dishes and soups.

Other cheeses made locally include *marzolino*, a ewe's milk cheese made in March when milk is most plentiful in the Chianti valley; *mucchino*, a cow's milk cheese made in and around Lucca by the same procedure as *pecorino*; *Brancolino* from the town of Brancoli; the delectable *formaggette di Zeri*, made with half ewe's and half cow's milk in Massa Carrara; and all the local rustic *cacciotte* and *ricotta* made with cow, goat and ewe milk. Hunting is a popular local sport (though tourist participation is discouraged) resulting in plentiful supplies of *cinghiale* (wild boar) and numerous small birds, from sparrows to quail.

Sweetmeats: Siena is famous for the *Palio*, for its ethereal Renaissance beauty, and for its incredible selection of pastries and sweetmeats. *Cavallucci* are delicious little hard biscuits which are served at the end of a meal and dipped into glasses of sweet Vin Santo.

Panforte has been made since the 15th century and is sold the world over, an Italian Christmas speciality, unmistakable in its brightly coloured octagonal cardboard box. It is a rich sweet cake of candied fruit, nuts, spices, honey and sugar, sandwiched in be-

cake of chestnuts called *torta garfagnina*; on the borders with Emilia Romagna they make a delicious apple cake, *torta di mele*.

Pistoia produces the pretty *corona di San Bartolomeo* for the feast of St Bartholomew on 24 August, when mothers lead their children to church wearing this cake necklace around their necks for a special blessing from the Saint. Prato has *biscottini di Prato* made from almonds, eggs, flour and sugar, delicious dipped into the fragrant amber-coloured local Vin Santo. In Livorno they make gorgeous light, golden buns called *bolli*. A speciality of Lucca is a ring-shaped plain cake called *buccellato*, and an unusual sweet tart of spinach and chard with pine

tween two sheets of rice paper.

Ricciarelli are delightful, diamond-shaped almond cakes, also saved for the Christmas celebrations, along with the delicious, golden rich rice cake called *torta di riso*. The local *pasticcerie* are filled with these and many other delectable varieties.

In other areas of the region, other sweet specialities appear. At Castelnuovo della Garfagnana they make a wonderfully simple

nuts. Florence is famous for *sticciata*—a type of rich, sweet bun flavoured with Marsala and orange flower water.

But the pride of place amongst all Toscana's sweet specialities is the incredible *zucotto*, a sponge cake mould with a filling of almonds, hazelnuts, chocolate and cream - once eaten, never forgotten. It is called "small pumpkin" because the segmented cake looks like a bright yellow pumpkin.

Mountain harvest: Chestnuts are a staple of the region, particularly in mountain areas, where they are made into flour, pancakes, soups and sweet cakes like *castagnaccio*, flavoured with rosemary and pine nuts.

In the autumn, when the rains fall, the hills become a target for family outings. On the mountain sides and along the roads there are little groups of people equipped with baskets and sticks, searching for the harvest of chestnuts and *funghi*. The wild mushroom season is awaited impatiently, as the spoils are highly prized both for their pungent flavour and the price they will fetch in the market.

There are many different varieties of wild mushrooms, growing in abundance amongst the trees in the hills—the type of mushroom found will depend very much upon the type of tree it is growing next to or under—but the most sought after is the perfect *porcine (boletus edulis)* which grows to enormous size and thickness. These are often served simply grilled with olive oil and salt—just like a steak.

You need to be an expert if you decide to go mushroom picking, each year during the season the newspapers are filled with horror stories about families poisoning themselves with their own hand-picked mushrooms and it is easy to make a dreadful mistake. Some local authorities have passed laws preventing people from picking the mushrooms unless they have paid for and been issued with a licence.

Yet, despite the restrictions imposed by the licence, the dangers of picking the wrong thing and the short season, wild mushrooms are widely available at restaurants, in the markets and at roadside stalls from late August to early October. The wild mushroom season coincides with the start of the wine harvest, the olive oil harvest and the snail season. It is a time of plenty, when much eating and drinking and celebrating goes on in the countryside and on the many farms and vineyards.

Tuscany has everything to offer the visitor in terms of food. There is a rich selection of fruit and vegetables from the wide, prolific countryside, a fantastic bounty from the sea—everything from red mullet to mussels, sweet and tender beef and pork, excellent oil with which to dress it and superb wines with which to wash it down, and to finish off hearty cheeses and divine cakes and desserts. But this is not the region to seek out complicated or intricate dishes; the food of Tuscany is a pure and simple art.

Fruit and vegetables in the market in Pescia.

110

FESTIVALS

Festivals are Tuscany's richest theatre, ranging from the simple *sagra* (feast) to the most complex Italian festival of all, the *Palio*. In a sophisticated festival, scenes of high drama or contemporary relevance can recall a pagan or medieval past, succumb to Bacchic indulgence or soar to mysticism and magic.

Even the most ordinary festival reveals an unbroken tradition, a curious competition or a rustic delicacy. There are *feste* in honour of fire and water, *ravioli* and wine, historic football jousts, saints and witches. Every conceivable animal is celebrated, from the thrush to crickets. Even the Virgin's Holy Girdle is worshipped.

It is difficult to avoid such small festivals in Tuscany. Any of the following signs suggest the unfolding of a secret rite: a parish church decorated with banners and snapshots of horses; huddles of town dignitaries plotting in corners; agile boys tossing flags; and a trestle table set for 200. Inevitably, the table is piled high with stodgy chestnut *polenta*; wizened old men are "helping" uncork the local wine.

In the background, yesterday's motorbike daredevil is today's Renaissance courtier in harlequin tights. Somewhere, a mechanical donkey fails to start but the fireworks explode anyway. Ask anyone what the festival is "about" and the innocuous reply will be *allegria*, "fun".

But *allegria* belies the seriousness of intent. Festivals are a distorting mirror to Tuscan life, projecting the rawness and romanticism of civic pride onto a citizen's individualism. Even if there is no overt competition, each participant expects the finest horse, the most lavish costume, the biggest bonfire or the longest *contrada* procession.

This expectation usually crystallises around the *contrade*, cities within a city. These emerged in the 12th century "communes" when a particular square, church and fountain became associated with a local area and character. The *contrada* spirit, particu-

larly marked in Siena, Arezzo and Lucca provinces, inspires most of Tuscany's festivals. Without such passion, many would have degenerated into tourist displays. With it, the survival of *palio* and *giostra* rivalries is ensured.

In Siena, the archetypal *contrade* city, each of the 17 *contrade* has its own organisation, church and even a museum housing the *Palio* memorabilia. This announces births, marriages and deaths: marriage is celebrated with a flag-waving display and

funerals are attended by a *contrada* page. Children are enrolled at birth and membership is for life.

Children learn *Senesita*, the city's proclaimed values of freedom, friendship and altruism. They are also gently indoctrinated in *contrada* folklore, *Palio* triumphs and disasters. The boys practise the noble arts of flag-waving, drumming and nobbling the enemy *contrada*'s horse while the girls learn how to cook *risotto* for 100 *contradaioli* on feast days. Both sexes absorb *contrada* values: stealth, diplomacy and single-minded victory. At its highest, the *contrade* spirit fosters individual excellence and a striving

Preceding pages: watching and winning the **Palio**. *Left, in full rig for the* **Palio**. *Above,* **buttero** *winner in a Maremma horse race.*

towards collective perfectionism.Even the humblest *palio* races reflect local *contrade* traditions and are not a mere parody of the Sienese model. Asciano and Querceta always race donkeys rather than horses. Likewise, Livorno's *palio marinaro*, a regatta along the atmospheric canals, is a natural choice for a sea-faring city. Jousts or *giostre* are a rougher variant on the *palio* theme.

The origins lie in medieval fist fights and the jousts are still a safe way of reliving and relieving ancient rivalries. At moments, the *giostre* have the fervour of a war ceremony, or the finality of a farewell service for crusaders. Although the buffalo races and bullfights have died out, real or mechanical fal-

rival fans stamp, whistle, scream and wave. The guiding spirit is anti-Olympiad: winning, not taking part, is what counts.

Arezzo runs an elaborate *giostra* with a more complex scoring system and greater rewards and punishments. The winner receives a gold lance, adulation from one *contrada* and hatred from the three losers. A knight missing the target can be knocked off his horse by a savage "cat-of-three-tails".

Each *contrada*, ensconced on its own side of the Piazza Grande, is engrossed in the accompanying procession which is a contradictory mix of medieval costume and modern sentiment. As Archibald Lyall wrote of Arezzo, "Beautiful ladies ride in the proces-

cons, bears, donkeys and horses "joust" regularly.

Two dramatic jousts at Arezzo and Sarteano re-enact local feuds disguised as the ritual savagery of medieval Crusaders. The Jousts centre on charges at a dummy representing the "Saracen." In Sarteano, a cortege circles into the medieval square and bows to the *notabili*, the stand packed with local dignitaries. The segregated members of the five opposing *contrade* explode in a riot of drumming and banner-waving. In turn, the knights try to hit and carry off the ring on the Saracen's shield. As each knight gallops up to the Saracen, supporters are quiet while

sion, their make-up by Elizabeth Arden and their costumes out of the Duc de Berry's book of hours."

The religious festivals range from simple homage to obscure saints to Grassina's elaborate "Way of the Cross", a re-enactment of the ascent to calvary and the Crucifixion. Prato's "Display of the Virgin's Holy Girdle" is certainly the oddest.

According to legend, Doubting Thomas could not accept either the Resurrection or Mary's Assumption until he found roses in Jesus's empty tomb and then saw the Virgin in heaven removing her girdle for him. The girdle eventually reached Prato Cathedral in the 12th century via Thomas and the Holy Land Crusades. Pratese merchants, conscious of their priceless relic, display it five times a year to incredulous crowds.

The fullest religious festival is Florence's "Exploding Carriage", *Lo Scoppio del Carro*, celebrating the Resurrection and the success of the First Crusade. On Easter Day, citizens excitedly squeeze into the Piazza del Duomo to catch a glimpse of a mechanical dove or a miracle. The essential elements are: a tense wait for an uncertain fire, intense children who believe in magic and a suspension of adult disbelief that a firework dove is the Holy Spirit.

The ritual began when Pazzino de' Pazzi

first simple *carro* built to bring the holy fire to the City and successive Popes made more opulent carriages. The present one, dating from 1700, resembles a Japanese palanquin on wheels. In a moment of inspiration, Leo X added the dove to the ritual.

As High Mass in the Duomo comes to an end, children outside eye the magic box of flowers and fireworks and will it to explode. Inside the Duomo, children gaze at the firework dove suspended on a wire above the high altar. At the intoning of the *Gloria*, the dove, fizzing with sacred fire, swoops through the open doors and ignites the triumphal carriage. Amid the chiming of bells, shrieks and fireworks, the dove fizzles out,

returned from the First Crusade to Florence in 1305. Legend has it that he was the first to scale the walls of Jerusalem and seize a piece of the Holy Sepulchre. Every year, these precious chips are taken from San Miniato to the Baptistry where a spark from the stones lights the holy fire. The fire, carried in procession to the Cathedral, is later used to ignite the dove.

Six white oxen drag the creaking, gilded carriage into the square. De Pazzi had the

its mechanical miracle accomplished.

Although today's participants are more likely to be shopkeepers than peasants, the sense of relief is just as great. The liberated crowds spill over the Ponte Vecchio, wander to lunch near the Boboli Gardens or watch the foolhardy dive into the river. The atmosphere is one of exhilaration. A successful ritual means a joyous release of tension.

The simplest and most dramatic festival is held in Monte Amiata. Abbadia di San Salvatore's *Fiaccole di Natale* or "Christmas Torches" is a mountain festival built around towering, conical bonfires. Originally a pagan mid-winter festival, its medie-

Left, blessing the *Contrada* horse. Above, everybody joins in the celebrations.

val roots lie in the vigil kept by villagers and shepherds as they waited for Midnight Mass on Christmas Eve. Carols, storytelling, feasting and fires helped to drive away the cold. In the gathering of shepherds, the long wait, the ritual worship, the cold of the mountains, there are echoes of Bethlehem.

Today, pyramids of fire are still used to rekindle memory and collective faith. The fire-making is a male art and village boys compete in building the most graceful fire to adorn their local piazza. The surrounding forests, in common ownership since 1300, symbolise local pride and the fires are a seasonal thanksgiving. The bonfires of chestnut wood from Monte Amiata illuminate the Town Hall, squares and alleyways. Torchlit processions and dancing to mandolins only die out with the fires at dawn. The dying embers signal the explosion of the winter sports season: skiing, nature trails and New Year balls.

Despite pagan or seasonal labels, many festivals are really a pretext for gastronomic delights. One tiny village near Florence holds a festival to celebrate the broad bean harvest in early May. Radicofani unashamedly holds a *Ravioli Festa* while Montale and Montalcino ennoble and eat the thrush in *Sagra del Tordo*. Consumption is not limited to locals: casual visitors can also enjoy a dip in the pot. If the bean, thrush or white truffle does not appeal, *porchetta* (roasted pig) is usually on sale.

But for uninhibited merrymaking there is nothing to equal *Carnevale*, a pagan spring carnival with a Christian veneer. Arezzo, San Gimignano and Piombino compete with allegorical or *Commedia dell'Arte* floats followed by processions of harlequins, courtiers, jesters and Popes. Viareggio's pre-Lenten carnival offers an unequalled display of political satire and burlesque. It is the time to discover the masked desires of close friends and colleagues.

The last word belongs to Horace Walpole, writing in Florence in 1740, "The end of carnival is frantic bacchanalia; all the morn one makes parties in masque to the shops and coffee houses and all the evening to the operas and balls. Then I have danced, good gods! How I have danced!"

Right, triumph and unbearable happiness at the *Palio*.

PLACES

Sometimes the delights of Tuscany all become too much, and a curious disease afflicts visitors, known as the Stendhal Syndrome. It manifests itself in sensitive visitors so overcome that they sometimes faint away completely. Stendhal recorded his own experience: "The tide of emotion which overwhelmed me flowed so deep that it scarce was to be distinguished from religous awe. As I emerged from the port of Santa Croce, I was seized with a fierce palpitation of the heart; I walked in constant fear of falling to the ground." Wagner was similarly affected, bursting into tears at the sight of the Duomo in Siena.

Tuscany has always been a favourite destination for travellers and pilgrims. But there is a risk of becoming so surfeited by the richness of the artistic inheritance of Tuscany that you may find yourself exclaiming with Mark Twain: "Enough! Say no more! Lump the whole thing! Say that the creator made Italy from designs by Michelangelo!"

The poet Laurie Lee fled to the hills after a visit to Florence. "I'd had my fill of Florence," he wrote, "lovely but indigestible city. My eyes were choked with pictures and frescoes, all stamped one on top of the other, blurred, their colours running. I began to long for those cool uplands, that country air, for the dateless wild olive and the uncatalogued cuckoo."

The truly wonderful thing about Tuscany is that its artistic riches are fully matched by the radiance of nature, and the grace of the people who live there. As E. M. Forster observed, "The traveller who has gone to Italy to study the tactile values of Giotto, or the corruption of the Papacy, may return remembering nothing but the blue sky and the men and women who live under it." And there's nothing wrong with that.

Preceding pages: the band takes a break; Badia a Passignano, Chianti; the roofs of Florence.

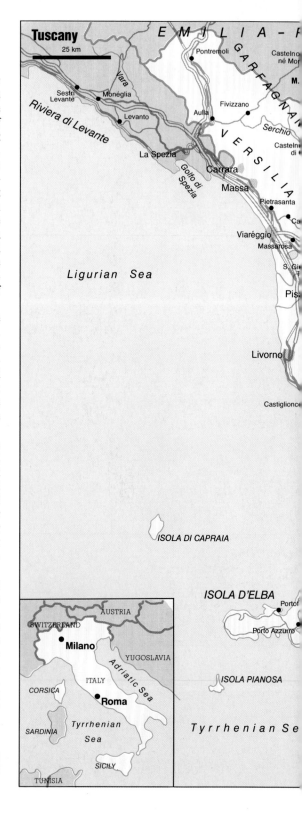

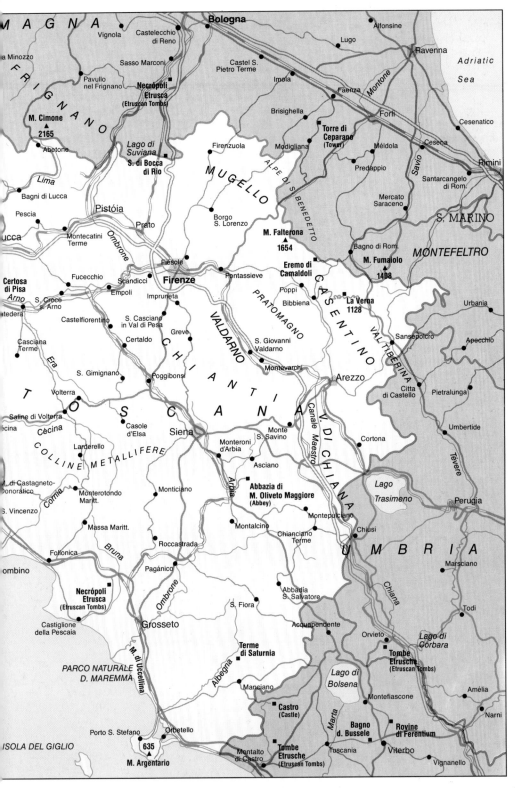

129

THE CITY OF FLORENCE

In a country of spectacular sites, the site of Florence is outstanding. Viewed from the surrounding hills, the city seems to be floating in a bowl which, at dusk, is tinged violet. The honey-coloured walls and myriad, rose-coloured roofs of the city combine to make a unity which is dominated by a single, vast building, the cathedral. It is still the biggest building for miles around, with its roof and dome in the same colour-range as the surrounding smaller buildings above which it seems to float like a liner among tugs.

There are few towers or spires. Giotto's multi-coloured Campanile next to the Cathedral, plain in outline but intricate in detail, and the thrusting tower of the Palazzo Vecchio, elegant and sombre, soar above a generally low profile. The overall impression is not that of a city, composed of tens of thousands of units, but of one single, vast building, a majestic palace.

This is symbolic of Florentine history: unity in diversity, a mansion occupied by a single family. Frequently there are family quarrels: members are even prepared to make common cause with foreigners to get the better of a neighbour, but they are still one family in one abode.

Close contact with the city can be at first disconcerting, even disappointing. The first impression is claustrophobic. The streets are narrow, hemmed in by towering, plain buildings. There is no delicate filigree, as in Venice, or cheerful baroque, as in Rome, to tempt the eye.

Some of the buildings resemble 19th-century warehouses, grim structures erected at a time of social unrest and so discharging the primary function of fortresses. In any case, Florentine taste runs to the understated, the restrained, the prudent, as befits a race of farmers.

But gradually, the visitor comes to terms with a city which, though sharing basic characteristics with the larger family of Italian cities, is unique in its mixture. The banning of traffic from the historic centre has given the city back again to pedestrians. The streets, instead of being conduits for lethal streams of fast-moving metal, are again part of the city's fabric, simultaneously discharging the role of stage-set and communication link. The visitor is free to wander, and stop, and wander again absorbing.

Overwhelming riches: It is perfectly possible to spend a lifetime studying Florence. Scores have done so in the past; scores will do so in the future. For the visitor to attempt a comprehensive survey on one single visit will simply invite fatigue, then boredom. The monuments and localities which figure in the following bird's-eye view are chosen on a necessarily arbitrary basis. Some, of course, automatically select themselves; others have been included because they can stand as an example for their class as a whole, or illustrate some particular point of the Florentine story.

The city has been grouped into four

Left, Florence duomo. Right, River Arno.

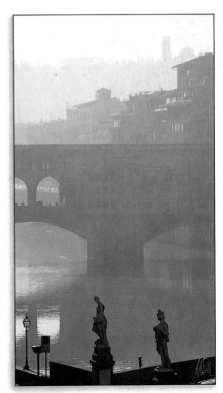

Florence

500 m

132

sections: starting with the area around the Palazzo Vecchio; followed by the area around the Cathedral; and then by three important religious foundations, (which, for reasons which will be explained have been grouped together in the narrative though physically scattered around the city). Finally the river Arno and beyond. Nearly all the places are within easy walking distance of one another.

As Florence is a small town, it is possible to walk its entire width, from the Porta Romana in the south to the Porta San Gallo in the north, in half an hour or so. During World War II, an aircraft dropped a stick of three or four bombs to the west of the town on a line running roughly north-south. Had the pilot corrected his course by a fraction to take him over the centre, then that small stick of bombs would have taken out almost everything we think of as "Florence".

The civic heart: The Piazza della Signoria. Of all the great Italian city squares, Florence's is the most perversely irregular. There's nothing here of the harmony which makes Venice's San Marco a vast, unroofed hall. There's nothing here of the grace of Siena's curved Campidoglio, or the simple majesty of Rome's Capitol. Instead, buildings follow each other around the perimeter of the Piazza in any sort of order.

Tucked uncomfortably on one side is the **Palazzo Vecchio**, the seat of government for the past six centuries. Next to it is the elegant **Loggia dei Lanzi**, crammed with statues, which doesn't seem to relate to anything in particular. The huge fountain in the centre is the subject of amiable mockery by the Florentines themselves and no two buildings in the Piazza seem to have the same facade.

With a despot's love of order, Duke Cosimo I tried to impose an artificial unity on the square, and Michelangelo even came up with a scheme to continue the shape of the Loggia all the way round. Happily, such schemes came to nothing—happily, because the Piazza della Signoria is a perfect illustration of Florentine "unity in diversity".

Despite the absence of an overall plan, despite the bristling individuality of the buildings, the Piazza as a whole does come together. How little it has changed over the centuries can be seen by comparing the contemporary painting of the execution of Savonarola in the Piazza in 1498 and today.

The narrow platform in front of the Palazzo sums up the function of the Piazza della Signoria. The platform is all that remains of the original *Ringheria*—literally, the "haranguing place" where orators could address the assembled citizenry.

The statues upon it are not simply decorative, but have profound political significance. Here stood the *Judith and Holofernes*, restored here in 1919 after many migrations, but now housed for safety in the Palazzo itself. Here is the **Marzocco**, the lion symbol of the city which prisoners were forced to kiss. Michelangelo's immense statue of David is a second copy of the first, commissioned in 1501 to mark another important change in the constitution.

Cellini's *Perseus* during restoration of the Piazza della Signoria.

Nearby is the statue of the first Medici duke—and the first Medici to so aggrandise himself—Cosimo I. In the **Loggia dei Lanzi** (named after the *landsknechts* or mercenaries employed by Cosimo) the beautiful headless body of the Gorgon spouts black blood, while Perseus triumphantly displays her head. Cellini was commissioned to do this disturbing group by Cosimo—perhaps as a riposte to the *Judith*.

The **Palazzo Vecchio** itself, begun in 1299, has changed its name many times over the years, each change signifying a change in the city. Originally, it was the Palazzo dei Priori, the priors being the heads of the Guilds who formed the government. In the 14th century it became the Palazzo del Popolo, then the Palazzo dei Signoria when the government of the city fell into the hands of commercial magnates (*Signori*). It became the Palazzo Ducale when the first Medici duke moved into it from the old family palace and finally, when he moved out to the splendid new palace on the other side of the river, it became simply the Palazzo Vecchio—the Old Palace.

Its interior belies that grim exterior. The flower-bright courtyard with its copy of an enchanting fountain by Verrochio, is a delight. The portentous **Salon dei Cinquecento** was built for the republican *Council of 500* introduced by Savonarola in 1496. It was transformed into a throne room for Cosimo I by Vasari, who produced those vast, rather tasteless but historically fascinating frescoes lauding the exploits of the Medici, and finally it served as the first parliament of a united Italy when Florence was briefly the Italian capital in 1863.

Because the Palazzo is still Florence's "city hall", admission tends to be erratic. But most of the historic rooms, including the Medici suite and the grim little cell where Savonarola was held before his execution in the Piazza below, are usually open to the public.

Adjoining the Piazza are the immense galleries of the **Uffizi**, running round the entire **Piazzale degli Uffizi** to link up with the Loggia dei Lanzi back in the Piazza della Signoria. Mental indigestion is an inevitable hazard in any Italian tour. It achieves acute form in Florence, acutest of all in the Uffizi. The only possible cure is avoidance, to fight down the temptation to look at every picture, every statue in the galleries' dozens of rooms, which are, themselves, rather confusingly, often re-arranged and re-numbered.

The overall scheme, however, is chronological, thus making it possible to pick out groups or periods. Which to chose can only be a matter of opinion and personal taste.

The Uffizi does present an unrivalled opportunity to follow the development of Renaissance art from Cimabue (whose *Virgin in Majesty* was painted when Giotto was still a little boy) onward through to the mannered works of the late Cinquecento.

Chronologically, the Palazzo Vecchio is the second city hall of Florence. Its predecessor, the **Bargello** (in the Via del Proconsolo) was built 50

Hanging out the washing in the streets of Florence.

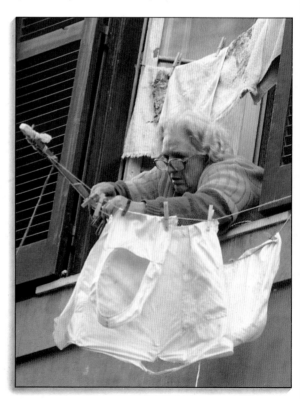

years earlier, in 1250, as the seat of the chief magistrate, the *Podesta*. The office of *Podesta* was common in all medieval republics and was an attempt to check the endlessly warring factions within a city. He was always a foreigner—that is, from a city at least 50 miles (80 km) away—appointed for one year only but given supreme power in that year.

The Bargello was therefore, in effect, police headquarters—reflected in its forbidding exterior. The elegant, but grim, courtyard was frequently the scene of public executions. Here they followed the curious custom of painting the effigies of criminals with details of their crime, sometimes in doggerel verse. The Bargello is now a museum specialising in sculptures; it has a rich collection with works by artists like Brunelleschi, Michelangelo, Cellini, Donatello among many others, but it is not nearly as bewildering as the Uffizi museum.

Four centuries of history: Just west of the Piazza della Signoria is a loosely associated group of three buildings which takes you across some four centuries of Florentine history, from the embattled Middle Ages to the era of ducal control. The **Palazzo di Parte Guelfa** (just off the Via del Terme), the headquarters of the all-powerful Guelf Party which, after the defeat and expulsion of the Ghibellines, completely ruled the city. The Palazzo was built in the 13th century, but subsequently enlarged many times—an indication of its expanding status in Florence.

The **Palazzo Davanzati** in the Via Porta Rossa is the earliest example of a patrician's home adapting to a more comfortable and safer age. Built about 1330, its painted walls and ceilings are excellent examples of Trecento work serving to soften and brighten domestic architecture, turning a fort into a home.

Nearby, the lively **Mercato Nuovo** belongs to another world. "Nuovo" is only relative, for the elegant covered market was built around 1550. It is still a popular shopping place, particularly for visitors looking for some genuine

View of
Brunelleschi's
dome.

memento (high quality leather goods, for example) instead of tacky souvenirs. Here is the **Porcellino**, the amiable bronze boar, whose snout is polished to gleaming gold by the rubbing of visitors who touch it as a means of ensuring a return to the city on the Arno.

The religious centre: It is characteristic of the Florentines that the main artery of their city, the street which links the two great monuments of the Palazzo Vecchio and the Cathedral, does not bear some grand impressive name. It is still known as the Street of the Hosiers—Via Calzaiuoli—after the trade of the stocking-knitters who were concentrated here. It still specialises in footwear. The Guilds were concentrated in this area: on the left of the street is **Orsanmichele**, the Guild church. Its exterior is an open-air art gallery: each guild made itself responsible for one section and commissioned an artist to decorate it.

The enormous size of **the Cathedral** (it can hold 20,000 people) is emphasised by the smallness of the square in which it is placed, and the narrowness of the streets which enter it. At no point can one take in the whole: instead there are a series of glimpses—blinding, multi-coloured glimpses, for in decorating the exterior the Florentines departed from their usual restraint, and indulged themselves in a riot of coloured marbles.

Despite the Cathedral's dominating presence, the little **Baptistry** in front of it easily holds its own. The Florentines particularly revered the Baptistry, the oldest building in the city. It was built on, or reconstructed from, a seventh-century building sometime between the years 1060 and 1120 and served as the Cathedral of Florence until 1228 when it was relegated to the role of Baptistry.

Dante was among the eminent Florentines baptised there (he nearly drowned in the great font) and the wealthy Wool Guild *(Calimala)* lavished vast sums on its interior. In particular, they commissioned the superb Venetian mosaics for the interior of the cupola.

The *Calimala* then turned their atten-

tion to the three great doors, first commissioning a Pisan to create bronze doors for the south entrance, then Lorenzo Ghiberti for the other two doors. There is no mistaking the second pair of doors, which took Ghiberti 27 years to create and which Michelangelo described as the "Gates of Paradise", for there is always a little knot of people standing staring at them. Florence must be the only city in the world to have a work of art of this nature on permanent outdoor display and if you want to get a chance to study it in detail, it's best to get there early in the morning.

The two doors are divided into 10 panels, each representing a scene from the Old Testament. Round the panels are heads representing the Sibyls and the Prophets. To get an idea of the incredible detail, and the precision to which Ghiberti worked, look for his self-portrait. It is half-way down on the right-hand side of the left-hand door and, though only a few inches high, is a perfect portrait—a little, balding man peering knowingly out like an inhabi-

Narrow streets of Florence.

tant from another dimension looking into our world.

It took the Florentines over 400 years to decide just what kind of facade they wanted for the West Front of the Cathedral—the side immediately facing the Baptistry. Again and again both artists and the City Fathers came up with some scheme which satisfied nobody (when the first Medici Pope, Leo X, visited his native city in 1515 they even erected a cardboard front for it). The present front was designed in 1887 and has inevitably come in for criticism.

After the multi-coloured splendour of the exterior, the interior of **S. Maria del Fiore** (the cathedral's official name) comes at first as a disappointment. Many of the treasures have been removed and are now in the **Museo dell' Opera de Duomo** (on the eastern side of the Piazza). The overall colour scheme of the interior is muted, rather muddy, coming to life only at the time of religious festivals when immense crimson banners are hung on the walls and pillars.

But the relative lack of architectural detail allows the eye to pick out the remaining treasures which highlight the city's history. High on the wall immediately to the left of the entrance are two large murals of soldiers. The right-hand one is of an Englishman, John Hawkwood, a mercenary soldier or *condottiero* who first attacked Florence for his paymasters and then became the city's Captain-General in 1375. It was intended to erect a monument to him, but thriftily the Signoria settled for this clever *chiaroscuro* imitation which gives the impression of a three-dimensional monument, painted by Paolo Uccello in 1436.

Further along the same aisle is the painting *Dante Declaiming the Divine Comedy* by Michelino. On Dante's right in the painting is Hell and Purgatory (the latter looking rather like a wedding cake) while on his left is a contemporary view of the city's major monuments, looking exactly as they do today. For many years readings from the *Comedy* used to be given in the

Duomo across the roof-tops.

Cathedral at Lent, a fact which would doubtless have given Dante wry amusement, and in 1465 this painting was commissioned to mark the second anniversary of his death.

The cathedral's greatest treasure is the *Pietá* by Michelangelo, which is now in the Museo. He sculpted it for his own tomb in 1550, though it was never finished. It is entirely different from his earlier, and perhaps more famous *Pietà* in St Peter's in Rome; where that is all calm, resigned acceptance, this is simply the utter defeat of death.

In the nearby **New Sacristy**, Lorenzo the Magnificent took refuge on Easter Sunday morning in 1478 when the Pazzi Conspirators murdered his brother Giuliano during High Mass, and wounded him. (One of the murderers was later hanged from a window of the Bargello and Leonardo da Vinci painted the dangling corpse, carefully noting the clothes it was wearing.)

If time permits and you have a head for heights, ascend to the gallery of the **dome**. A head for heights really is needed for the gallery is narrow and the balustrade low, but only here can Brunelleschi's stupendous achievement be fully appreciated. It was originally intended to cover the interior of the dome with mosaic, which would have emphasised its soaring majesty; instead Vasari was commissioned to cover it with dull allegories, which visually reduces its size.

Memories of the Medicis: A few streets to the northwest of the Cathedral is the heartland of Medicean Florence. Here is the **Medici Palace** and the church of **San Lorenzo** with the Medici tombs. The main facade of the palace is on the Via Cavour, one of the few street names in Florence to have changed its name— it was the Via Larga at the time of the Medici.

The palace (now known as the **Medici-Riccardi** from the name of the family to whom the Grand Duke Ferdinand sold it in the 17th century) is dignified but not ostentatious. It still has the look of a fortress about it, particularly in the facade of the ground floor with its

Statues in the Piazza della Signoria.

massive blocks of "rustic" masonry. It is today the Prefecture of Florence but the Medici chapel and the Medici Museum are open to the public.

The museum contains various mementoes of the family, including the poignant death-mask of Lorenzo, but it is the chapel which contains one of the brightest jewels in the Medici crown, the *Procession of the Magi* by Benozzo Gozzoli, painted in 1469. This is a painting which has been reproduced again and again, for it breathes the essential spirit of the Florentine Renaissance in its mixture of real figures of identifiable people, historical re-creation and sheer delight in colour.

The immense procession, winding its way through a delightfully improbable landscape, is led by a handsome richly dressed youth on horseback—the young Lorenzo. Behind him comes his grandfather, Cosimo, soberly dressed, attended by a black servant. Other members of the family are in the group—which includes the painter himself, with his name inscribed on his

hat. In the distance is the Medici country villa Cafaggiolo—and a couple of camels to remind the observer that the picture is set in the Middle East!

To go from this painting in the chapel to the **New Sacristy** in **San Lorenzo**, which Michelangelo designed, is to go from dawn to sunset. This is not simply because the colours in the Sacristy are muted, or that it is a mausoleum for the Medici. It is because Michelangelo created his incomparable commemorative sculptures in bitterness and defeat, mourning that the republic he worshipped had been destroyed by the Medici Pope Clement VII. Under this Pope's orders, he was executing memorials not to the great Lorenzo the Magnificent, his old patron, but to a worthless young man who was a nephew of the Pope and another insignificant member of the younger generation.

The two tombs are graced with the extraordinarily symbolic figures of *Dawn, Dusk, Night* and *Day* conveying to the observer an unforgettable feeling of uneasiness, of sadness, of loss. In one

The Franciscan church of S. Croce.

of his sonnets, Michelangelo put these words into the mouth of *Night*:

> *Sweet is sleep to me and*
> *even more to be of stone,*
> *while wrong and shame endure.*
> *To be without sight or sense*
> *is a most happy chance for me.*
> *Therefore do not rouse me.*
> *Hush! Speak low.*

Black and white friars: The three great buildings of S. Maria Novella, S. Marco and S. Croce are widely separated in the city. **S. Maria Novella** is the first major building encountered by a visitor coming in by train, being opposite the railway station. When first built, it was in vineyards outside the city walls. **S. Croce** is on the far eastern side of the city, a little beyond the Palazzo Vecchio while **S. Marco** is in the north.

They are grouped together here because they illustrate a truth about Florence, in the absence of which even the most splendid buildings lose something of their significance. The truth is that religion was a driving force probably even stronger than commerce or the

desire for self-aggrandisement—a force so strong, indeed, that on more than one occasion it nearly drove the city to destruction.

S. Maria Novella and S. Marco are Dominican foundations, S. Croce is Franciscan, and the difference between them illustrates the two sides of the Latin character. The Dominicans, taking after their harsh, intolerant Spanish founder, were great persecutors of heretics. They delighted in the Latin pun on their name—*Domini canes*—the "hounds of the Lord," symbolised in paintings and stained glass by black and white dogs. The Franciscans also followed their founder, Francis of Assisi, but achieved their objectives not by fire and sword, but by persuasion and love.

The church of **S. Maria**, begun in 1246, is probably the most important example in Florence of Italian Gothic, the style which preceded the Renaissance. Designed by Dominican monks, though dignified and indeed majestic, it reflects their gloomy preoccupations: striped like a tiger, the family chapels are sombre and overwhelming, their murals little more than illustrations of sermons. The **Spanish Chapel** carries this to extremes, with its murals dedicated to the 13th-century theologian, Thomas Aquinas—a Dominican, of course.

Decorations in the church were carried out well into the Renaissance, with work by Brunelleschi among others, so there is a lightening of the spirit. But the overall impression is something of gloom, touched with threat. It was in S. Maria, incidentally, that Boccaccio's seven young maidens met in the spring of 1348, where they were joined by three young men and launched the comedy of *The Decameron*.

Ironically, the convent of **San Marco** was almost entirely rebuilt with money provided by Cosimo de' Medici—ironically, because San Marco became the headquarters of the friar Girolamo Savonarola, who was the greatest and most determined enemy of Cosimo's grandson, Lorenzo. Cosimo engaged his own favourite architect, who had designed the Palazzo Medici, to build

Feeding the birds outside S. Croce.

San Marco and eventually spent more than 50,000 florins upon it, as well as presenting it with a magnificent library.

The Bonfire of the Vanities: Savonarola was Prior of San Marco from 1489 until his execution in 1497. In those eight years he totally dominated Florence, nearly overthrew the Medici and challenged the Papacy. He was prepossessing in neither appearance nor speech. The vivid portrait of him by Fra Bartolommeo, which hangs in San Marco, shows a forceful but ugly face with a great beaked nose and burning eyes.

Contemporary reports of his sermons show that they were regarded as only average in both content and delivery. It was their burning sincerity which moved his audience, coupled with the fact that his prophecies of damnation seemed to come true with the French invasion of Italy, and occupation of Florence in 1494.

The Florentines, ever responsive to novelty, responded to this harsh, austere retainer. When he ordered them to cleanse their bodies and homes of the Devil's frivolities, they burnt their precious ornaments on a vast bonfire in the Piazza della Signoria. The great pile represented not only a fascinating cross-section of contemporary art, but also a substantial cash value, and a Venetian merchant, who happened to be present offered 22,000 florins cash for the objects. The Florentines responded by throwing his own portrait on the pile before setting alight to it.

There was, naturally, a strong reaction. Just a year after that triumphant *auto-da-fe*, Savonarola's power crumbled. The people abandoned him to the powerful enemies who had been waiting for this moment. He confessed that he had been deluded and his visions false. They hanged him, with two of his disciples, in the Piazza della Signoria and burnt the bodies afterwards.

The **Convent of San Marco** is now a museum. The prize exhibits are, perhaps, the murals of Fra Angelico, himself a Dominican but bringing a delicacy to his work quite at variance with the austere tenets of that order. Each of

Souvenir stall.

the friars' cells is graced by one of his murals and at the head of the stairs is the most famous of them all, the *Annunciation*, where he almost achieves the impossible in showing how a young girl receives the news that she is to be the Mother of God. Savonarola's cell is laid out as he knew it, complete with desk and elegant, but decidedly uncomfortable-looking chair.

The great **Piazza** in front of Santa Croce was a particularly favoured place for such large-scale activities as horse races and tournaments. It was here that Lorenzo de' Medici held the most sumptuous tournament of all to mark his marriage.

"To follow the custom, and do like others, I gave a tournament on the Piazza Santa Croce at great cost," he recorded complacently. "I find that about 10,000 ducats was spent upon it". The square is now dominated by a statue of Dante, whose monument was erected within the church.

S. Croce, begun by Arnolfo di Cambio in 1294 and with the lightness and elegance associated with Franciscan churches, is the Pantheon of Florence. And, indeed, a pantheon of Italy since so many of Italy's illustrious dead now rest here. The tomb of Michelangelo is here, designed by Vasari and invariably with a little bunch of flowers laid upon it. Here are the graves of Ghiberti and Galileo; of Machiavelli, who died in 1527, and the dramatist Vittorio Alfieri, who died in 1803.

Among these great Italians is a solitary Englishman, John Catrick, Bishop of Exeter, who came on an embassy from King Henry V in 1419 and died in the city. And crowning all, are the frescoes of Giotto.

Across the river: The Florentines look upon their river with decidedly mixed feelings. It has brought wealth but it has also brought danger for it is entirely unpredictable.

In summer it can shrink to a trickle along a dried-up bed. As Mark Twain put it: "It would be a very plausible river if they would pump some water into it. They all call it a river, and they honestly

Entertainer outside Palazzo Vecchio.

think it is a river, do these dark and bloody Florentines. They even help out the delusion by building bridges over it. I do not see why they are too good to wade."

In winter, however, the Arno becomes a raging brown torrent. As recently as 1966 it flooded the city, causing great damage—probably the worst flood since the great flood of 1330 destroyed the ancient Roman bridge.

The present bridge, the **Ponte Vecchio**, was erected by Taddeo Gaddi some time after 1360 and has become virtually a symbol for Florence itself. Fortunately, the Germans spared it when they blew up every other Florentine bridge in their retreat to the north during World War II. It bears, therefore, the same appearance that it has borne for centuries; even the goldsmiths and jewellers who throng it today were first established there in the time of Duke Cosimo I.

It was for this same Medici that Vasari built the extraordinary gallery that runs from the Uffizi to the Pitti

across the Ponte Vecchio, making a physical as well as symbolic link between the two centres of Medicean power. In his film, *Paisá*, Roberto Rosellini shot an unforgettable sequence of the fighting that took place along this gallery during the German retreat, which caused damage so severe that the gallery has been closed until recent years.

Opposition to the Medici: The part of Florence beyond the river, the **Oltrarno**, has a character all of its own. It was not even a part of the city until an expansion of the walls in the 12th century encompassed it. Here the nobles gathered in the 14th century to make their last stand against the victorious populace who would henceforth run the city until the Medici grip tightened.

Here, in the 15th century, was centred the opposition to the Medici, spearheaded by the Pitti family. It was they who built the **Pitti Palace**, the most grandiloquent of all Florentine buildings which, by the irony of history eventually became the seat of government

Benozzo Gozzoli, *Journey of the Magi,* **1459-61. Fresco, in the chapel, Palazzo Medici-Riccardi.**

for the Medici dukes themselves.

The Pitti Palace flaunts itself, a vast cliff of golden-brown stone enclosing on three sides an equally vast cortile, the whole being the antithesis of Florentine restraint. The visitor, crossing that arrogant, shadeless approach on an Italian summer's day, might well feel that there is a lot to be said for Florentine restraint.

The Pitti was built after 1440 to the design of the Medicean architects Brunelleschi and Michelozzo, but it was specifically planned to eclipse Medicean grandeur. According to Machiavelli, Luca Pitti had no scruples about laying his hands on public funds to build his palace, and even offered asylum to criminals who could either pay or work.

The Medici, however, triumphed over Luca Pitti; he was pardoned, but ruined and the palace was still unfinished when his descendants sold it to the Medici in 1549. It was then completed to an immense design and in due course became one of the royal palaces of the kings of Italy.

It is today a museum and art gallery on probably an even greater scale than the Uffizi with its magnificent art collections, and many sumptuously decorated rooms.

An excellent antidote to the overwhelming splendours of the Pitti are the enchanting **Boboli Gardens** attached to them. Begun by Duke Cosimo in 1549, they are not only an attraction themselves with their fountains and grottoes and shady walks, but provide exquisite views of Florence from gradually rising ground. The grottoes have statues by Bandinelli and Giambologna, and there is a 17th-century amphitheatre behind which is Neptune's pond with bronze statue by Stoldo Lorenzo.

The **Via Romana**, which runs past the Pitti Palace, goes to the **Porta Romana**, providing an artery from the centre of the city, via the Ponte Vecchio, to the outside world. The gates of Florence were more than a means of entry and exit. The larger ones, like the great Porta Romana, built in 1328, were both a garrison and a customs post, **Boboli Gardens**.

144

collecting dues from all goods that came into the city whether they were silks from far Cathay or farm produce from down the road.

The 14th-century writer Franco Sachetti tells a tale of a farmer who tried to smuggle eggs, hidden in his baggy breeches. Tipped off by the farmer's rival, the gate guards courteously insisted that he should be seated.

The southern section of Florence outside the remainder of the city wall is doubly poignant; it was here that the republic of Florence came to an end in 1529 when the combined armies of Pope Clement VII and the Emperor Charles V besieged the city. The area is a reminder though, alas, a rapidly fading reminder, that Florence is a country town. A brisk walk of 15 minutes or so will take you from the very heart of the city out into vineyards, olive groves and maize fields.

Threading its way through this rural scene is the last remnant of Florence's **city wall**, golden-brown among the green. Michelangelo acted as defence

River Arno crossed by the Ponte Vecchio and Ponte S. Trinita.

adviser during the last, frantic days of the republic.

The story goes that he hid in the belfry of the Church of S. Niccolo when the city capitulated, but gave himself up when Pope Clement offered to pardon him if he would complete the Medici tombs.

And here, just outside the walls of Florence, is Florence's great set piece, the city itself, viewed from the **Piazzale Michelangelo**. You can get to it from the Porta Romana along the enchanting Viale dei Colli, constructed in the 19th century, or by climbing up from the river, past the Porta S. Niccolo up by winding paths through the gardens to the Piazzale.

Another 19th-century construction, adorned with bronze copies of Michelangelo's statues, the Piazzale is the one place no visitor should miss. From it is visible the entire panorama of the city, looking much as it would have done in the time of the Medici, despite the vast convulsions of the intervening centuries.

A DAY IN THE LIFE OF THE CITY

Restless Florence wakes up to the soothing whirring of the "Pulizia Stradale" water machines. At 6 a.m. abandoned cars are towed away from the Piazza del Duomo so that the street cleaning can begin. The bars gradually fill with a democratic mix of Florentines enjoying a coffee, brioche and a glance at *La Nazione*'s entertainments page. Just before 8 a.m., students gather around Piazza San Marco in the vain hope of squeezing into an inadequately small lecture hall.

In fine weather, students and executives alike weave into work on *motorini*, far easier to park than cars. Thanks to an extension of the *Zona Blu*, the partial ban on city centre traffic, Florence is a pedestrian's paradise and a driver's nightmare, at least during the day. The traffic may all run in the opposite direction once Florence's satellite city is built: its part-sponsor, Fiat, should ensure adequate parking.

As the early cool turns humid, the air-conditioned shops near Via Tornabuoni open their elegant doors for business. Even for those who choose to patronise home-bred designers, the choice is dazzling: under a Raspini coat, a sombre Coveri suit can be paired with Ferragamo shoes, a Pucci headscarf and a Gucci bag and belt. By eleven, the smart morning coffee crowd surges into Giacosa.

Those with *tanto da fare* (lots of work to do) opt for repeated trips to more plebeian establishments where local or international affairs can be picked to pieces over an *espresso* or four. Over in Via Cavour, the *funzionari* (civil servants) from the provincial administration may be swapping insults over more *espressi*. Outside the post office, the senior citizens are gathering by the "Toto Lotto" stand to while away the morning in idle but impassioned debate.

The peckish sneak into nearby *Cantinetta Antinori* for an early rustic lunch in palatial surroundings. Like most of the Florentine nobility, the Antinori are no longer *rentiers* but entrepreneurs, consolidating empires in wine, food, fashion or crafts. To the Tuscan aristocracy, their produce is sacred: when a foreign neighbour accidentally damaged a few Antinori olive trees, the family sued.

On a warm day, office workers are inspired only by an ice cream in the shade while overheated tourists swelter in the midday heat of the Ponte Santa Trinità. The Ponte Vecchio is left to *giovanotti* hunting for naive foreign art students. Florentines with more than an hour to spare voluntarily double their daily travelling time by heading home for *pasta* and *riposo*, variously interpreted as anything from watching TV cartoons to simply sleeping. At the tail end of the rush come hordes of starving school children: no packed lunches here since school finishes at 1.30.

For those who are stuck in town, lunch is a *pasta primo* at the counter or a *crostone ai carciofi* eaten in a *birreria*. In Giubbe Rosse in Piazza della Repubblica, employees, entrepreneurs and local politicians grab a quick *ravioli* in a restaurant which was once the haunt of *Risorgimento* revolutionaries and later a salon for Futurist painters.

Around two o'clock, disconsolate tourists discover they have just missed both Michelangelo's and Donatello's *Davids*, plus everything in San Marco. The centre by now is semideserted; the only shop still open is the *Upim* department store.

Fortunately not all culture comes to a halt in the afternoon: colourful street banners advertise the latest exhibitions. Art lovers are drawn to the magnificent sculptures of nudes and horses at the new Marino Marini museum or to the latest photography exhibition at the Rucellai's frescoed palazzo. Florentine cultural influence may have declined of late, but the city is still a major displayer of works of art. Florence held the greatest exhibition of Henry Moore's sculpture and, more recently, displayed Robert Mapplethorpe's photography and the *Bronzes from Riace*.

The third rush hour gets under way. In sleepy Oltrarno, gallery attendants and shopkeepers wake up over a coffee and a conversation about the next Florence-Juventus football clash. If business is slack, Santa Croce leather workers and San Frediano silversmiths abandon shop and head likewise for the nearest bar. There they complain about the decline of Florence as a cultural centre and the failure of the local left-wing coalition to promote tourism.

By early evening, people watchers are already sipping *aperitivi* in Piazza della Repubblica or, if Piazza della Signoria is not under archaeological rubble, in *Rivoire* bar. A furious battle recently divided Florentines. The *Comune* wished to recover the Piazza with grey paving stones, while traditionalists favoured the *Cinquecento* red herringbone design. Emilio Pucci, leading the campaign, argued against "a sad grey stone blanket."

After seven o'clock, the City again becomes a traffic hazard. Piazza della Repubblica is the first stop on the youth circuit of *pizzerie*, *gelatterie* and video bars. Workers head home to Campo di Marte or Sesto; bank managers and retailers to

homesick soldiers prowling the streets. After failing to find civilian companionship or thrills, they congregate in the Central Post Office and make sad calls home to Naples or Milan.

Natural culture vultures, Florentines of all classes buy season tickets to the theatre, opera and music seasons. Although based on a conservative repertoire, Florentine theatre combines foreign classics and Florentine favourites in the newly-restored Teatro Verdi and Teatro della Compagnia as well as in the grander Teatro Comunale. As for opera and ballet, Florence used to be considered a "cold piazza" but the Mayor has used his experience at the Paris Opera to inject some warmth. In Fiesole, summer crowds gather to see international opera and ballet companies perform in the atmospheric Roman the-

Bagno a Ripoli; wealthy entrepreneurs and designers to Bellosguardo or the slopes of Fiesole.

Around nine, the streets empty as Florentines disappear into cramped *trattoria*, discreetly elegant *ristoranti* or the white minimalist interiors favoured by Tuscan *nouvelle cuisine* restaurateurs. After dinner, bustling Via Calzaiuoli attracts impromptu mime artists, puppeteers and comedians. A tatty cardboard box signals a new delivery of fake Lacoste T-shirts or African trinkets sold by Senegalese students.

Since Florence is a large garrison town, Florentine evenings need to accommodate hordes of

Preceding pages: Piazzale Michelangelo. Left, Florence's elegant shops. Above, sipping *aperitivi* in the Piazza della Repubblica.

atre. In the city below, students flock to Forte di Belvedere's open-air film festival.

Less "cultural" but equally active are the Viali, the streets which replaced Florence's town walls. Driving along them at night, try to avoid the inside lane or you may find yourself in a queue for a transvestite rather than the traffic lights. Happily married Florentine men occasionally prefer the services of a luscious transvestite to those of the distinctly mundane female prostitutes.

By this time the *giovanotti* are watching a light show or American students at the Space Electronic disco; Florentines drink a final Fernet Branca *digestivo*, the *borghesi* at home and the yuppies at a jazz club. Arty eccentrics linger on at Garga's *trattoria* where poems and paintings are created late into the night.

FLORENCE PROVINCE

The province of Florence is full of towns and villages perched on steep, cypress-covered hills. Below them, straggling down to the bottom of the valleys, are the vines that have been producing some of the most famous wines in Italy since the Renaissance— red Chianti and Carmignano and white Malvasia and Trebbiano.

This delightful legacy from the past is almost as important as the historical and artistic heritage of the people of a region that was the most advanced in Europe throughout the Middle Ages and the Renaissance.

North of Florence: The best place from which to observe the mountains of the Mugello is a seat in the Roman amphitheatre at **Fiesole**. These mountains to the north of Florence once provided hideouts for ruthless medieval barons who occasionally descended into the valleys from their fortified lairs to sack

Preceding pages: Piazza della Signoria; the Roman amphitheatre at Fiesole. Left, Franciscan monk at the Convent of San Francesco, Fiesole. Below, stained glass window.

and pillage.

At first Fiesole could fend for itself. But in 1125 it was the Florentines who attacked the city and completely destroyed it, leaving only the Duomo and the bishop's palace. In its heyday as one of the chief towns of the Etruscan Confederacy, secure on its hilltop, it could claim to be the mother of Florence itself; now it is little more than a highly refined and slightly subdued suburb, protected from the urban sprawl surrounding Florence by the steep hill on which it stands.

From Florence the Via Bolognese, the SS65, climbs up to Fiesole past many villas built on sites attractive for their magnificent views down into the valley to Florence, and for the cool breeze, the lack of which makes Florence so unattractive during the hot summer months.

On the Via Vecchia Fiesolana is the **Villa Medici** which was built on Cosimo il Vecchio's instructions for his youngest son Giovanni by Michelozzo between 1458 and 1461. The villa was favoured particularly by Lorenzo Il Magnifico who entertained his humanist friends here.

Today the interior of the villa no longer retains its original decoration; much of it was swept away in 1772 and replaced with the English Chinoiserie style by Robert Walpole, Earl of Oxford. But the terraced gardens retain their original lines; these can be visited though the villa is closed.

The road climbs on up to Fiesole's centre, the lively main piazza, named after Mino da Fiesole, a *Quattrocento* sculptor and a native of the town. Bars and *pizzerie* surround the Duomo which contains some of the best examples of Mino da Fiesole's works—the tomb of the Bishop Salutati and an altar front in the Capella Salutati. The **Duomo** itself dates from 1024-1028 and contains a great variety of frescoes and sculpture by lesser known, though excellent, artists.

On the west side of Piazza Mino da Fiesole is the 11th-century bishop's palace and the Seminary, both with fragments of the Etruscan acropolis wall in their garden, and to the east is the Palazzo Pretorio. The Piazza itself was once the site of the Roman Forum and a road leads from it to the Roman Amphitheatre which was excavated in 1911.

Behind the Duomo, in Via Dupre, is the tiny Bandini Museum containing an art gallery with a fairly wide and representative selection of paintings from the early and middle Renaissance and some School of della Robbia terracottas.

The route to Fiesole passes through the village of **San Domenico**. Apart from its magnificent view of Florence, it is well-known for its monastery and church of San Domenico di Fiesole. Both contain important remains of an art collection much vandalised during World War II. In the first chapel on the north side of the church is *Madonna with Angels and Saints* by Fra Angelico, who lived in the monastery; in the chapter house is his *Crucifixion*.

The Via Badia leads to the Badia Fiesolana which was the cathedral of Fiesole until 1028. The present building was left unfinished in 1464 and it incorporates the facade of a smaller Romanesque church embedded into it. This earlier facade is an excellent example of the Florentine Romanesque style which uses as surface decoration layers of green and white marble. There is a tiny open piazza in front of the church where you can sit and admire the view of Florence.

On the northern side of Fiesole, on the road that winds through the olive groves to Olmo, is a turning on the right to **Settignano**. It may be easier to reach this village, straggling around its hillside, from Florence from the Lungarno del Tempio, though the road from Fiesole is more diverting, with views of the Tuscan countryside—rows of cypresses, oak woods and old terraced olive groves—vanishing into the hot, blue afternoon haze.

Settignano has been home to many illustrious people. At the Villa Buonarroti, Michelangelo spent his youth. At the Villa I Tatti lived Bernard Berenson, who restored the villa to house a large collection of Renaissance paintings

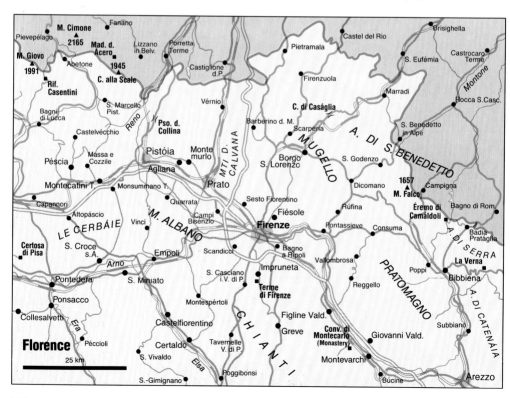

eventually inherited by Harvard University. Other well-known residents of Settignano included Desiderio da Settignano, an important Renaissance sculptor, Tommaseo, D'Annunzio and Eleanora Duse.

A fine Renaissance villa which survives here with most of its original garden intact is the 15th-century Villa Gamberaia. The spirit of this remarkable survival was inspired by Pliny and was consciously modelled on descriptions of his own Tuscan villa. It also exploited descriptions of the ideal garden as advocated by Alberti, on whose advice it was thought best to build a house on a light, airy and breeze-swept site.

All around are small wayside shrines and broken-down fences; buy a bottle of the local farm wine and a hunk of pecorino cheese and spend a lazy afternoon looking down at the view over the village.

Settignano is also richly endowed with ecclesiastical treasures: Santa Maria has a 16th-century pulpit by Buontalenti and a white terracotta *Madonna with the Child and two Angels* by Andrea della Robbia. San Martino a Mensola contains a triptych by Taddeo Gaddi.

The SS65 from Fiesole climbs northwards to Pratolino and to the **Parco Demidoff**. At one time the park (in fact, a vast garden) contained the Villa Pratolino, later named the Villa Demidoff, which was built in 1569 and demolished in 1820 as a misguided economy measure.

Practically nothing of the gardens of the former Medicean villa survive except Giambologna's massive statue *The Appennine*. This huge stone monster was once an important feature in an arrangement of watercourses and fountains which lead down the hill behind the house.

Today the garden is wild and unkempt and in dank corners under thick undergrowth can be found the remains of stone terraces, broken statues and old urns. Be warned: the custodian here keeps strange hours so be sure to find

Romanesque facade of Badia Fiesolana.

out the opening times well in advance of a visit.

The Mugello Valley: Above Pratolino is the Servite monastery of **Monte Senario**. Built in 1233 it was a retreat for wealthy Florentines who had renounced the material world, preferring to live a contemplative life of fasting and prayer. Magnificent views over the valley to the River Sieve make the isolation of the local hotels more attractive.

The Mugello has great associations with the Medici; it is the region from which they come and it is one of the regions on which they lavished a lot of their attention. In 1451 Cosimo di Medici had Michelozzo alter the old fortress of **Cafaggiolo** in **Val de Sieve**, creating a country retreat. He did the same at the old castle of Il Trebbio, slightly further to the south.

The run-down appearance of the exterior of Cafaggiolo, which has lost one of its towers, hides a magnificent interior (open by appointment). Most of the interior is used for the storage of hay—a strange use for such an important building. It suffers more today because of the siting of a major sliproad to the main Bologna-Florence motorway just in front of the building. How the mighty have fallen.

Il Trebbio, by contrast, has a much more satisfactory existence. It has been extensively restored over the years and, perhaps, more than any other 15th-century Tuscan villa, retains the feudal atmosphere of a Medici villa. Large parts of the gardens are still intact—due possibly to the remote siting of the villa on a hill in the middle of a large private estate.

Facing Villa Cafaggiolo, high on a thickly wooded outcrop is the Medici fortress of **San Martino**, built in 1569 by Lanci and Buontalenti for Cosimo I to defend the Florentine state. Today this massive pentagon-shaped castle at the end of a rough track outside San Piero di Sieve is completely derelict. Like Cafaggiolo, a minimum of effort would be needed to restore and repair this building, part of which is open to the public.

Statue of Giambologna's *L' Appenino*, Villa Demidoff.

Just north of San Piero di Sieve is **Scarperia**, a pristine little town, its clean streets and tidy houses the epitome of civic virtue. Its spotless monuments are rarely visited by outsiders, yet there is much to see. The **Palazzo Pretorio** in the main street is one of the finest examples of 13th-century civil architecture in Tuscany.

The outer facade, decorated with the coats-of-arms of local notables, carved in stone or worked in della Robbia terracotta, faces the Oratorio della Madonna della Piazza in the small rectangular piazza. The latter is a tiny darkened room in which, over the altar, is a *Madonna and Child* by Taddeo Gaddi.

At the bottom of the main street, near the entrance to the town is the Oratorio dei Terremoti which contains a fresco also of the *Madonna and Child*, said to be by Filippo Lippi. In a way, it is a good thing that not very many people visit Scarperia. An air of calm hangs over its monuments which gives the visitor a chance to contemplate the paintings and the architecture in silence.

A turning on the left of the southern approach to Scarperia wends its way through dense woodlands to the remote convent of **Bosco ai Frati**. This Franciscan retreat retains the peace and solitude of the Franciscan ideal that places like Assisi lack; no touring hordes, no postcard sellers, only the peace and simplicity offered by a church and its convent buildings in a clearing in the woods.

These buildings were restructured by Michelozzo around 1440 for Cosimo il Vecchio. They house a little-known large wooden crucifix, gessoed and painted, by one of the greatest masters of the Italian Renaissance, Donatello.

West of Florence: Prato, to the northwest of Florence, directly half-way between Florence and Pistoia, possesses an extraordinary relic: in the Duomo, in Piazza del Duomo, is what is believed to be the girdle of the Virgin Mary. The legends surrounding this relic have been celebrated by Agnolo Gaddi, whose frescoes cover the walls of the Chapel of the Holy Girdle and

there is a sculpture by Giovanni Pisano with a statue of the *Madonna and Child* on the altar.

Outside the Duomo is the Pulpit of the Holy Girdle, designed by Donatello and Michelozzo, where on Christmas Day the girdle is exhibited to the faithful.

The daily activities of Prato are more prosaic than this, however: today the city is renowned for its textile manufacturing industries. Although the trade has made contemporary Prato a rich city, it was already an important centre for textiles in the 12th century and its magnificent monuments are evidence of its former great wealth.

The small ancient centre of Prato, enclosed within its medieval walls, contains—apart from the Duomo—the **Church of Santa Maria delle Carceri** behind the **Castello dell'Imperatore**. It was begun by Giuliano da Sangallo in 1485 in a Brunelleschian style—an attempt on this architect's part to emulate the great Duomo of Santa Maria del Fiore in Florence. The Castello was built by Frederick 11 Hohenstaufen in the first half of the 13th century and is unique in Tuscany, taking as its model the Norman castles of Apulia.

In the Via Rinaldesca is the **Palazzo Datini** (c1350), former home of the man who invented the promissory note and founder of the city's riches in the wool trade in the 14th century. His story is told in *The Merchant of Prato* by Iris Origo. Further north in the Piazza Commune is the **Palazzo Pretorio**, Prato's seat of government in the days of its independence and now housing the Galleria Communale.

To the west of Florence along the Pisa-Florence highway, the first major stop is **Empoli**. The main piazza in this country town is named after Farinata degli Uberti who made a speech to the Ghibelline Parliament in 1260, saving the town from destruction after the Battle of Montaperti. As a result Empoli retains at its centre, around the church of Sant'Andrea, its earliest buildings, some of which were constructed in the 12th century.

Like so many other Tuscan towns it

Hunting for *cinghiale* (wild boar) and small birds is a popular local sport.

has a great quantity of religious paintings now housed in the **Museo delle Collegiata**, a collection which ranges from Masolino to Pontormo.

A few miles west of Empoli is **Fucecchio**, another fairly typical ancient Tuscan town the core of which is surrounded by more modern outskirts. A variety of buildings including the remains of Castruccio's Tower are worth visiting.

From Empoli, it is fairly easy to visit two important Medici residences, **Villa Poggio a Caiano** in the town of **Poggio a Caiano** and the **Villa of Artimino** outside the hilltop village of **Artimino**.

Poggio a Caiano is one of the most magnificent buildings of the 15th century. It was converted by Giuliano da Sangallo for Lorenzo de' Medici between 1480 and 1485, and from its position above the town it dominates the surrounding flat countryside. The entire building sits on a continuous loggia which surrounds the house and which supports the piano nobile. Lorenzo's son, Giovanni who eventu-

ally became Pope Leo X, continued the building work, commissioning from the della Robbia family a frieze for the entrance pediment.

Some of the internal decoration is proof that the Florentine leader and his circle were very conscious of modelling themselves on the ancients. Two of the main rooms have scenes from Roman history painted by Andrea del Sarto and Pontormo, into which have been injected matching scenes from the history of the Medici family.

In the 19th century the gardens were converted according to the fashionable English style. They were given romantic temples, an aviary, fountains and a mock-Gothic ruin. Most recently, the villa was used as a country residence by King Umberto of Italy and the few remaining furnishings date from this period.

It was also the scene of the ghastly double murder of the Grand Duke Francesco and his wife in 1587. Now the huge bare rooms are sad and desolate and the villa has been converted

Coaxing a new-born lamb to its feet.

into a somewhat tawdry museum.

The walled village of **Artimino** is about seven miles (11 km) away from Poggio a Caiano. Its huge villa was built by Bernardo Buontalenti as a hunting lodge for Ferdinand Medici 1 in 1594. It stands on a rise connected to the village gates by a tree-lined avenue. A bucolic vapour hangs over Artimino itself, owing to the many small local wine *fattorie*, seemingly the only means of support in this remote and rustic environment.

Half a mile down the hill on the other side of Artimino is the Etruscan cemetery from whose stones the nearby church of Pian di Rosello was built in the seventh century.

From Artimino a tortuous road leads via Carmignano to **Vinci** on the southern slopes of Monte Albano and to the village of Anchiano, the latter the alleged birthplace of Leonardo da Vinci. The entire *raison d'être* of Vinci is a celebration of the great Italian genius.

The medieval castle of the **Conti Guidi** houses the **Museo Vinciano**, a museum which exhibits a vast selection of mechanical models built to the exact measurements of Leonardo's drawings. There is also the **Biblioteca Leonardiana**, devoted to the documentation of his life and work. In **Anchiano**, near his rustic birthplace, is another museum featuring the more prosaic mementoes of his life.

Valdarno: To the east of Florence, off the SS70 which goes to Consuma, is a narrow pass which climbs tortuously up the western slope of the Pratomagno hills to the monastery of **Vallombrosa**—958 ft (292 metres) above sea level in the central Appenines. Founded by S. Giovanni Gualberto in the 11th century, this monastery, the first house of the Vallombrosan Order, is surrounded by magnificent woodland of oaks, pines and firs, many of which were planted by the monks themselves.

By the time Gualberto had died in 1073 the Vallombrosan Order, part of the Benedictine Rule, was spreading all over Italy. Their power became so great that in 1866 the Order was suppressed

Restaurant on the Chianti road.

and today only four monks remain to say the offices of the church.

In the vicinity of Vallombrosa are Romanesque churches worth visiting— **S. Pietro** in **Cascia**, **S. Agata** in **Arfoli**. There is also the tiny village of **Saltino**, handy in the winter for the ski runs of **Monte Secchieta** which lie above Vallombrosa.

The Chianti: In 1716 a decree issued by the Grand Duke of Tuscany defined the boundaries of the area known as Chianti and established the laws governing the production and sale of wine. Chianti wine became popular in the 15th century, and by the 1700s it was very well-known.

Today this is the world's oldest wine-producing league. The Chianti Classico area includes the communes of **Barberino Val D'Elsa**, **Impruneta**, **Greve**, **San Casciano** and **Tavernelle Val D'Elsa**.

Closest to Florence in this area is the town of **Impruneta**, an important sanctuary in the early medieval period when a shrine was erected here to house an image of the Virgin Mary, supposed to have been the work of St Luke and believed to be able to perform miracles. This shrine, the **Basilica di Santa Maria**, with its terracotta tabernacle by Luca della Robbia in Michelozzo's Chapel of the Cross, underwent numerous alterations throughout the centuries, until it was finally decimated by a bomb in World War II.

Subsequent restoration and repair to this and to other pre-17th century buildings have meant that Impruneta has retained a great deal of its early character, though without the patina of age. Brunelleschi insisted that the tiles for the roof of the Duomo in Florence be supplied by Impruneta, which is still important as a centre for terracotta production. Vases, bricks and roofing materials are still made here.

South of Impruneta, in the centre of the Chianti area, is **Greve** whose annual September *Mostra Mercato del Chianti* (Chianti Classico Fair) in Piazza Matteoti attracts much attention. Fairs have been held in the marketplace since the Middle Ages and today the market also does an excellent trade in the Chianti's other main products—extra virgin olive oil, traditional boar sausage and a variety of local handicrafts.

San Casciano in Val di Pesa, another quiet old Chianti town a third of the way along the highway connecting Florence and Siena, is enlivened every February by a Carnival. The town's reputation today rests solely on the great quantity of art works held by the Collegiata Church, the Convent, the Church of St Francis and the Church of the Misericordia—paintings by Simone Martini, Ugolino di Neri, Taddeo Gaddi and Fra Bartolomeo.

The Valdelsa: Because the town of **Castelfiorentino** in the Valdelsa is split between two sites, it has two centres. The older of the two has its origins in the Middle Ages and is located around the Piazza del Popolo.

But now the town's former beauty is somewhat lost among the sprawling modern outskirts while the hill town of **Certaldo**, further to the south, has been saved from being swallowed whole because its upper part, **Certaldo Alto**, is fairly inaccessible. It straddles the summit of a steep hill and is reached by a narrow winding road. Consequently the integrity of the medieval townscape has survived virtually intact. It consists of nothing more than a central street, off which are a series of alleyways.

It is built predominantly of red brick and its claim to fame is that towards the end of his life it was the home of Boccacio—in fact he died here in 1375—and today his alleged home, restored in 1823, bombed during World War II, has been rebuilt and can be visited.

The differences between Certaldo Alto and Certaldo Basso are marked by the silence of the former where, on summer afternoons, the only sounds are footsteps and the distant music of a radio. The town is crowned by the 15th-century Palazzo Pretorio, the front facade of which is studded with terracotta coats of arms. Exploration around the back of the town will reveal the early gateways, the portals of which are still intact and which lead down to steep, narrow approach lanes.

PISTOIA

Pistoia is the smallest province of Tuscany, sandwiched between Lucca and Florence and fought over for centuries by both. It is part fertile plain and part mountains, bordered in the north by the Appenines where Abetone, a popular ski resort, is little more than an hour's drive from the city of Pistoia.

The other major town in the province is Pescia, cradled in the plain of the Valdinievole and famous for its flower production. The province is also important for railway construction, embroidery, furniture making and shoe manufacture. Here too is Montecatini Terme, an elegant international spa town.

Pistoia (population 94,000) is only 22 miles (37km) from Florence and rather unfairly neglected as a result. Its historic heart is a delight and well worth negotiating the surrounding industrial suburbs, and it has enough good hotels tucked away in the medieval streets, as well as excellent restaurants and elegant shops, to make it an attractive alternative base.

If you stay in a hotel in the centre of Pistoia be sure to get a sticker which entitles you to park; otherwise it can be a problem and you would be well-advised to leave the car outside the old city and walk 10 minutes or so to the centre.

The citizens of Pistoia take great pride in their many historic monuments and churches but there is little in the way of the more tawdry tourist trappings. There are shops as glamorous as Florence or Lucca and the traffic could compete with any town in Italy; but when dusk falls, the lamp-lit shadowy streets of Pistoia still have an authentic medieval atmosphere. Church bells peal, Franciscan monks stride along in their unmistakeable brown habits and rope belts and the stone slabs outside the shops are laid out with goods for sale just as they were in the Middle Ages.

Pistoia was originally a Roman town, founded as a staging post on the Via Cassia, but it was razed to the ground in A.D. 400 by the invading Longobards.

It flourished as an important banking centre during the Middle Ages when most of its important architecture was built, but suffered during the wars between Florence and Lucca, eventually falling under the dominion of Florence. The word pistol apparently derives from Pistoia, named after the daggers known as *pistolese* worn by the local soldiers.

The impressive trapeze-shaped walls with bastions and four gates that still encompass the centre of the city were built by the Medici during the 15th century. The central **Piazza del Duomo** is banned to traffic and, when not full of bustling market stalls (Saturdays and Wednesdays), is a good place to quietly take stock of Pistoia's riches. (Pick up a city map from the tourist office in the Palazzo dei Vescovi in the Piazza.)

The **Cathedral of San Zeno** is originally fifth century but was rebuilt in the Romanesque style in the 12th century with a splendid facade of green and white marble stripes. A marble porch was added later and decorated with an

Preceding pages: Villa Garzoni and gardens at Collodi; San Giovanni Fuorcivitas, Pistoia. **Left,** 12th-century Romanesque facade of Cathedral of San Zeno, Pistoia. **Right,** terrace of a Tuscan country villa.

exquisite blue and white Andrea della Robbia bas-relief.

Inside are many medieval frescoes and Renaissance paintings, the tomb of poet Cino da Pistoia, and—most glorious of all—the massive silver altar in the chapel of St. Jacopo, decorated with bas-reliefs and statues over a period of two centuries by many different artists, including Brunelleschi. It is a priceless work and usually the chapel is kept locked; so ask the sacristan if you want a closer look.

Next to the Duomo is the soaring campanile, originally a watchtower, to which have been added three tiers of green and white Pisan arches reflecting the Duomo facade. Opposite is the 14th-century octagonal **Baptistry** of San Giovanni in Corte, designed by Andrea Pisano. It has the most wonderful high brick ceiling and a huge font of many different coloured marbles, recently restored.

The Piazza is completed by a number of fine Renaissance palaces, including the **Palazzo del Podesta** which is still the city's law court. Opposite is the **Palazzo del Commune** built in the 13th and 14th century with a harmonious facade of arches and delicately pointed windows, decorated with the ubiquitous Medici crest and a grim black marble head.

Inside is a courtyard and sweeping stairway and sculptures by celebrated modern artist Marino Marini, many of them based on his favourite theme of riders and horses. At the foot of the stairs is his *Rider Miracle* from 1953. Upstairs in the first and second floor rooms is the impressive art collection of the new **Museo Civico**, which includes a rare 13th-century painting of St Francis, a number of 15th-century altarpieces from churches in Pistoia and many delightful polychrome wooden sculptures, such as the 15th-century *Angel* by Francesco di Valdambrino and an exquisite 16th-century *Madonna and Child*, as well as works by many later artists.

To the north of the Piazza Duomo in Piazza Giovanni XII is the **Ospedale**

Octagonal Baptistry of San Giovanni in Corte, Pistoia.

del Ceppo, named after the offering boxes in which alms for the poor were collected. It was built in the 14th century and still functions as a hospital. Above the portico is a brilliantly coloured majolica frieze by Giovanni della Robbia worth observing in detail. In rich blues, greens, yellows and browns it depicts the *Seven Acts of Mercy*: worthy citizens handing out food to the poor, comforting prisoners and the sick, washing the feet of dusty travellers and minstering to the dying. The figures are realistic, and even humorous, despite the gravity of their occupations.

Pistoia has a large number of churches, many of great architectural interest, some with notable artworks—in particular the Pisano pulpits, which are the great pride of the town. A few of the churches are neglected or under restoration, some are closed, some so badly-lit it is impossible to see anything, and some have been so altered and embellished that their interest lies mainly in the way they reveal the different styles and tastes that have emerged over the centuries.

Most are within easy walking distance of each other and a rewarding selection could be visited in a morning's tour, bearing in mind that most will close at midday until three or four o'clock. Alternatively, just drop in whenever you happen to pass one as a brief respite from the busy streets and traffic.

Sant Andrea in the Via Sant Andrea, is flanked by an enormous spreading pine tree. It has an arcaded facade and reliefs above the central door. Inside is a richly painted wooden ceiling and narrow nave well-lit from the upper clerestory. Here is one of the famous pulpits by Giovanni Pisano, created in 1298 and modelled on the Nicola Pisano pulpit in the Pisa Duomo. The sharply carved marble reliefs border on the melodramatic in their depiction of the life of Jesus and the Last Judgement. In the right of the nave hangs a wooden crucifix, also by Giovanni.

San Bartolemeo in Pantano, in the Piazza San Bartolomeo, is one of Pis-

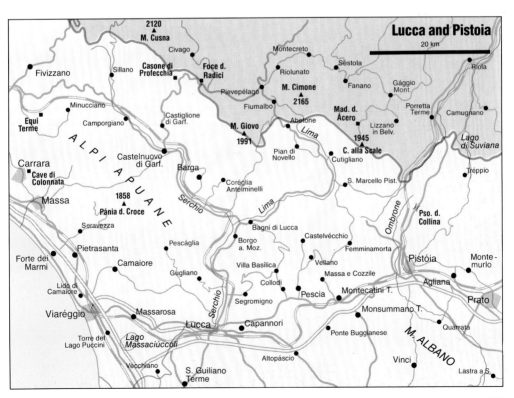

toia's oldest churches, built in the 12th century with a five-bay facade and rich in marble carvings and reliefs; those above the door are based on Roman sarcophagi. Inside is a reconstructed pulpit by Guido da Como (1250) with marble reliefs of Christ's nativity, the whole massive construction resting on the backs of men and lions carved out of marble.

In the Via Cavour is the church of **San Giovanni Fuorcivitas**, thus named because it was built in the 12th century outside the city walls. It has an elaborate green and white striped marble facade and walls in the Pisan style, and inside is light enough for a good view of some fine works of art including the pulpit created in 1270 by Fra Gulglielmo da Pisa, a water stoup by Giovanni Pisano and a touchingly beautiful white glazed terracotta of the *Visitation* by Luca della Robbia.

The church and monastery of **San Domenico**, in the Piazza Garibaldi, is an example of 13th-century Gothic style and a good illustration of what not to do

to a church, with its original windows filled in and new ones inserted, and huge paintings unaccountably chopped about. But inside are a number of colourful original frescoes and works claimed to be by Rossellino and Bernini.

Opposite San Domenico is the former chapel of Antonio Tau. It is no longer a religous building and is currently under restoration as an artistic monument, containing many darkly dramatic Gothic frescoes on its walls and vaulted ceilings.

Other churches worth including in a visit to Pistoia are Santa Maria del Grazie, San Francesco, San Paolo, and San Spirito. But at almost every turn there is *some* architectural find to enrich a meander through the narrow streets, from a fine palazzo to a carving over a doorway.

The main shopping streets with excellent clothes, shoes, leather and jewellery stores are the Via Cavour, Via Cino, Via Ateo Vannucci and Via Orafi, and it is here that the evening *passeg-*

Majolica frieze of *Seven Acts of Mercy* by Giovanni della Robbia, Ospedale del Ceppo, Pistoia.

giata takes place. In July the *Giostra dell'Orso* (Bear Joust) is held in the Piazza del Duomo, a colourful costumed display of a joust between 12 knights and a bear though the bear is now a prosaic wooden model. About three miles (five km) outside of the town is Pistoia's famous zoo, set in a large pine forest.

The spa towns: West of Pistoia, and most easily accessible via the A11 autostrada are the spa towns, the grandest of which is **Montecatini Terme**, famed throughout Europe for its elegance and luxury. It was rebuilt by the Grand Duke Leopold of Tuscany in the 18th century and has since become a company town with whole avenues of huge spa buildings dispensing waters to drink and treatment ranging from baths and inhalation to the famous mudbaths. You can stroll through the magnificent parks, or sip the waters in marble pavilions—or, of course, commit yourself to a complete cure.

Montecatini Alto is the original medieval fortified town above the ther-

mal springs, and can be reached by funicular railway or by road. Although full of wealthy tourists in high season, it is still a charming restful place to visit, with a shady walk of chestnut trees around the lower terrace of the village and panoramic views of the plain of the Valdinievole.

The main square, Piazza Guiseppe Giusti, has large open cafés. Little remains of the original fortress, although its walls and towers are being restored. It is surrounded by a quiet little park of pine trees with a moving war memorial of cannon and barbed wire. The adjacent church of St Peter has Romanesque origins, but has been hideously restored with its columns and exquisitely carved capitals barely visible for sheets of cheap marble veneer.

Monsummano is the birthplace of the poet Guiseppe Giusti (1809-1850) and the site of a particularly extraordinary spa, a thermal grotto, Grotta Giusti, where the steam treatments are actually taken deep in underground caves.

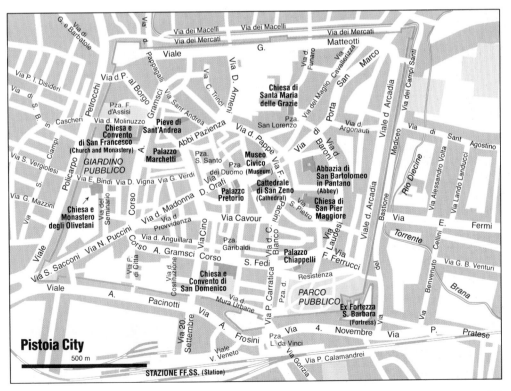

Pistoia City

500 m

Taking The Waters

Spa treatment in Italy is available on the country's National Health Service, and many Italians are firm believers in the benefits of taking the waters. The spa cure has remained virtually unchanged for hundreds of years, since Papal couriers used to carry the waters to Rome, and Ugolini di Montecatini wrote his treatise on mineral waters in the 14th century.

The initiates bathe in the spa waters, inhale them, steam in underground grottoes, or merely stroll, elegantly slipping in the marble halls of spa towns like Montecatini Terme.

Tuscany is the location of a large number of different spas, ranging from open air hot springs used by local people to luxuriously equipped and medically regulated residential establishments. Most can be visited for a few hours or a day and make a very pleasant diversion during a holiday; but less dilettante practitioners would recommend taking a full cure, which can last for a week or 10 days and is regarded very seriously. The most appealing aspect is that you don't really need to have anything wrong with you to take a cure, and it is an excellent restorative way to spend a vacation.

There is plenty of medical evidence for the physical benefits of mineral waters taken externally and internally; thermal treatments are prescribed for skin problems, digestive, urinary and gynaecological ailments, rheumatic problems and respiratory diseases, but it is the concept of the complete cure that is so attractive. All the spas are in the middle of beautiful countryside, surrounded by parks, mountains and lakes and an essential part of the treatment is calm and rest and long gentle walks.

Like the Ancient Romans before them, whole families or groups of friends go off to the spa together, all equipped with voluminous towelling bathrobes and plastic slippers. At Saturnia, near Grosseto, is a newly developed spa on an original Roman site. Now modern Romans come over from Rome for the day to take the waters.

There are large swimming pools, waterfalls and fountains for drinking, all overhung with the acrid smell of sulphur. Visitors spend the day bathing, sitting in deck chairs and snoozing in the sun. Floating in the water are large clumps of slimy green seaweed which the truly dedicated smear over their face and body.

In summer it can be an enervating experience since the water here is very warm; perhaps the best time to go to Saturnia is in winter when it is quiet and the pools steam gently in the frosty air, the cold providing a welcome contrast to the warm waters.

Montecatini Terme is by far the most spendid of all the spas, famed throughout Europe along with Marienbad or Baden-Baden, and frequented since the 18th century by the grand and leisured, from European royalty to Hollywood stars. It comprises whole avenues of huge spa buildings dispensing waters to drink and treatments from baths and inhalation to the famous mudbaths.

The Leopoldina pavilion is the most magnificent, a baroque 1920s edifice of rose marble, with fountains gushing the healing waters and an orchestra playing. Glamorous women sip coffee and eat pastries served by formally attired waiters, and romantically pale *Death in Venice* types waft through the marble columns, glass in hand.

The different waters, prescribed for varying ailments, are dispensed with great formality from elaborate brass taps over marble basins worn smooth with use. It is recommended to drink the waters in the morning on a empty stomach, preferably while walking.

But the most bizarre spa treatment must be the Grotta Giusti, near Monsummano Terme. The spa offers a complete range of treatments from thermal baths to hydro-massage but the hot thermal springs themselves are deep underground, fed by an eerie green thermal lake. White hooded figures shuffle down a rocky winding passage of stalagmites and stalagtites into a dimly lit cave where rows of chairs and shrouded sweating wraiths look like a scene from a Fellini movie. The further you descend the hotter it gets and the different levels are appropriately named Purgatorio and Inferno. No wonder Guiseppe Verdi called it the eighth wonder of the world when it was discovered in 1849.

Driving north of Montecatini along the N633, you arrive at **Marliana** via a stunning mountain road that winds steeply upwards through chestnut trees and olive groves with views of a much darker and more rugged Tuscan landscape. Marliana has the remains of a castle, and a campanile from which there are magnificent views.

A little further on is **Vellano,** a hilltop fortified village, and well worth exploring. It is still a working village little changed since medieval times, although there are now washing machines along with the stacks of wood for winter tucked beneath the ancient portals. As you climb the little twisting streets to the campanile, the town becomes more ruinous, but every tiny piece of land is cultivated, and pumpkins and courgettes sprout among the ruins. It's a handy place to break for lunch as Vellano has a number of good family restaurants with windows overlooking the valley slopes and olive terraces.

Pescia itself is best known for its flowers with the largest flower market after Holland, specialising in carnations, gladioli, lilies and chrysanthemums. The market itself, now in a vast new building, can be visited but it is necessary to get there early - it's all over by 8 a.m. Pescia is a prosperous town, surrounded by nurseries, greenhouses, olive groves and acres and acres of flower gardens.

Elegant villas, sheltered by cypresses, are visible in the hills beyond, many of which can now be visited or rented as part of the current drive towards "agri-tourism". The town itself, most of which is 13th-century in origin, is divided by the River Pescia, and at its centre is the Piazza Mazzini, dominated at one end by the Oratory of the Madonna di Pie di Piazza, which dates from the 17th century. It has a finely carved wooden ceiling, richly embellished with gold leaf by Giovanni Zeti, and there is a delightful little painting beneath the altar showing Pescia as it looked in the 17th century.

At the opposite end of the Piazza is the Palazzo Communale with its forti-

Left, sipping the waters in the marble halls of Montecatini Terme. Below, visitors to Montecatini at the turn of the century.

Bagni di Montecatini - Piazza Umberto I

VAT 679

fied tower, still used as the town hall. On the other side of the river is the 17th-century Baroque cathedral which still retains its 14th-century bell tower but has a modern facade.

Pescia's most prized works of art are the earliest known paintings of St Francis, to be found in the church of San Francesco in the Via Battisti. Buonaventura Berlinghiero painted them in 1226, only nine years after the saint's death. In the church of Sant'Antonio are frescoes by Bicci di Lorenzo. In the hills above Pescia is the Convento di Colleviti, a peaceful Renaissance monastery, accessible by footpath from Pescia.

Just to the south of Pescia are two villages worth visiting, though they are in dramatically different states of repair. **Uzzano** is a pretty hill village with winding streets, but it is not in good shape and many of the houses are in danger of imminent collapse. However, it has an interesting gateway and a curious church right at the crest of the hill; it has a rose window and an elaborate Pisan doorway.

Buggiano, by contrast, has been carefully though not over-restored, many of its stuccoed houses painted with a coral red wash. If you head towards the church and campanile you will find a very fine palazzo, and a proud caretaker will appear showing you round for a small consideration. The building has massive oak beams and lovingly preserved frescoes on the walls, and a store of town documents dating back to 1377.

The village of **Collodi** is famous for the magnificent Villa Garzoni and its gardens and the Parco di Pinocchio. The village itself, once part of Lucca province, was the scene of fierce fighting during the wars between Lucca and Florence. Today it straggles up the hill behind the Villa Garzoni, with only a few ruins of its original fortifications remaining. It is worth climbing up the winding stone steps of the pretty streets to be rewarded with wide-ranging views of the plain below. In the church of San Bartolomeo are wooden sculptures, 15th-century frescoes and terracotta statues.

The **Villa Garzoni** can be visited; access is through the 18th-century neoclassical gardens, which are enchanting. Fountains and flower beds are laid out in an elaborate formal pattern with parterres and pools, behind which is a complicated series of interconnecting stairs and terraces leading to waterfalls, hidden statues, grottoes and a maze. To the left the path takes you through a bamboo grove, up to the great wooden doors of the villa itself, and through into the inner courtyard. Although still in private hands it is open to visitors.

Within the 17th-century villa are grand reception rooms, bedrooms and galleries decorated with flowery frescoes, polished terracotta floors and charming, if faded, furnishings.

But the most appealing room is undoubtedly the kitchen with its huge fireplace, cast-iron cooking utensils and well-scrubbed pine table, where Carlo Lorenzini wrote *Pinocchio* using the pen name of *Collodi*. The local people are very proud of Pinocchio and complain that the rest of the world believes

Statue of Fame in the garden of Villa Garzoni, Collodi.

that the famous puppet was created by Walt Disney.

Proper tribute is paid in nearby Pinocchio Park, full of bronze monuments of *Pinocchio* characters and a square of mosaics by Venturino Venturi depicting episodes from the story. There is also a good restaurant on the site, the *Gambero Rosso*, designed by modern Italian architect Giovanni Michelucci.

Mountain pursuits: The drive up into the mountains to the north of Pistoia, the **Montagna Pistoiese**, is stunningly beautiful, with sunlight slanting through tall slender birch trees. It is perhaps at its most intense in autumn when the colours of the trees rival New England—but winter sports enthusiasts will probably prefer it with a good covering of snow.

The main town of the Montagna Pistoiese is **San Marcello Pistoiese,** functioning primarily as an administrative centre and tourist base. It is traditionally known for the *Mongolfiera*, or hot-air balloon, which is launched every year on 8 September to mark the end of the summer. According to local legend, if the balloon rises higher than the bell tower, there will be a good harvest. Near to San Marcello, at Mammiano, is a spectacular suspension bridge, a footbridge 720 ft (220 metres) long connecting the village with the road across the rushing waters of the River Lima.

Cutigliano, further down the valley, is a typical mountain village, quiet with the all-pervading scent of woodsmoke in the air and surrounded by fir trees. Limited skiing and a cable car service is available, but the more dedicated will probably prefer Abetone. Cutigliano has a surprisingly grand 14th-century Palazzo Pretorio with numerous shields emblazoned on the facade, including the ubiquitous Medici coat of arms. Opposite is a quiet village loggia, with arcading and stone seats.

Abetone, about 90 minutes' drive from Pistoia, is 4,660 ft (1,400 metres) above sea level and is the most important ski resort in central Italy, with ski lifts, cable cars and chair lifts to a wide range of *pistes*, catering for intermediate and advanced skiers. It has two ski schools and wide variety of accommodation, as well as cinemas, clubs, discos, swimming pools and ice rinks. It is a centre for international skiing with competitions including "Pinocchio on skis" a mini-Olympics for children which takes place every April.

In the summer it's a good centre for climbing and walking expeditions in the surrounding forests of pine and chestnut trees—a favourite pastime of Puccini. *Rifugi*, or mountain shelters, are dotted around the area, supplying basic shelter and sometimes restaurants as well. Abetone is also well supplied with mountain restaurants which command wonderful views of the dramatic landscape and supply hearty food and restorative drinks—a local speciality to try is the *Grappa di mirtilli*, made from mountain bilberries.

Abetone is basically a mountain pass, not a town, and has little else in the way of cultural attractions. Two pyramid-shaped milestones in the centre of the town mark the original border between Tuscany and Liguria.

Terraces and waterfall in the Villa Garzoni gardens.

MASSA-CARRARA

Massa-Carrara is the northernmost province of Tuscany bordering on Liguria. It has been part of Tuscany only since the mid-19th century and is very different from the archetypal image of the Tuscan landscape.

Inland, Lunigiana is a little known region of pine-covered mountains, craggy ravines and remote castellated villages. The coast is a predictable, over-developed continuation of the Versilian Riviera, but overshadowed by the marble industry. The beaches are dominated by the majestic marble peaks of the Apuan Alps glittering deceptively like snow in bright sunshine.

The towns of Massa and Carrara have both prospered as a result of the marble trade, although the resulting industrial development has blighted great swathes of the surrounding area. **Marina di Massa** is a popular resort with fine wide sandy beaches interspersed with groves of pine trees and a promenade of pretty pastel-shaded holiday villas. The ribbon of development extends up to and beyond **Marina di Carrara**, where the beach is divided by the sight and sound of the mighty port out of which ships carry marble all over the world.

Massa is a busy modern town but has a well-preserved medieval centre, built by the Dukes of Malaspina who ruled Massa for three centuries, holding sway over the entire region. The core is the Piazza degli Aranci, edged with orange trees and presided over by the elegant 17th-century Palazzo Cybo Malaspina, with airy courtyard loggias where cultural events are staged in summer.

Beyond a cluster of narrow winding streets stands the Duomo above a wide flight of steps. It was begun in the 13th century but now has a Baroque interior and a modern marble facade. The crypt, where the Malaspinas were entombed, is a museum.

Massa is dominated by its magnificent Castello. Beyond the narrow old streets of the town, walk on up through leafy lanes past decaying villas dotted over the mountainside. The walls of the old fortress provide marvellous views and welded onto it is a graceful Renaissance palace, its delicate marble pillars and frescoes providing a powerful contrast to the grim towers of the original castle. After World War II it was used as a prison but is now slowly being restored as a cultural centre.

Disaffected air: The main evidence of the marble quarries in **Carrara** is the river of white mud that flows though the town, which has a dusty disaffected air about it. It is very much a working town, not a monument to marble and there are few fine marble statues to be seen. Even the Duomo—with distinctive features like its 14th-century rose window, Pisan-style facade and, inside, the 14th-century statue of the *Annunciation*—is in serious need of cleaning.

The interesting sights are within a few streets of one other and are adequately signposted. Worth visiting is the Accademia di Belle Arti, a 16th-century Malaspina residence built around an older medieval castle. To

Preceding pages: Carrara marble caves. Left, cutting giant blocks of marble in Carrara.

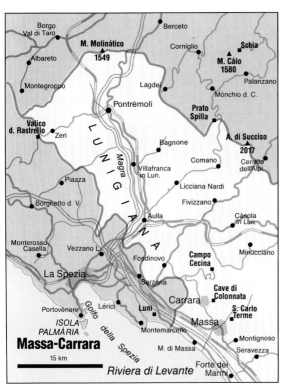

view the galleries you need permission from the director but a brief reconnoitre will reveal splendid marble bas-reliefs on the walls and sculptures from the Roman site of Luni as well as a Roman altar found in the marble quarries.

In nearby Piazza Alberica are two imposing 17th-century palaces and here every July there is a massive symposium of work in marble. Carrara also holds a biennial sculpture exhibition and an annual International Marble and Machinery Fair.

Of particular interest in Carrara are the marble ateliers, of which there are a number in the Piazza XXVII Aprile. Atelier Niccoli is full of marble craft-workers and sculptors, hair protected from dust with newspaper hats, all intently carving and drilling to produce a huge range of marble statues, friezes and ornaments.

The quarried marble was originally dragged down to this square by oxen, "pulling as though to break their hearts under the tyranny of the stones," as Edward Hutton described it. Later the huge blocks were brought by train and truck from the nearby quarries. The marble caves are fascinating to visit; you can either take a guided tour or, better still, drive up there yourself and wander around, taking obvious safety precautions.

The fine-grained pure white marble for which Carrara is renowned has been quarried here since Roman times, and has supplied artists from Michelangelo to Henry Moore with raw material. It is still the world's most important source of marble.

There are 300 quarries scattered throughout three steep valleys, the Colonnata, Fantiscritti and Ravaccione. Here the villages cling on to sides of mountains which have been sliced away like chunks of cheese. Dusty little houses have washing flapping from the windows, tomatoes and beans lovingly planted in any available crevice, and little marble exhibits carved by the quarry workers themselves.

Hutton, writing earlier this century, captures the drama of the caves,

Marble polishing in Carrara.

"...glens of marble that lead you into the heart of the mountains, valleys without shade, full of a brutal coldness, an intolerable heat, a dazzling light, a darkness that may be felt."

There are extraordinary views down into the quarries where the marble has been excavated deep into the ground. Precarious-looking staircases are strung across the sides, and massive trucks look like dinky toys as they trundle across the smooth marble surface far below. Modern equipment such as wire saws and compressed-air drills substitute for a time when marble blocks of 25 tons were transported manually on rollers lubricated with soap, and two men took an hour to saw through one centimetre of marble.

There is a marble museum, the Museo del Marmo, on Via XX Septembre between Marina di Carrara and Carrara. Displays include a gallery of many different varieties of marble and granite and geographical and historical exhibits, although no information is available in English.

Just on the border of Tuscany before heading inland is **Sarzana,** a bustling market town which has been colonised by artists and is being carefully restored. There is a large market in the Piazza Matteotti which is surrounded by arcades of Romanesque arches sheltering smart little cafés.

Finally in a scruffy area off the Via Aurelia north of Carrara there is **Luni,** the original Roman settlement from which marble was shipped. Here there is an amphitheatre and museum, and ongoing excavations have revealed columns, capitals, mosaic floors and tomb fragments.

Land of a hundred castles: Luni gave its name to **Lunigiana**, "the land of the moon", an almost undiscovered part of Tuscany which sees few tourists and makes little provision for them. It has always been a main trading route, however, and its many castles were built to extract tolls from pilgrims and merchants by the powerful Malaspina family who controlled the region.

Lunigiana was in the front line of

Marble atelier in Carrara.

fighting at the end of World War II, which has left its mark. Since then there has been inevitable rural depopulation with many emigrating to the United States. Now an enlightened attitude to tourism promises new hope for the area, villages and castles are being restored and the roads are in good repair. There are enough hotels, *pensions* and local restaurants to make a visit comfortable but its attractions are unlikely to ever generate mass tourism.

It is a mountainous region of steep winding roads, deep wooded valleys and unpolluted rushing streams. On the lower slopes are vines and olives. Higher up are forests of oak and the chestnut trees which have provided a staple of the local diet for centuries, and there are deer and wild boar in abundance.

The terrain ranges from the busy, productive flat valley of the River Magra to the profound silence of deep river gorges. Narrow valleys are dotted with tiny villages, quiet except for the sound of cowbells, dogs barking and the occasional gunshot.

The region is famous for its Romanesque churches and intact medieval villages as well as its castles, many of which are in the process of restoration through government grants. A number have been taken over by artists and sculptors and are used both as private homes and cultural centres.

The inhabitants of Lunigiana are proud and insular, in rural areas still growing most of their own food and wine and olives and regarding all other produce with some suspicion. They will buy in grapes from Chianti, making the wine themselves rather than buy an unknown finished product from foreigners.

Lunigiana is becoming a popular area for property hunters, although the locals still find it hard to understand the fascination of a ruined farmhouse. One English purchaser, deciding that the farmer's cowshed spoiled his view, offered to buy it along with the farm. But the farmer wanted more money for the shed than for the farm; the house was

Villa near Sarzana.

his grandparent's, falling down and no use to him, he explained, but the cowshed was his livelihood!

Fosdinovo is the first fortified village you arrive at as you drive towards Aulla on the winding road from Sarzana. Its little piazzas are shaded by huge chestnut trees and the steep twisting streets are dominated by the magnificent castle. It is one of the best preserved castles in the region, despite being damaged by Allied fire during World War II. The Germans had a command post there, exploiting its superb strategic position with views from all sides.

It was constructed by the Malaspina family between the 13th and 14th centuries with a complicated network of corridors and loggias. Beautiful frescoed walls and ceilings and furniture have been restored; it is sometimes used for cultural events and is one of the few castles with an interior open to the public on a regular basis.

Aulla itself is the gateway to the region where the rivers Magra and Taverone meet but much of it is war damaged. Of the 10th-century Abbey of San Caprasio only the original apse survives. The Fortezza of Aulla, **Brunella** broods over the town, originally built in the 15th century as a defensive rather than residential castle with walls 10 ft (three metres) thick, narrow windows and vaulted ceilings. It was restored earlier this century by Montagu Brown, the British consul in Genoa, and is now a natural history museum, accessible up a steep driveway off the main Via Nationale from Aulla, and surrounded by a large park of holm oaks and purple heather.

Fivizzano is a few miles west of Aulla along the 63 road, a busy attractive market town full of elegant Renaissance palaces and with a distinct air of pride in itself. The young people of Fivizzano are prominent in the movement to revive folk traditions with colourful flag-waving performances, dancing and mock duels, and they travel all over Tuscany giving demonstrations.

Nearby is the enchanting castle of

The hills of Lunigiana.

Verrucola, a completely fortified settlement on the banks of the river which has been superbly restored. Little red-roofed houses and narrow medieval streets cluster around the fortified square keep, with geraniums spilling from window boxes and gardens full of courgettes, beans and tomatoes crammed right down to the river's edge.

The castle is thought to date back as early as the 11th century and is distinguished by its two separate fortified towers, erected when the town was divided between two rulers. The castle and the 15th-century church with its peaceful arched loggia can be visited at some periods of the year.

To the north of Fivizzano is **Licciana Nardi**, an 11th-century fortified town. Much of the town wall is still visible with narrow passageways running through immensely thick walls into the village. In the Piazza del Municipio the 16th-century castle dominates the square, and is joined to the graceful baroque church by a small bridge spanning the narrow street. There is a small market once a week in the leafy main square.

Above the nearby Taverone river are the hill villages of **Bastia** and **Cisigliana**, a good base for walking with high meadows and wonderful views out to sea, perfect for picnics and mushrooming. Bastia has a 15th-century square bodied fortress, with cylindrical turrets at the corners, built by the Malaspina and now privately owned.

Along the valley from Licciana is **Crespiano** with a Romanesque church, Santa Maria Assunta di Crespiano, which was *restored* in 1079.

Comano is an important base for walking and riding, and nearby is the Castello of Comano, a ruined malevolent-looking tower surrounded by a tiny farming community, with ducks and chickens wandering the streets, and steep steps up to the tower.

At the end of the valley is **Camporaghena**, the last outpost before the Appenines, where there is a sad war memorial in the church. When German soldiers came hunting escaped prison-

Springtime Wisteria blossom.

ers of war and partisans, the priest rang the church bell as a warning and was summarily shot for his brave deed.

Monti is a tiny village with a particularly charming domesticated castle, complete with geraniums, lace curtains and even a street number on the door. It is well restored with its original gateway, keep and towers and is still apparently used as a summer residence by a surviving member of the Malaspina family. The church of Santa Maria Assunta di Venelia has an apse in *pietra serena* (the local grey "sacred stone") dating from the 12th century.

Pallerone is most famous for its crib, which can be seen in the church on request. It is an extraordinary clockwork nativity scene which changes from night to day and has a huge cast of busy clockwork characters, the Holy family, angels, millers, blacksmiths, and fishermen. It is touching, sentimental and very Italian.

A 10-mile (16-km) drive south of Fivizzano will bring you to **Equi Terme,** a popular spa resort, smelling strongly of sulphur, with waters that are claimed to have radioactive properties. If you follow the path through the old village tucked into the mountain gorge, you will reach a bridge and a waterfall and the high-roofed caves called Buca del Cane, because the remains of paeleolithic men and dogs were found here. Guided tours of the caves are available at certain times.

Close to Aulla is another fine castle, **Podenzana,** a well-proportioned, triangular white building, massively restored in the 18th century after an explosion in the powder room. The castle is at the top of a steep hill and nearby is an excellent local restaurant, *Gavarina d'Oro*, which specialises in the regional dish of *panigacci*, small chestnut flour pancakes cooked over an open wood fire and served with creamy cheese and home-cured meats.

Quiet villages: Along the main road (SS62) up the Magra valley between Aulla and Pontremoli are many fascinating villages and castles, all within just a few miles. Few of the small vil-

lages have facilities such as shops, restaurants or even bars, so if in need of refreshment try Villafranca or Bagnone.

Villafranca in Lunigiana lies in a strategic position near a ford over the River Magra and, has some remaining medieval streets. But its 12th-century castle is in ruins, destroyed during the war, and only parts of the keep and outer walls remain. The church of San Francesco has a terracotta of the school of della Robbia, and there is an interesting Ethnographic Museum in an old water mill near the river, which specialises in exhibits of typical local rural activities such as weaving, crafts and woodwork.

Bagnone is a large attractive town of Renaissance palaces, wide streets and cool shady arcades with many little bars and cafés. A honeycomb of houses, arches and passageways leads down to the river bank and tiny gardens. The 15th-century village of Bagnone is clustered on the hillside above, surrounding the cylindrical tower of the Castello and a fine 15th-century campanile. There is

an exquisitely carved wooden pulpit in the church of Santi Nicolo da Bagnone.

Nearby **Filetto** is a delightful, totally symmetrical square walled village with a tower at each corner. Almost every street is linked by covered overhead passages or bridges. Originally a defensive structure, it is now quite cosy, with cats snoozing in corners and village women sitting on the steps sewing and gossiping. Filetto has two piazzas overlooked by palaces, also connected with the rest of the town.

Malgrate and **Filattiera** are also worth a detour and nearby, next to the main highway is a magnificent Romanesque church, **Pieve di Sorano.** The nave is ruinous and has been turned into a cemetery but in the main apse is a very simple and beautiful little chapel.

Mulazzo was headquarters of a branch of the Malaspina family which had territories to the west of the River Magra; their arms are emblazoned over a fine arched doorway which guards the steep steps up to the town. Fragments of the original walls are left and in the upper part of the town the narrow streets widen into charming little squares overlooked by elegant loggias and their inquisitive inhabitants.

Pontremoli The town was originally divided into two halves to separate the warring factions of the Guelfs and Ghibellines and the Castruccio Fortress, built in 1332, cuts the town in two. There are many rich medieval town houses and the Church of the Annunziata has a 16th-century octagonal marble temple by Sansovino. To the north is the Castello del Piagnaro which was part of the original fortifications, and now houses the Archaeological Museum with its unique collection of *menhirs*, prehistoric and Bronze Age stone statues. Pontremoli is also famous for its travelling booksellers and awards the Bancarella literary prize every July.

At almost every turn there are more medieval villages, more castles, more breathtaking views. One of the best ways to see this rich and varied region is to take the little train between Aulla and Lucca on its slow journey through the mountains.

Left, Romanesque church of Pieve di Sorano, near Filattiera. Right, crushed grapes and new wine on offer in Malgrate.

LUCCA

To the west of Lucca province is "Tuscany by the Sea", a broad strip of land between the sea and the Appennines which contains a rich playground of villas and hotels. To the north is the steeply mountainous Garfagnana region, popular in the past for its variety of spas—a more remedial kind of playground—now more or less forgotten and hardly ever visited by tourists.

The city of **Lucca** has a more realistic outlook on life, with its renowned olive oil industry and increasingly important wine production.

Driving west along the A11 towards Pisa and the sea, you could be forgiven for thinking that Lucca was one Tuscan city which doesn't merit inspection. Yet to miss Lucca is to miss one of the least appreciated Italian—let alone Tuscan—cities, with its wonderful tree-topped walls, its enchanting Gothic and Romanesque churches, but above all the ease with which life is lived. More perhaps than Siena, its ambience is "*sympatico, molto sympatico*", making it one of the best places to bring a comprehensive tour of Tuscany to an end.

The walls were built at the height of the 16th-century revolution in warfare, when the nature of fighting moved from the offensive to the defensive. Largely inspired by Michelangelo's designs for the defence of Florence, the walls of Lucca are the only major city walls in Italy to have survived 19th-century destruction and are an excellent place to conduct *passeggiata* at dusk and to catch the last glimpse of the sun before it sets behind the Pisan mountains.

With its well-kept chestnut trees, already a part of the Luccan walls in the late 17th century, it is not surprising to discover that this continuous, circular avenue was to be the model for the larger-scale Tuileries at the Louvre in Paris.

For the people of Lucca however, the walls represent a fierce fight to preserve their independence. Until the 11th century, Lucca had been the capital of Tuscany. Then, for 400 years it defended itself against an ever more belligerent Florence and, even though the Florentines won the title of capital of the region, Lucca never ceded its political and economic autonomy. It remained an independent republic, apart from a brief period of Pisan rule, until the Napoleonic invasion of 1799.

At the other end of the historical scale, Lucca was the most significant Tuscan town in Roman times. The legacy of this history is seen in a plan of the city with its grid iron pattern of streets—so typical of any Roman habitation—and more obviously in the elliptical Piazza Amfiteatro around which houses were subsequently built. Caesar, Pompey and Crassus, the three most influential figures in the last years of the Roman Republic, met here in 56 B.C. to patch up their differences and to grant Rome a few more years of Republican rule.

The wealth of Lucca, like Florence, was based on banking and, from the late 14th century, its extensive silk industry.

Preceding pages: Lake Massaciuccoli at Torre del Lago. Left, the promenade at Viareggio. Right, Via Fillungo, Lucca.

As early as the 12th century, bankers from the "*banchi grossi*" were plying the waters of the Mediterranean or travelling north to Bruges, Antwerp and London, buying and then selling silk and woollen cloth. Successful bankers, like the Guinigi family, built substantial city homes. To demonstrate their prosperity they erected towers, although only one of these, the Torre Guinigi remains, distinguished by the oak trees sprouting from the top.

But the Guinigi were not the only ones to visibly display their wealth in the creation of towers as a picture in the Villa Guinigi (home of Lucca's principal art gallery) shows. It was, like San Gimignano, a forest of towers which illustrates just how wealthy late medieval Lucca was.

Villa Guinigi, not far from the Palazzo Guinigi, originally lay outside the medieval walls of the city. Among its treasures, which date mainly from the pre-1475 period, is a wonderfully pious *Madonna and Child* in bas-relief. The artist was Matteo Civitalli, a contemporary of Donatello and Lucca's most renowned sculptor.

Walking back into the centre of the town—walking is the only way to see Lucca unless you adopt the Luccans' preferred means of transport, the bicycle—you'll pass the delightful extended piazza of San Francesco with the simple facade of the church at one end and the 17th-century column with the Virgin Mary on top. If the area immediately around the column suggests a picaresque scene from an opera, one's senses are being led in the right direction: Lucca was the birthplace of Puccini, who is commemorated with a plaque outside his house in Via di Poggi.

But Lucca's chief attraction is its particularly interesting and beautiful churches. **San Michele**, built on the site of the old Roman forum, has one of the most spectacular Pisan Romanesque facades in Italy. The four stories of intricate arcades rest above some splendid examples of blind-arcading, and the delicate motifs and allegories carved

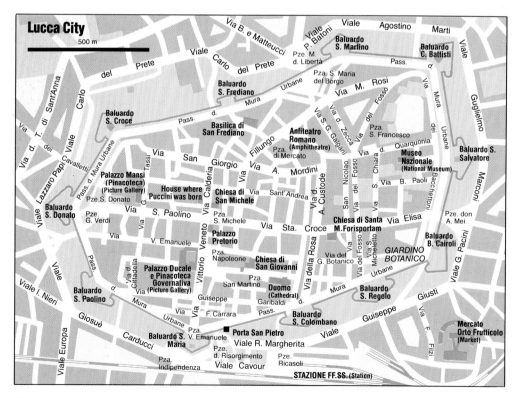

above each arch are especially noteworthy.

The **Cathedral of San Martino**, if you haven't got waylaid in *Il Giglio*—an attractive restaurant with excellent fresh-water fish close to San Martino—is also splendid, enhanced by its tower and the particularly attractive piazza in front of it. The facade was built in the 12th century, and the Gothic interior took 100 years to complete. So Romanesque and Gothic are combined and work surprisingly well together.

Inside there is the mysterious 13th-century labyrinth, symbolizing Life, and Lucca's masterpiece, the tomb of Ilaria del Carretto by Jacopo della Quercia. Staring at her face is to be transfixed by a sense of quietude and devotion rarely felt in any other sculpture.

The church of **San Frediano** is at the north end of the Via Fillungo, a street redolent of the city's medieval past. It's rare to find a mosaic on any church, let alone a Romanesque one, and represented is the *Annunciation of the Virgin*.

Inside it is supremely simple, practically austere. There is also an intricate and unusual font.

Round the corner is the **Palazzo Pfanner**, built in 1667. With its large 18th-century garden and its well preserved staircase, it's a perfect contrast to the medieval and religious architecture that so dominates the centre of Lucca. John Ruskin was so inspired by the architecture of Lucca that he declared that this was where he "literally *began* the study of architecture." He wrote, "Absolutely for the first time I now saw what medieval builders were and what they meant."

Villas and gardens: Outside Lucca itself are even stronger contrasts: the Villas **Mansi** and **Torrigiani**, both of which are open to the public. Mansi, with its statues and busts dotted above windows, in niches, on pediments, looking almost like candles from a distance, is close to fantasy, so ornate is the Baroque decoration. Villa Torrigiani, if less beautiful, has a strong patrician feel. Both are set in large open parks.

Pisan Romanesque facade of San Michele, Lucca.

Villas And Gardens

The idea of a country retreat, so popular in Tuscany today, originated with the Romans who built *villa suburbana* where they could escape to the peace and quiet of the countryside, usually only a few miles from the city. The villas were either working farms, which supplied the townhouses with produce, or were planned purely for pleasure. They would be visited for a day's outing and many did not even have bedrooms.

In the 15th century the idea of the country villa was revived by the Medici, who commissioned magnificent residences and elaborate gardens, modelled on classical ideas. Leon Battista Alberti laid down in his *Ten Books on Architecture*, the essential ingredients for a truly well-appointed country retreat: it had to be on a slope, full of light and air, with rooms grouped round an inner hall, "the harmony and concord of all the parts achieved in such a manner that nothing could be added or taken away or altered except for the worse."

Some are relatively simple structures, with gardens more lavish than the house; others are more extravagant, with whimsical additions, colonnades, domes, even mock antique ruins and statuary. Often they were copied by visiting Europeans, who applied principles intended for the sunny Mediterranean to more northern climates, with romantic but chilly results.

The Medici villa at Fiesole, which has has been described as "the first true Renaissance villa," was designed by the architect Michelozzo for Cosimo the Elder between 1458 and 1461. The villa was favoured particularly by Lorenzo Il Magnifico who entertained his humanist friends there. The design of the hanging gardens, in particular, was very influential and the villa commands a superb view of Florence.

The villa at Poggio a Caiano, near Pistoia, was converted by Giuliano da Sangallo for Lorenzo dei Medici between 1480 and 1485 and it dominates the surrounding countryside. It is characteristically Palladian in style; strictly symmetrical, with a classical temple front of colonnades and pediment added to the villa facade. In the 19th century the gardens were converted according to the fashionable English style, with romantic temples, an aviary, fountains and a mock Gothic ruin, and it is now undergoing restoration.

The 15th-century Villa Gamberaia has retained most of its original 18th-century garden and is considered by Harold Acton to be "the most poetic garden in Tuscany" with its fountains, statues, geometrically planned pools and parterres, secret grottoes, bowling alley and arcades of clipped yew and cypress.

The area surrounding Lucca is rich in villas: the Villa Torrigiani, the Villa Mansi and the Villa Reale at Marlia are all surrounded by beautiful parks and are open to the public. Marlia was created by the Orsetti family who were responsible for the gardens, and it was substantially remodelled by Elisa Bacciocchi, Napoleon's sister. There is a lush park of shrubs and lake which surrounds the formal Italian gardens. Box parterres lead to shady damp grottoes, a large fishpool adorned with swans, a garden of lemon trees in terracotta pots, fountains and—most wonderful of all—the *teatro di verdura,* an outdoor theatre sculpted from yew, a supreme example of the art of topiary.

Both the house and gardens of the Baroque 17th-century Villa Garzoni, near Pescia, can be visited. The gardens in particular are extraordinary: fountains and flower beds are laid out in an elaborate formal pattern with parterres and pools, behind which is a complicated series of interconnecting stairs and terraces leading to waterfalls, hidden statues, grottoes and a complicated maze. To the left the path takes you through a bamboo grove, over a rickety bridge to the adjoining villa, which was built in the 17th century by the Garzoni family from Pescia, fleeing Ghibellines who found refuge in Lucca.

Most of these villas are still in appreciative private hands, and often the gardens can be visited even if the house is closed to the public. Wandering through fragrant shrubbery and cool grottoes, past whimsical statues and fountains, can be recommended as an especially delightful diversion on a hot Tuscan summer's day.

The Versilia: This coastal region of Italy has always attracted the attention of scholars, poets, writers and artists. It is the area west of Lucca, squeezed between the Apuan Mountains in the east, the sea and the mouth of the Cinquale River in the north, and Lake Massaciuccoli in the south.

The flat landscape covered in pine trees has lost a lot of its earlier rustic and remote appeal now that it has been built on so heavily. The sea can be reached only if you are prepared to pay an entrance fee and actually want to lie on a sunbed on sand carefully raked and flattened for your added comfort.

Viareggio is the oldest of the coastal towns in the Versilia. Its origins are Roman and in the Middle Ages it was most important as a sea landing for the Republic of Lucca. In the 19th century, as the capital of the Versilia, it acquired a reputation for building some of the best boats ever launched on the Tyrrhenian Sea.

It was also in the 19th century that areas were established along its coast where men and women could bathe separately—though today it is a popular mixed bathing resort.

Today Viareggio is best known for its February Carnival. Vast hangars at the end of the Viale Marco Polo are set aside for the preparation of floats which are built to a specified theme and which are usually spiced up with political satire and irony. The whole town joins in and there are football matches, masked balls and fireworks.

To English visitors however, Viareggio is the place where in 1822 the drowned corpse of Percy Bysshe Shelley was washed up after a particularly lethal squall out in the Tyrrhenian Sea as he and a friend were on their way from Leghorn (as they called Livorno) to La Spezia. The two bodies were eventually cremated south of Viareggio, near the mouth of the Arno.

Viareggio reached its heyday at the turn of the century and there are a number of buildings of this period remaining in the town, such as the **Bagni Margherita** on the seashore, as

Left, gardens of Villa Garzoni at Collodi. Below, Cathedral and campanile of San Martino, Lucca.

well as a great many huge *art nouveau* hotels located on the seafront boulevard. During the summer months there is a very lively atmosphere here; not many foreigners tend to visit and the stretch of coastline going towards Forte dei Marmi is well-known as the playground for people from the north, in particular the Milanese.

A lot of factors have made Viareggio so popular. It has a wide sandy beach, there are plenty of trees and originally the promenades along the seafront were quiet places to stroll and relax. Nowadays strollers dice with death if they attempt to cross the main seafront road and it is extremely difficult to find a patch of beach that hasn't been colonised by a bathing establishment.

Puccini's lakeside retreat: Just south of Viareggio, along the Viale dei Tigli, is **Torre del Lago Puccini**. The approach to this lakeside resort passes through one of Viareggio's two pine forests and this one, the **Macchia Lucchese** or *Pineta de Levante*, is the most beautiful.

On **Lake Massaciuccoli** at Torre del Lago Puccini, is Giacomo Puccini's villa in which were written all his operas except *Turandot*. The area has been rather over-popularised but when Puccini first came here it was a peaceful backwater where he was able to indulge not only in composing but in his other favourite pastime, shooting birds and animals. His villa is open to the public in the mornings and on show are his musical instruments as well as his guns. Puccini, his wife and his son are all buried in the nearby chapel and Torre del Lago holds a festival of his operas each August in his memory.

Continuing north from Viareggio, the resorts fall into line in quick succession. **Lido di Camaiore** is slightly more downmarket than the other places further north but then access to the beach is easier—being virtually free of pay-as-you-enter stretches of sand. From this part of the shore it is easy to reach **Camaiore** (to the Romans, *Campus Major*), which is about four miles (seven km) to the east, and has an interesting range of architecture, of which

Torre del Lago.

the eighth-century **Badia dei Benedettini** with a monumental 14th-century portal and the Romanesque **Collegiata** are the most important.

From Lido di Camaiore the subsequent pocket of watering holes are collectively known as Marina di Pietrasanta. **Pietrasanta** itself is about five miles (eight km) inland from the sea; its name, "Holy Stone", refers to the town's chief product, marble.

Not much happens in Pietrasanta today except for the celebration of the town's main product. It is the Tuscan centre for stone sculptors who come here in droves to work the marble in the privacy of rented studios—private or commercial. Each year it has a large sculpture exhibition which is held in the Consorzio Artigiani and in the old Istituto d'Arte is a permanent exhibition illustrating the various ways of working marble. A fine white dust covers everything in Pietrasanta, even the wine glasses in the bars of the Piazza Carducci.

While this town has some of the loveliest monuments in the Versilia, including the 13th-century **Duomo** and the ninth-century **church of SS Giovanni and Felicita**, the **Marina** down below on the shore is bland and unexceptional. The two are joined by a tree-lined avenue which reaches the Marina at Fiumetto. The Marina is really a series of former villages—**Fiumetto**, **Tonfano**, **Montrone** and **le Fucette**—and each offers something different. Fiumetto has a pretty park with an ancient bridge in it, the "Ponte dei Principi".

But the gem of the Versilia today is **Forte dei Marmi**, still further to the north. Here the rich old villas of the late 19th century are still occupied as private residences, some *art nouveau*, some ornate and ugly, a suitable backdrop to lives of the utmost luxury. The Agnellis, owners of the Fiat car factory, live here. So do holidaying industrialists from Turin and fashion magnates from Milan, and the number of expensive sports cars seen cruising the streets at the hour of *passeggiata* in the early

Sunset at Forte dei Marmi.

evening is directly proportional to the number of bullet-proof vests required by the drivers and their bodyguards.

Forte dei Marmi grew up around a fort built in 1788 by Leopold I of Tuscany, the remains of which still survive in the main square of the town. The shops and cafés around the square still retain something of a small-town atmosphere even if they do sell some of the most expensive items that money can buy.

There are no high-rise buildings, unlike Lido di Camaiore. The highest things are the pine trees in the gardens of the villas, and in the back streets there is still the quiet and solitude that artists, writers, poets and scholars found here in the late 19th century.

Patches of beach are freely accessible while the rest is made up of smart bathing huts and tropical-style bars with palm-frond roofs, perched on the fine pale grey sand. Here the shore slopes gently into the water and bathing is very safe.

In most Italian towns, life is led conspicuously out in the streets—shopping, walking or simply sitting about in cafés. At Forte dei Marmi it happens on the beach. Along the sand at the water's edge there is an endless parade of nearly naked bodies strolling languidly up and down in the sun, chatting or simply sporting a fine figure.

Many of the holidaymakers stay in villas over the road from the beach, behind high wooden fences that shield private gardens with swimming pools from prying eyes. These people cross the road in the morning and late in the afternoon simply to stroll; swimming in the sea is out, that's what the private pool is for and at lunchtime the beaches are deserted.

Garfagnana: The landscape changes dramatically east of Pietrasanta. On the other side of the Alpi Apuane is the **Garfagnana** region, through which runs one major road once very popular with travellers wanting to avoid the risk of catching malaria in the formerly mosquito-infested Versilian lowland by the sea.

Beach at Forte dei Marmi, gem of the Versilia.

The centre of the Garfagnana is the town of **Castelnuovo di Garfagnana**, about 40 miles (64 km) north of Lucca. This fortress town once controlled the route from Genoa to Lucca and Pisa and was under the rule of the Este family of Ferrara until the Italian Unification. The town also had strategic importance during World War II; it suffered most during this period and a great deal of its town centre was destroyed.

But the Duomo survived and so did the town walls which surround the church of San Michele, which contains a 14th-century *Madonna* by Giuliano di Simone da Lucca. Part of the Rocca, or governor's palace, which dates from the 12th century, also survived.

In the Rocca, in the 16th century, lived Ludovico Ariosto, the epitome of the Renaissance man—successfully combining his talents as a poet with the functions of soldier and statesman. The Este appointed him Governor of the district, a post which he evidently hated and some of the murkier passages in his *Orlando Furioso* may have been influ-

The rugged hills of Garfagnana, painted by Adolfo Tommasi.

enced by his time at Castelnuovo.

Just north of the town, at the foot of the pass which leads up through the rugged heart of the Garfagnana, are the thermal springs of **Pieve Fosciana** which produce radioactive water. This concept is another variety of therapeutic spring, with which the area is prolifically endowed. The treasures of Fosciana are displayed in the church, including a terracotta *Annunciation* by Luca della Robbia.

Continuing over the pass for about 11 miles (18 km), the first stop is **San Pellegrino in Alpe**, where there is a museum of peasant life of the Garfagnana. But **Barga** to the south is by far the most interesting town in the district. The passing of time forgot to take Barga with it and today there is a curious silence in the lanes and alleyways behind its walls.

The Romanesque Duomo contains a 12th-century marble pulpit carved by a sculptor from Como called Guido Bigorelli. The pillars supporting the pulpit rest on the backs of lions while the inlaid

decoration and the panels of the pulpit itself, on which are scenes from the scriptures, make this work one of Tuscany's finest early Renaissance altars.

However, the real tourist attraction of the area, apart from the July/August opera festival held annually at Barga and the house and tomb of the poet Giovanni Pascoli at Castelvecchio Pascoli, are the subterranean caves at **Grotta del Vento**, near the village of **Fornovolasco**. Nearly three quarters of a mile of caverns wend their way through the ground, surrounded by stalactites and stalagmites, every inch of it looking like an elaborate stage set from a horror movie.

The cold clammy atmosphere is very slightly repugnant, but compelling nevertheless, and an added theatrical dimension is obtained by the use of coloured lights and echoes. Each visitor must be a part of a guided tour because it is fairly easy to lose the way as only a fraction of the caves are lit.

The terrain is steep and barren and offers the possibility of excellent, but rather dangerous, walks. The caves themselves are only open at certain times (from April to September).

San Romano in Garfagnana is an interesting town on the way to Bagni di Lucca. It has a large medieval castle and stunning views across the Alta Garfagnana, whose barren beauty is best appreciated with a visit to the nearby **Parco Naturale Demaniale dell' Orecchiella**. This is the preserve of rare flowers, wild boar and deer and all around are the grandiose peaks of the Alpe Apuane.

Near this spot, in a valley where the river Lima and Serchio meet, is the spa town of **Bagni di Lucca**. The town has always been known as a source of hot spring water, which contains sulphur and salt. It was very fashionable around the year 1800 when Byron, Shelley and Elizabeth Browning visited it, but since then it has been quietly forgotten. It has retained however, an air of quiet respectability and faded elegance and is worth a visit.In the 19th century the bathhouse was in the Palazzo del Bagno which is now in a rather neglected state. There are 19 springs in the town as well as two steam vapour grottoes which quite easily sustain temperatures of up to 47C (118F). The open season for the springs lasts from May to September and they are good for anyone suffering from arthritis and rheumatism.

From Bagni di Lucca the road continues along the banks of the River Serchio to **Borgo a Mozzano**, a hamlet well-known for its Magdalen Bridge, dating from 1322. The other name for this bridge, which spans the Serchio, is *Ponte del Diavolo* because, as the story goes, the devil is supposed to have built it for the villagers in return for the first soul to cross it on its completion. The crafty villagers cheated the devil by sending over, by night, a pig with which the devil had to be content.

In reality, this bridge, with arches of five different sizes, was built by Countess Mathilde of Tuscany. Her generosity was also responsible for the construction of the Romanesque churches of Diecimo, Pieve di Brancoli and Villa Basilica.

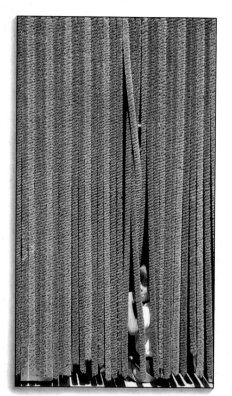

Left, cooling off in the shade. Right, Cypresses march down a Roman road.

PISA

The Leaning Tower draws tourists to Pisa like a magnet, many of them pausing to appreciate the surrounding religious architecture, others to enjoy the glorious art and history of this Tuscan city.

Once a thriving Roman port, Pisa's harbour silted up in the 15th century and it now stands on the Arno river, six miles (10 km) from the coast. Great sea battles were fought during the Middle Ages, with the city-state of Pisa first allying then becoming rivals of a number of other states including Genoa, Lucca, Venice and Florence. At its height, Pisa's power extended to Sardinia, Corsica and the Balearic Islands.

During World War II the city was heavily bombed and has been working ever since to restore its buildings. Pisa is halved by the gently curving River Arno, its steep stone banks coloured by floating green algae. Elegant 16th-century palaces along the banks hide the less imposing buildings and general decay in the narrow streets and alleys behind. Two-horse carriages lazily clip-clop along the quiet banks in the middle of the day, when most Pisans take their siesta.

The Church of Santa Maria della Spina sparkles in the distance. The statues on the sides were carved by followers of Giovanni Pisano, while the central statue of the *Madonna and Child* came from the workshop of Nino Pisano. The chapel once guarded what was believed to be a (*spina*) thorn from the crown of Jesus but that relic, plus the original statues, are in the National Museum.

Crossing the original city bridge, Ponte della Citadella, the Via Nicola Pisano leads to the Campo dei Miracoli—Field of Miracles, probably the most perfect assemblage of religous buildings anywhere on earth.

The secret of enjoying Pisa is to see the monuments for the first time from the right place. For the Leaning Tower, the first sight should be through the archway of the Porta Santa Maria, otherwise known as the Porta Nuova. When the sun is shining, the whiteness dazzles; when raining, it glistens.

The best time to visit Italy's most famous landmark is in the early morning when it opens. Then the crowds have not arrived, the air is fresher and it provides a magical introduction to the historic buildings.

Visitors come from all over the world to marvel, if only once, at the phenomenon of the 12th-century Campanile or Leaning Tower. The sensation on making the sloping ascent up 294 steps, balancing precariously on narrow, worn ledges, is one that will stay in the memory for ever.

It was begun in 1173 by Bonnano Pisano, the designer of the bronze south transept doors of the cathedral, but almost immediately began to tilt because the alluvial subsoil was unable to take its great weight. It now leans 13 feet (4 metres) out of true at the top.

Various proposals have been made to stop it leaning any further; removing the

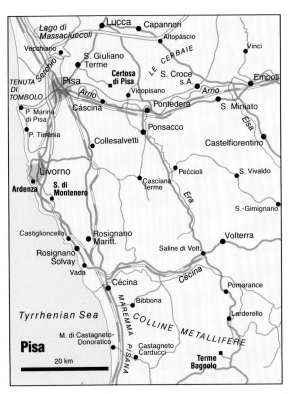

belltower which was added in 1350 and is about 5% of the total weight of the tower; inserting steel girders; injecting concrete under the foundations—and even dismantling it and starting again.

Il Duomo: The **Cathedral**, built between 1068 and 1118, is one of the major monuments in Italy. The beautiful white marble facade, the model for the Pisan Romanesque style is set with mosaics, inlaid marble and glass stones. The tomb of Buscheto, the architect of the building, is on the left of the facade which was designed by Rainaldo and built in the early 13th century. The central bronze doors, designed by Giovanni da Bologna in 1602, gleam from the caresses of thousands of fingers stroking a lizard, the head of Mary; the naked baby Christ, the pointed headdress of an attendant, the back of a dog, two frogs, the head of a woman, a pointed helmet, the round upturned hat of a guard, and four noses on the faces of heads in the friezes.

The main entrance to the cathedral was intended to be through the bronze transept door of the Porta di San Ranieri, near the Campanile. These panels of the life of Christ date from 1180 and show the Greek and Roman influences in the work of Bonanno Pisano.

On entering the cathedral the visitor is immediately drawn to the height of the nave, with its ornate golden coffered ceiling, rebuilt after a fire in 1596. Hanging in the centre on a long corded chain is "Galileo's lamp". The bronze chandelier with balancing *putti*, supposedly helped Galileo understand the theories of movement of the pendulum.

The nave, 312ft long, is supported by 68 Corithinian columns. The interior is impressive, not only for its huge spatial effect but also for the originality of its black and white striped marble walls.

The magnificent pulpit, sculpted by Giovanni Pisano between 1302 and 1311, was damaged by fire and removed in 1599, and not reconstructed until 1926. The five detailed reliefs show scenes of the birth of John the Baptist, the life of Christ and the Last Judgment. The six supporting columns

Pisa cathedral seen from the leaning tower.

are decorated with lifelike statues of biblical figures. The pointed arches draw the eye to a lighted stained glass window of the Virgin Mary.

Across from the Rainaldo facade is the third building of the cathedral complex—the Baptistry, begun in 1153. It is unfortunate that time and pollution are beginning to take their toll. Statues and busts by Giovanni Pisano, his father, Nicola and Arnolfo di Cambio are being removed from the second tier to the Museo dell'Opera Duomo while the four massive doors already have wooden replacements.

The spacious interior, with its eight stained glass windows, holds in the centre the 1246 octagonal font of Guido Bigarelli da Como, decorated with squares of ornate black, white and russet oriental design.

The carved pulpit, by Nicola Pisano, has, around the centre column, which is supported by three sculptures, six others—each alternate one resting on a lion's back. The five exquisitely sculptured panels depict scenes of the nativ-

ity, the message to the shepherds, the Adoration of the Magi, the presentation of Jesus in the temple, the crucifixion and the Last Judgement.

A visit to the Baptistry is not complete without a guide or chorister singing a single note which echoes several times over around the building, lifting even the most atheistic spirit. "Go by night into the Baptistry, having bribed some choirboy to sing for you, and you shall hear from that marvellous roof a thousand angels singing round the feet of San Raniero." wrote Edward Hutton.

The fourth element of the cathedral group is the Camposanto, the "sacred field", a cemetery consisting of cloisters surrounding a field of earth taken from the Hill of Calvary by the Crusaders. A fire bomb in 1944 destroyed most of its celebrated frescoes. However the most famous, *The Triumph of Death,* as well as those depicting *Hell* and the *Last Judgement* were saved and are now on display in a room off the north cloister.

Sinopie Museum: The Sinopie Museum is housed in what was one of the

Kiss of Judas, detail from cathedral doors.

THE PISAN STYLE

In 1062, in a sea battle fought off Palermo, the Pisan navy won an overwhelming victory over the Saracens of Sicily. The next year, the Pisans used their fantastic spoils to begin work on the foundations of a mighty cathedral. It was designed by one Buscheto (or Buschetus) in what became known as Pisan Romanesque—a style which spread across the country and greatly influenced the early Tuscan Renaissance. Its distinctive marble stripes and arcading are to be found all over Tuscany, pre-dating Gothic and Renaissance additions.

The Cathedral was consecrated in 1118. It was soon joined by a Baptistry, a bell tower (the celebrated leaning tower) and the Camposanto, making it the best example of grouped cathedral buildings in the world and a grand monument to the splendour of the Pisan republic.

Stylistically the buildings showed many influences, but all were faced with marble panelling and featured arcades and colonnades. The blind arcades—a row of filled-in round arches—on the outer walls of the cathedral were very distinctive, as were the four tiers of arcading on the facade, designed by Rainaldo, with a facing of alternating dark and light marble. Marble arcades, filled-in or left open to make a colonnade or gallery, became the style manual of the Pisan school. Another distinctive element at Pisa is that the curved tympana at the top of the blind arches contains an inset square diamond. These are all features of the Pisan style.

The facade of San Paolo a Ripa d'Arno (begun in 1210) in the city of Pisa itself is a good example, as is Santa Maria della Spina (1325), also in Pisa. This church has different layers of marble facing striped like a zebra—a feature to be found on many Pisan school churches. In addition to stripes, the different tones of marble are often used to make other geometric patterns, squares and circles in combination with the arcading and windows. Sometimes the stripes are all that remain after a façade has been rebuilt.

An excellent example of the Pisan school is the cathedral at Lucca; San Martino, which has a fine Pisan Romanesque facade by Guidetto da Como, dated 1204 and an almost exact imitation of the first three tiers of colonnades on the cathedral facade at Pisa. There are more columns and arcades surrounding the apse. Other examples in Lucca include San Michele in Foro (begun in 1143), which is surrounded on all sides by blind arcading, including the base of the bell tower. The four ranges of galleries on its amazing facade dwarf the nave which was intended to be raised. The arcading on the facade has the characteristic insert square panels, as has Santa Marie Forisportam (late 12th century) which was based directly on the cathedral at Pisa. More colonnades can be found on San Pietro Somaldi (rebuilt 12th century) and on the apse of San Frediano (1112).

The influence of the style spread far beyond the Pisan republic itself and can be seen in the blind arcading on the facade of the cathedral of Troia in Apulia (1093), San Giusto at Bazzano in the Abruzzi, and the cathedral of Massa Marittima which was begun in 1228 in the Pisan Romanesque style with blind-arcading across the lower part of the facade.

Parts of the cathedral of Genoa (1199) are Pisan-influenced and the church of San Giovanni Fuorcivitas in Pistoia displays three stages of purely Pisan arcading along its flank, complete with square insert panels and exuberant green and white zebra stripes. Next door, across an alley, there are more zebra stripes embodied in a commercial building that was clearly originally part of the San Giovanni Fuorcivitas group. Pistoia has many Pisan Romanesque churches including Sant' Andrea and San Bartolomeo in Pantano. Santa Maria della Pieve in Arezzo (1216) has three ranges of colonnading on its Pisan Romanesque facade.

The style also influenced a number of churches in Sardinia—in particular, San Gavino at Porto Torres (1111). Finding traces of striped marble or a row of small columns giving a complex interplay of light and shadow among the pointed arches of Italian Gothic is a rewarding exercise, and a particularly pleasant occupation while seated outside a café on the piazza of a Tuscan village.

wards of the "New hospital of Mercy" (Ospedale Nuovo di Misericordia), which was built between 1257 and 1286. Sinopias are preparatory designs which were carried out directly onto walls on a special kind of rough plaster, known as *arriccio*.

After preparing the outline of the design, the painter would gradually cover over and paint various parts of it, using a different kind of plaster which was richer in lime (*grassello*) until he had finished the whole work, so the sinopias were destined to disappear for ever.

The fire which followed the bombing of the Camposanto destroyed some of the frescoes and left the others in so precarious a condition that it was necessary to remove them—but that was how the immense sinopias lying beneath the frescoes came to light and were salvaged, and have now been carefully restored.

Last on the itinerary of the Piazza is the **Museo dell'Opera Duomo**—the Cathedral Works Museum.

The exhibits are all from monuments in the Cathedral square. The main items of the collection can be seen on the ground floor; these are sculptures dating from the llth, 12th and 13th centuries and are evidence of the artistic currents present in Pisa when, as a Republic, it was at the height of its power.

The precious objects in the museum collection—the Cathedral treasure and plate—are to be found in Room 9 and in the Seminary chapel, together with some very old ecclesiastical garments, dazzling rich silk robes, heavily embroidered in white, gold, red and black. Here too is Giovanni Pisano's famous *Madonna and Child* in ivory. There is also a fragment of a famous belt that once was the length of the Cathedral perimeter, encrusted with enamelled plaques, gemstones and silver crosses.

The archaeological section demonstrates the reuse of Etruscan and Roman material taken from the ancient settlements of Pisa and Volterra to decorate the city's new buildings. In Room 1 the 12th-century sculptures taken from the

Left, Pisan Romanesque style. Pisa cathedral with blind arches, colonnades and inset square diamonds. Below, Campo dei Miracoli, Pisa.

cathedral allow a full appreciation of the artist's work and a clear diagram shows where the fragments originated in the facade.

Another unusual art form, in Room 13, is wood marquetry, of which Cristoforo da Lendinara was the greatest master of the 15th-century school of inlaying which developed in the Po valley. His two intarsias are, together with Guido da Seravallino's six panels of animal figures, one of the favourite themes common to the Pisan intarsia workers.

From the Museo dell'Opera Duomo the Piazza dei Cavalieri is a short walk, but the best viewpoint for this spectacular square is opposite the Palazzo dei Cavalieri at the exit from Via S. Frediano. From here the whole of Vasari's glorious facade may be appreciated. In six niches above, the Grand Dukes of Tuscany gaze over the central steps and the fountain topped with Pietro Francavilla's sculpture of Cosimo the First.

Vasari (1511-74) designed the tower of the **Church of Santo Stefano dei Cavalieri** where trophies and spoils of war are displayed. In 1606 Giovanni de' Medici added the marble facade and placed the Knights' emblem above the doorway.

The large, irregular square is sometimes called Piazza dell'Orologio from the porcelain clock above the archway which has cool, stone benches beneath it. In 1284, when the Pisans lost the Battle of Meloria, the Podesta, Count Ugolino, suspected of treachery, was starved to death in the Palace of the Clock.

From the Field of Miracles, you can follow the banks of the Arno as far as the Piazza Garibaldi. From here it is a short walk along the river to the **Museo Nazionale di San Matteo**. Pisa's National Museum is housed in the converted ex-convent of the Sisters of Saint Matthew, and is renowned for its panel paintings with gold backgrounds, including one of Saint Paul by Masaccio, wooden crucifixes, altar-pieces and medieval Islamic and Pisan pottery.

There is a unique collection of an-

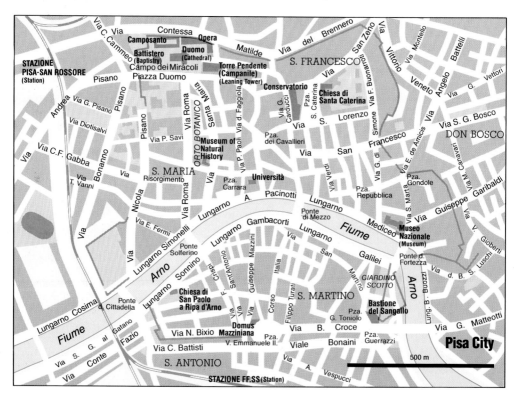

Pisa City

tique armour used in the *Gioco del Ponte* (The Bridge Pageant), which comprises about 900 pieces ranging from breastplates to helmets dating from the 15th and 16th centuries. There are also many wooden shields, painted with the colours of the city quarters, for use in the fight and during the parade.

The contest takes place each year on the last Sunday in June, together with the Historical Regatta and other celebrations. The historical procession which precedes the tournament, is composed of 750 people in medieval costume. A crowd of 100,000 people gather along the banks of the Arno to watch this spectacular event each year.

Marina di Pisa and Tirrenia: The pretty road out of Pisa to the coast pauses here and there at railway crossings as it follows the River Arno to the sea. It passes the San Piero a Grado Basilica where legend has it that Saint Peter landed when he reached Italy.

At Bocca d'Arno the hanging trawlnets from fishing boats and the rods of silent fishermen evoke the at-

mosphere captured by artists like Nino Costa, Gabriele d'Annunzio, and Giuseppe Viviani.

On both sides of the mouth of the Arno the coastline boasts miles of sandy beaches. Beyond the river mouth is the regional park of San Rossore, with its busy race-course and enchanting woods. Just in front of the former Royal Estate, lies the seaside resort of Marina di Pisa with its variety of architectural styles. Concerned newspaper reports of the pollution on this part of the coast are probably true, since industrial waste from the Arno and the sewage of seaside towns fill the Tyrrhenian Sea at this point, but the beaches are kept clean.

Natural barrier: A kilometre or so down the coast at **Tirrenia** is the remaining stretch of Mediterranean pine forest—the one place where no building has been allowed on the shore. The evergreen trees act as a natural barrier against the *libeccio*, a strong southwest wind. Thanks to the trees, the strong wind is reduced to a light, scented breeze of pine and juniper which cools the air on hot, summer days.

A much larger resort than Pisa di Marina, accommodation in Tirrenia varies from luxury hotels to clean homely boarding houses. Night clubs, restaurants and numerous sporting facilities for golf, tennis, horse-riding, underwater fishing, windsurfing, sailing and rowing are enjoyed by Tuscans but few foreigners stay along this coast. Each year colourful regattas and boat races are held and the training centre for the Italian National Olympics is based in Tirrenia.

Spa town: Midway between Pisa and Lucca, at the foot of the Pisan mountains, is the spa town of **San Giuliano Terme**. The Palazzo Termale (spa building), set in private grounds guarded by high walls is a national health hospital. Arrangements are made by the Albergo Terme di San Giuliano for private patients but anyone requiring treatment must be recommended by their own doctor.

Olives, chestnuts and pines grow in the surrounding fertile countryside and wild horses roam the hills. A number of

Dining al fresco.

ruins are dotted among the valleys and at Capoluogo in the Caldaccoli region are eight stone arches remaining from the acqueduct built by Mediceo di Asciano in 1592.

Certosa di Pisa: Set in lush green countryside, the **Charterhouse of Pisa** was founded in 1366. From the end of that century modifications and additions were continually made until the final touches to the interior decoration were finished in the early 18th century.

The Carthusians were one of the new strict orders who believed that the increasing prosperity of the Clunic orders was accompanied by a decline in religous observation. Their architecture reflected this; the monks lived in separate cells within a main enclosure, and took their name (anglicised as Charterhouse) from La Grande Chartreuse in Dauphiné. The centre of monastic life was the Great Cloister of which the Certosa di Pisa has a fine example.

Artists and craftsmen worked on the frescoes of the church walls from 1701-3; Angelo Maria Somazzi from Livorno added fine stucco work to the church, chapels, guest quarters and boundary walls and in 1718 workmen from Carrara carved the marble and renovated the church facade. In 1981 a part of the Charterhouse was allotted to the University of Pisa to house the Museum of Natural History and History of the District.

Entering **Cascina** past fields of sunflowers, grapevines and maize, the roads are lined with plane trees. Cascina is proud of its solid stone walls dating from 1142, which are depicted in Vasari's energetic painting of the Battle of Cascina, now hanging in the Palazzo Vecchio in Florence.

The town is centred round the making of wooden furniture. At the end of the main street, Corso Matteotti, with arcades each side, is a large factory building with *MOSTRA DEL MOBILI* displayed in huge letters, with furniture on permanent exhibition to visitors. Although the exhibition building is prominent, most of the workshops are tucked away in the pretty side streets, fes-

Umbrella pines at dusk.

tooned with seasonal flowers.

Leaving the Mostra and walking up Corso Matteotti, the tiny chapel of Suore di Carmelitane di Santa Teresa is on the left. It has beautifully detailed frescoes depicting the creation of the sky and the earth, the expulsion of Abel, the Tower of Babel and St John the Baptist. The nearby Church of the Saints Casciano and Giovanni, dating from 970, is a graceful arched building with a starkly simple interior.

Casciana Terme, less than 25 miles (40 km) from Pisa, lies 160 metres above sea level and is surrounded by flourishing vineyards, olive groves and peach orchards. The beautiful hillsides and the mild climate all the year round create a relaxing atmosphere for visitors.

The town exists solely for the spa, which is open from April to November, and the pace of life is leisurely yet clinical. The powers of the Casciana thermal waters have long been appreciated with notes about them in ninth-century documents.

In 1870 Poggi designed the large spa building, but a bomb destroyed it in World War II, leaving only the facade and the hall intact. In 1968 the building was completely re-built around the remains of the famous architect's original structure.

The country around Casciana Terme is good for walking, especially in the nearby pine woods of Pineta della Farnia. The village of **Colle Montanino di Ceppato** with its 1,000-year-old tower and **Pariascia** with its fortress are also within easy reach and a visit to the **Sanctuary of the Madonnina Dei Monti** might serve to restore the spirit. At **Crespina** and **Fauglia** are several magnificent 19th-century villas as well as the Church of **Chianni** and nearby **Lari Castle**, heavily adorned with medieval coats of arms and family crests.

A few minutes' drive from Casciana is the co-operative wine cellar *Enoteca di Terricciola* well-stocked with local wines and those from other parts of Italy. The area around Casciana Terme

A curious onlooker.

is known for the production of *Chianti Colline Pisane*, while the Arno valley from Santa Croce to Cascina and south of San Miniato produces *Bianchi S. Torpe*. The third area of local wine is around the town that bears its name—*Montescudaio*.

Ancient town: In a stillness not usually associated with Italian cities, rests the ancient town of **San Miniato**, whose origins go back to Etruscan and Roman times. It is set on the top of three hills, 192 metres above sea-level, and gazes out upon magnificent views. On one side stretches the large plain of the River Arno with the Appennines towering over the Pisan, Pistoian and Florentine mountains. On the other side, Carducci's "wavy gracefulness of the hills" continues to San Gimignano and Volterra.

The nature and history of the town has always been closely linked to its geographical position, equidistant to the important cities that played a decisive role in the history of the times: Pisa, Florence, Lucca, Pistoia, Siena and Volterra.

High on the hillside are the two towers of the Rocca which was rebuilt in the 12th century by Frederick II. Torre di Federico as it became known was destroyed in World War II but has been faithfully reconstructed. Dante recounts that it was from this tower that Pietro della Vigna leapt to his death and as punishment was turned into a gnarled and twisted tree. The oldest tower of the fortress, the Torre di Matilde was restructured as a belltower when the cathedral was built onto it at the end of the 15th century. The oldest building in San Miniato is a church built by the Lombards in the 8th century dedicated to the Blessed Martyr Miniato.

The church of San Francesco was built in 783 and completely rebuilt in 1276. It is a magnificent example of a Franciscan building. The remains of a 15th-century fresco depicts Saint Christopher with the Child Jesus. The building, to which a convent was added (Chiesa e Convento di San Franceso), was in a state of constant transformation

The rocca at San Miniato.

until the 16th century. By using bricks made from local clay, the medieval construction and decorative traditions were continued.

The Diocesan Museum of Sacred Art (Museo Diocesano di Arte Sacra) in the old sacristy of the cathedral, exhibits art and sculpture from various churches of the diocese. The determined tourist who can gain entry can admire works by Lippi, Verrocchio and Tiepolo.

Many local traditions are still maintained. On the feast of St John, when winnowing is over, bonfires of ears of corn and cloves of garlic are lit on all the hills surrounding the town, to keep ill-luck away. From the middle of September to the end of Christmas is the season for white truffles (*tuber magnatum pico*). There is an "Association of Truf-flers of the San Miniato Hills" who issue a map of where to find the aromatic plant, which is dug out of the ground with a *vangheggia*—a type of pole. On the last Sunday in November a huge market and exhibition is held to display the catch of the season.

Majestic position: Volterra is one of the most important towns in Tuscany, it has a richly layered history with abundant evidence of its 3000 years of civilization. It commands a beautiful, wind-swept and majestic position on a steep ridge 1780 feet (545 metres) above sea level between the valleys of the Era and Cecina rivers. Walking round the ancient defensive walls is an excellent way to view the town and the Roman remains and the wide sweep of countryside below.

Volterra was the Etruscan city state of Velathri, one of the confederation of 12 city states which made up the Etruscan nation. It became an important Roman municipality (Volterrae) when Rome annexed Etruria in 351 B.C. It followed the new faith of Christianity and at the fall of the Roman Empire in A.D. 476, it was already the centre of a vast diocese.

Although predominantly medieval, the town still cherishes abundant evidence of the Etruscan period, including the massive stretches of the city wall. The Porta all'Arco (the Arch gate), is

The heights of San Miniato.

the best preserved Etruscan gateway in Italy, dating from the fourth century B.C. with sides of huge rectangular stone blocks and three mysterious carved stone heads above the gateway. The Acropolis in the "Enrico Fiumi" archaeological park on the Plain of Castello shows various periods of human settlements from prehistory to the Middle Ages; also preserved are a large number of hypogea, vases and cinerary urns.

The traditional craftsmanship in alabaster is a legacy from the Etruscans who made great use of it from the fifth century B.C. for their beautifully sculptured urns. Alabaster is one of the most typical products exported from the region, sold from many local workshops.

Examples of the Roman period include the remains of the theatre in Vallebona, started under Augustus but completed during the rule of Tiberius; the baths, an enormous rectangular water cistern, sculptures and mosaic flooring.

Evidence of the Middle Ages is demonstrated, not only in Volterra's urban structure but in its buildings, the most important of which are in the Piazza dei Priori. Here is the tall, 13th-century Palazzo dei Priori, whose facade with its iron flag and torch holders is decorated with coats of arms of the Florentine magistrates; to the right of the square is the Palazzo Pretorio, with its crenellated Torre del Porcellino (Tower of the Little Pig), the name adopted from its decorative bas-reliefs of wild boar.

Also of great architectural interest are the towers of the Buonparenti and Bonaguidi families united by a high arch; the house-towers of Toscano in the small square of the church of San Michele in the Via Guarnacci; the 12th-century Cathedral which houses works of art from the Middle Ages to the Renaissance; the Baptistry, an octagonal building of the 13th century streaked with Volterran stone with an elegant marble doorway; the church of S. Francesco with its adjacent chapel of the Croce di Giorno decorated with

Volterra cathedral with Romanesque facade.

frescoes by Cenni di Francesco in 1410.

The Renaissance buildings such as the Palazzo Minucci-Solaini, blend gracefully with the medieval Volterran houses. The Palazzo Inghirami is the work of Gharaldo Silvani and the conventual complex of San Girolamo has a splendid *Annunciation* by Benvenuto di Giovanni and della Robbia terracotta statues.

Volterra has three major museums; the **Guarnacci Museum** is one of the most important museums in Italy for its Etruscan-Roman exhibits, particularly for the outstanding collections of alabaster cinerary urns decorated with many different motifs and sculpted in a great variety of styles.

The Art Gallery and Civic Museum of **Palazzo Minucci-Solaini** houses valuable paintings of the Sienese and Florentine schools of art. Among the works of Taddeo di Bartolo, Benvenuto di Giovanni, Donato Mascagni and Baldassare Franceschini are such notable paintings as the *Annunciation* by Luca Signorelli and the *Christ in Glory* by Domenico Ghirlandaio.

The most famous painting in the collection is the *Descent from the Cross* by Rosso Fiorentino (1494-1540)—a work of considerable importance and innovation for the stylization of the figures and the striking tragedy of the composition. The Museum of Sacred Art has many ecclesiastical vestments, a collection of gold reliquaries and illuminated manuscripts and 13th-century sculptures of the Sienese school of art.

The countryside around Volterra is of gentle, undulating hills, interrupted in the west by the wild and awe-inspiring spectacle of abrupt crevasses known as the Balze (the crags)—a natural phenomenon created by the continual erosion of layers of sand and clay. Repeated landslides finally destroyed the Etruscan and early Christian remains.

Lardarello: This area is important as the centre of the borax industry and the landscape is dominated by borax fumaroles, which harness the volcanic energy of the local hot springs to generate electricity.

Defensive city walls of Volterra.

LIVORNO

Livorno Province is sweet wine, Elba, sandy beaches, Napoleonic myths and a few unfortunate industrial ports. With barely enough Renaissance art to enliven an overcast beach holiday, Livorno should be on the defensive. In fact, the province is as varied as its famed fish soup, *cacciucco*.

The fishy ingredients, a little of everything in the right proportions, apply to Livorno's seascapes. Captured in moody canvases by the Tuscan Impressionists, the rocky northern coast is as dramatic as the southern coast is soothing. The mainland stretches from wild, marshy Maremma to the rugged, hilly interior, or the Elban mountains.

Livorno is no architectural desert: a coastline of Pisan watchtowers and Medicean fortresses hides the occasional Roman villa or Etruscan necropolis. Inland, the neglected hilltop villages inspired equally romantic verse

from Carducci, Livorno's greatest poet. Livorno is rich in Romanesque and Baroque architecture but the lone sanctuary or homely red-painted farmhouse are truer to the province's individuality.

Livorno City: The city owes its existence to the silting up of Pisa in 1530, and the Livornese joke that, unlike their rivals, the Pisans, they will never be so careless as to let the sea slip away from them. In 1421 the Florentines paid the Genoese 100,000 florins for Livorno, a vast sum for such a malaria-infested and mosquito-ridden village.

It was the enlightened Cosimo I who transformed Livorno into the greatest Medicean port in 1571. Cosimo was aided by Buontalenti whose plan for the "Ideal City" envisaged the present star-shaped port with its five bastions.

Grand Duke Ferdinand employed Robert Dudley, the great naval engineer, to build the harbour walls and administer the port. Dudley benefitted from Livorno's status as an "open city" with free trade, tax exemption and shelter from persecution.

As late as the the 19th century it was an enterprising yet patrician city. Cosmopolitan salons, elegant avenues, Renaissance and Baroque villas made it a fashionable port of call for the "Grand Tourists". But after 80 bombing raids in World War II, Livorno resembles a modern necropolis.

Except for the oyster beds laid down by Cosimo, the Medicean port is unchanged. The crumbling red-brick Fortezza Vecchia is a patchwork of Livornese history: Antonio da Sangallo's and Buontalenti's masterpiece incorporates Roman remains in its vast Medicean dungeons; 14th-century Pisan walls enclose a small Medicean house and are topped by a Romanesque tower.

The Fortezza Nuova, built in 1590, completed the Medici's ambitious fortifications. The murky canals encircling it once led to Pisa. Now restored, the "New Fortress" is home to conferences, festivals and children's romps through the palm trees and gardens.

Between the fortresses is Venezia, an ill-lit, seedy area not unlike working class Venice. The canals are lined with

17th-century palazzi, crumbling warehouses, fish stands and workshops. The area comes alive in July with the *Carnevele Marinaro*, more of a water pageant than a race. Escorted by swimmers in carnival masks, bedecked boats follow the maze of canals between the two fortresses and sail under the main square, Piazza Repubblica. Visitors soon realise that the city lives on commerce, not tourism. An impossible one-way system, gruff hotel and restaurant service reflect the fact that most tourists only spend one night on their way to the islands, the hills or Florence.

Livorno is often described as a *citta particolare*, an unusual city, but it is a place to visit from afar, from a medieval town or an elegant seaside resort. Unless fascinated by naval engineering and military history, most visitors cannot bridge the gap between Livorno's glorious past and ordinary present.

The rocky north coast: Most of the city's artistic and literary pretentions lie in **Ardenza** and **Antignano**, now elegant coastal resorts. On the outskirts of Livorno, Villa Maria houses the Museum of Contemporary Art and is particularly good for 1930s art, especially Ottone Rosai's lyrical landscapes and shadowy depictions of Fascism.

Villa Fabbricotti houses a gallery to the "Macchiaioli Movement", the Italian counterpart to Impressionism. While a fuller collection exists in Florence's Pitti Palace, Lega, Signorini and Fattori are well represented.

This area was home to much of what the Livornese called "Leghorn's British Factory". In 1819 after the tragic death of their son, the Shelleys moved to Villa Valsovana, now a depressing villa in the suburbs. The sea views and the dramatic summer storms revived Shelley enough to work on his blank verse drama *The Cenci* and to write his famous *Ode to a Skylark*.

Mary Shelley's description of the villa reflected standard Romantic happiness: "The peasants sang as they worked beneath our window during the heat of a very hot summer; and at night the water wheel creaked and the fire-

The harbour at Livorno.

flies flashed among the hedges". Byron, living at Villa Dupouy in Ardenza, was a frequent visitor when not working on *Don Juan*. Ardenza is now a fashionable coastal resort flanked by palms, box hedges and Liberty villas.

From prosperous Antignano, once a mere creek at the foot of the Montenero hills, a road or rickety cable car climbs to the **Sanctuary of Madonna di Montenero**, the patron saint of Tuscany. For those who dare look, there are views of Livorno, Elba and even Corsica. Between 1345 and 1774 the original shrine was transformed into a church and monastery.

The church is always full of votive offerings from relics to crutches and gold hearts to handwritten promises. Beside the sanctuary is a deep series of watery grottoes. Outside, elixirs are on sale to gullible visitors from beyond the Madonna's parish. Ritual stroll and religion over, the locals head for **Castiglioncello**'s fish restaurants with a clear conscience but without elixirs. Dried cod, red mullet and a spicy ver-

sion of bouillabaisse are best eaten at inland rustic *trattorie*, cheap dockside bars not at exorbitant resort restaurants.

Out of season, the high coastal road from Ardenza to Castiglioncello is a delight, with spectacular views of the wildest coastline in the province. The coast becomes progressively more rugged as Ardenza's neat dwarf oaks give way to rocky creeks cut into deep pine woods.

The road winds past Medici castles, watchtowers and even follies. **Castello del Boccale**, encircled by gulls and rocky paths to the shore, is a Medicean fort converted into a villa. At **Calafuria**, an isolated Medicean tower and distorted rock formations provided the Macchiaioli painters with a dramatic setting. But their favourite spot was **Romito**, a Grand Ducal castle later occupied by the French in 1799. It looks like a whimsical folly, a miniature bandstand perched over the sea.

After exposed Romito, the coastline becomes wild and wooded. **Quercianella** comes into view: pine woods run

Ship painting, Livorno.

down to the water's edge; small coves, shingle beaches and a narrow harbour struggle for space.

The Lucchese, proud of their flat golden sands, wonder how the Livornese can neglect their own sands below **Cecina** in favour of **Castiglioncello**'s fashionable rocks. But the Livornese place adventure over comfort, just as they prefer a living city to a museum city, modern art to Renaissance art, "vernacular" theatre to classical theatre, the Risorgimento poet Carducci to Florentine Dante. The cunning Livornese also know that there are sandy bays tucked into the rocks.

Cosimo's fort, built on the pine-clad promontory, was designed to keep the pirates at bay but since the last century has drawn all the great Italian Impressionists.

In the 1930s Castiglioncello was popular with film stars and, although now less chic, it is still one of Marcęllo Mastroianni's haunts.

The Maremma: Ignoring **Cecina** and the vast **California** beach, take the inland road towards Bibbona and the real Maremma beyond. Quiet lanes trace through marshy countryside dotted with red farmhouses and occasional herds of placid white Maremman cattle.

The Grand Dukes drained the swamps in 1828 but the reclamation was only completed in Fascist times. The neatly parcelled countryside is a result of the 1950 land reforms designed to break up the *latifundia*, the old feudal estates. Expropriated land was irrigated and ploughed but also divided into uneconomical strips, each linked to a cooperative or to a local farmer. Unconsciously, these paternalisitic reforms drew on Fascist models of land settlement, creating a landscape of visually tranquil pastel-coloured homesteads but failing to stem the painful drift from the land.

Bibbona is a higgledy-piggledy medieval village traditionally linked to Volterra. One of its simple churches, Santa Maria delle Pieta, has the odd inscription, *Terrible Est Locus Ist—* either written after a touch of Livornese

The rugged coast road at Castiglioncello, painted by Adolfo Tommasi in 1880.

fever or because the church is built on a precarious slope.

Nearby is the **Oasi di Bolgheri**, a nature reserve and bird colony. It is a place apart, neither sea nor land. The "Oasis" is home to moorhens, wild ducks, herons, egrets and migratory birds which might otherwise end up as Bolgheri roast duck or thrush *alla Carducci*.

From Bibbona it is a short drive to the tiny chapel of **San Guido** and to medieval **Bolgheri**, the land beloved by Giuse Carducci, one of Italy's finest poets. Tuscans still see the intensely green valley through Carducci's brooding eyes. The landscape is a shrine to a poet loved as much for his revolutionary fervour and commitment to national unity as for his melancholic verse.

San Guido and Bolgheri are linked by a magnificent avenue of cypresses, almost three miles (five km) long, planted in 1801 by Camillo della Gherardesca. In Carducci's celebrated poem the tall flowing trees are *quasi in corsa giganti giovinetti*, "galloping young giants" or ranks of upstanding Tuscan soldiers waiting in double file for inspection.

The flatness beyond the trees is broken by low farmhouses, olive trees and the village vineyards. The gateway to the village is the ancient door to the Gherardesca castle. The poet's home was in the village as was the home of his first love, Maria Banchini. A square called Piazza Bionda Maria recalls his poem, *If Only I'd Married You, Blonde Maria*, a lament which sounds marginally more poetic in Italian.

Lines of Carducci's verse in Bolgheri are as common as Dante inscriptions are in Florence. Busts of Carducci are available at the local shop.

For the resolutely cheerful there is an austere cemetery where the poet's beloved "Nonna Lucia" is buried, "her white solemnity dressed in black" and the only provider of solace in his dismal childhood. For the faint of heart, Bolgheri's excellent wine will dispel Carducci's ghost.

Castagneto Carducci was once a

19th-century village life, by Adolfo Tommasi.

Gherardesca stronghold and a scene of more childhood misery for the young Carducci but is an attractive hilltop village in its own right. Superficially, little has changed since the Gherardesca lords drained the land, planted the vines and encircled the castle with high stone walls. From its rocky balcony, the town surveys pine forests, plains, golden beaches and two castles. On summer evenings the town is popular with *borghesi* families tempted by the views—and the aromas of sizzling sausages, roast pigeon and hare. **Sassetta**, a bird's nest of a village, was once accessible only to local warriors who thrived on feuds and a diet of game. The area was damned in Dante's *Inferno* as "an impenetrable thicket without paths, leafy patches or apple trees". Since then, Sassetta has sat on its mass of red marble and waited for visitors to penetrate the deep chestnut woods.

Despite the serenity, few have visited its medieval Castello, parish church and alleyways. The locals are no longer ferocious except towards their traditional enemy, Monteverdi Marittima, with whom they share a patron saint, Sant' Andrea, but nothing else. It is a hardy, self-sufficient community with a tradition of weaving, embroidery and pipe making. An injunction on the wall sensibly tells visitors, *Lavorate in Citta, Ristorative a Sassetta*, ("Work in the city, rest in Sassetta").

The *sagra del tordo* is a celebration of the thrush in a place where hunting is both a religious cult and a hobby, carried out in all seasons, legally or otherwise. The last Sunday of October heralds a torchlit procession, a *palio* in costume and a banquet of roast thrush with chestnut-flavoured *polenta*. The village displays signs of token tourism: a Zona Climatica board publicises the fresh climate while the summer "information office" is run by eager children.

From Sassetta a winding road through olives, oleanders and woodland leads to **Suvereto**. The well-preserved villages have much in common, including the same line in advertising. A battered sign encapsulates the re-

Tuscan cypresses.

gion's charm: *La Mattina al Mare, il Pomeriggio ai Monti* ("Mornings at the Sea, Afternoons in the Mountains").

Suvereto was the first "free commune" in Maremma and is proud of its 13th-century Palazzo Comunale with its intact loggia and crenellated tower. The early Romanesque church of San Giusto combines decorated Byzantine portals with a Pisan facade. Many churches and houses are decorated with the local red, brown or grey variegated marble which has been quarried since medieval times.

Suvereto's urban design, based on rising concentric circles, is simple but effective: each level corresponds to a street, from San Giusto to the towering Rocca above. The steep ascent is through a rabbit warren of covered passageways. The fortress itself was the scene of a great funeral in 1313: Harry VII of Luxembourg died at the Battle of Buonconvento in Siena province but was embalmed here and buried in Pisa.

The sedate village pours onto the streets for the evening *passeggiata* and for the *sagra del cinghiale*, a "wild boar feast" combining food, folklore and spectacle. Early December signals flag-waving displays and crossbow competitions between the rival *Rioni* or districts. It all culminates in a feast to and of the "King of the woods". The boar is washed down with the "Ghimbergo" wine locals claim is "as simple and honest as the people of Suvereto."

This is the heart of the **Val di Cornia**, an enchanted area of gently wooded hills, hot springs, lush valleys and old quarries. Wild orchids and anemones grow on the rocky areas while myrtle, broom and yellow saxifrage cover the slopes.

Towards **Monte Calvi**, the "Macchiaioli" artists liked to paint the cork trees: the contrast of the fragile leaves and gnarled branches occupied them for days. Wildlife often trotted into the picture, particularly white Maremman oxen and sad-eyed Chianina cows; today it is more likely to be foxes, porcupine and foolish wild boar.

At **Montioni**, a village and spa south

Geraniums adorn a village street.

of Suvereto, Elisa Bacciocchi, Napoleon's sister used to bathe nude in the hot springs. Pauline, his favourite sister, used to scandalise the Elban natives in much the same way.

The ancient baths at **Caldana Terme** are even more impressive. Both the natural lake and pool contain ferrous sulphates and natural radioactivity "guaranteed to restore youthful vigour in one session."

Despite its name, **Campiglia Maritima** is a small market and mining town set in the hills. As a "free" commune it was fought over by the Florentines, Pisans and Sienese, all of whom have left heraldic traces on the town walls, four gateways and imposing Rocca. Sixty coats of arms surmount the Gothic arches of the Palazzo Pretorio.

The Romanesque church of San Giovanni has an equally turbulent past. When San Fiorenzo's relics were found nearby, Piombino and Campiglia disputed ownership. A test was devised to establish the Saint's posthumous sense of home: the relics were put on a cart and the oxen, left to decide where to go, trudged uphill to the Saint's present resting place. Naturally the oxen were Campigliese.

Campiglia's mineral past is never far from the surface. Apart from viewing the permanent mineral display, visitors can visit a working quarry in **Madonna di Fucinaia**. The Campigliese boast that their marble contributed to Florence's Duomo is to be taken with a Tuscan pinch of salt: claiming ownership of national monuments is a common regional pursuit.

Just outside town is the **Rocca San Silvestro**, the centre of a site quarried since Etruscan times. Recent excavations have revealed traces of copper, lead, silver and tin and a minerological park is planned to show the historical development of Tuscan mining.

Although mining is an important cultural tradition, food plays a bigger role in the local economy. The simple peasant dishes reflect Campiglia's traditional poverty and dignity. Many dishes were imported by the so-called Lombardi, seasonal workers from the Emilian or Pistoian hills.

These shepherds and woodcutters lived in tenements near the swamps but came inland in the evenings to mix with the locals. In exchange for kindness and dinner, the Lombardi introduced those in the Val Di Cornia to chestnut *polenta*, rice soups and *raviolini*.

Local game, sausages and funghi porcini were easily incorporated and Campigliese cuisine has never looked back. The dynamic Suvereto and Campigliese tourist offices will suggest restaurants and *Agriturismo* farm stays where these delights can be sampled.

The Etruscan coast: For sightings of flamingoes sheltering under umbrella pines, the **Rimigliano** nature reserve hugs the coast between San Vincenzo and Populonia. If the coast beckons, San Vicenzo's metallic sands and endless bungalow colony can be sacrificed to Populonia's Etruscan city. The Etruscans considerably had themselves buried by a pine-fringed beach, reason enough to visit the only Etruscan city built on the coast.

Windswept bay of Baratti, near Populonia.

Behind the sweep of **Baratti Bay** lies **Populonia**, the last of the 12 Etruscan cities to be founded. The ancient city was divided into two parts: the "acropolis", the religious centre clustered high around the village; and the maritime and industrial centre around the bay. The necropoli cover the slopes between the two centres. When the Maremma revealed its treasures in the 19th century, the contrast between the desolate marshes and the sophisticated tombs stirred locals and scholars alike.

Thanks to its proximity to Elba and to the metal-bearing Campigliese hills, Populonia became a rich industrial city, often called "the ancient Pittsburgh". While Elban iron ore was smelted and then traded within the Etruscan League, minerals from Campiglia were shipped to Corsica, Sardinia and France.

Populonia's secure industrial base meant that, unlike most Etruscan cities,it flourished from 9 B.C. to the Roman Age without economic or political upheavals. In the ancient "industrial zone", excavations have uncovered a blast furnace and sophisticated metalworking equipment dating back to 6 B.C. Foreign slave labour was used to dig water channels, operate the furnace and mint coins. In 6 B.C. Populonia was the first Etruscan city to mint gold, silver and bronze coins, often featuring a lion's head. Since the main tombs were used continously, all periods and tomb types are represented; early oriental 'trench' tombs; cylindrical 'chamber' tombs; 'temple' tombs and tiny 'niche' tombs.

Sadly, many tombs lie buried or collapsed under the weight of the ancient slag heaps. Others have been looted, some recently.

Every few years a new tomb reveals tools, silver coins and bronze jewellery, often designed by resident Greek goldsmiths and gem cutters. Most of the tomb contents are now in Florence but a tiny Etruscan museum in Populonia contains a collection of sacred objects found in the unlikely "Tomb of the Harpy".

From Populonia there are smoky

views of **Piombino** but the most typical first view is from a hot traffic jam on the way to Elba. Sprawling iron and steel works continue Populonia's tradition. Piombino has been ruled by the Pisans, the noble Appiani family, the ignoble Cesare Borgia, and, most effectively, by Elisa Bacciocchi, Princess of Piombino and Lucca but better known as Napoleon's sister.

As befits a city which was once the capital of a tiny state, vestiges of old Piombino remain in Piazza Verdi's town walls and in the heavily restored Palazzo Comunale and fortress. Best seen on foot, the city's genteel, dilapidated charm lingers on in quiet squares and Art Deco bars.

The Island of Elba: Known to the Etruscans as *Ilva* ("Iron") and to the Greeks as *Aethalia* ("Soot Island"), **Elba** has exploited its mineral wealth for more than 3,000 years. As the European powers occasionally took an interest in Elba's strategic position, waves of Romans, Pisans and Genoese were followed by Spanish, Turkish and French invasions.

In 1548 Duke Cosimo I fortified the capital and named it "Cosmopolis" after himself. His great military architect, Giovanni Camerini, designed the star-shaped defensive system and the two defensive forts, Forte della Stella and Forte Falcone.

However, **Portoferraio** is inextricably linked to that other great modern Imperialist, Napoleon. He made his official home in two converted windmills above the charming Forte della Stella. Under the terms of the Congress of Vienna in 1814, Elba became a principality of the fallen sovereign.

Napoleon's great empire shrank to his faithful "old guard", pragmatic mother and libertine sister Pauline. Most Elbans were proud to have him improve the administration, build new roads, develop the mines and expand the fleet. The foreign Commissioners rightly feared the "Eagle" might spread its wings and after nine months Napoleon flew with the apparent connivance of the Elbans.

A variety of greens embroider the Tuscan landscape.

On the eve of his escape, he sent for the island Governor and reputedly confided, "I am leaving my mother and my sister in your care to show you how much I trust you. I am also placing in your charge this country which means so much to me". He escaped with 1,000 troops, the Elbans' affection, his sister's diamond necklace and his mother's curt blessing, "Go and fulfil your destiny."

His Palazzina dei Mulini was lined with silver and books from Fontainebleau and furniture from Elsa's house in Piombino. Most of its charm lies in the period furnishings and Italianate gardens. His country villa, San Martino, set amid woods and vine-yards, was purchased with with one of Pauline's handy diamond necklaces. There is a fine garden shaded by evergreen oaks and terraced vineyards. The 17th-century Misericordia church displays one of Napoleon's bronze deathmasks and a requiem mass is still said for Napoleon on 5 May each year. Napoleon used to say, "When I die, the world will heave a sigh of relief," a sentiment not shared on Elba.

To the east of Portoferraio is Elba's iron heart. Most minerals are concentrated around **Rio Marina** where open cast mining, polishing and jewellery making still exist. Surrounded by hills rich in ferrous oxide, the whole village has a pinkish hue, including the 16th-century tower of San Rocco.

Most are ferrous minerals including black loadstone, yellow pyrites and blackish-red ilvaites. Semi-precious stones are also worked, including green quartz, black onyx and pink or pale green beryl. More than 700 exhibits are on display in the Museo Mineralogica.

Inland **Rio Nell'Elba** is a strange, rather wild village perched on a couple of ledges among desolate mountain slopes. Seemingly untouched by tourism, its misfortunes can perhaps be traced to its destruction by Barbarossa's pirates and abduction into slavery of the entire population.

Many of the rocky beaches are mineralogical treasure hunts. A line of parked cars signals hazardous tracks

Farmhouse in the Maremma.

down steep cliffs to the sea. From Rio to Cavo in the northeast, the road cuts through woods and moorland. Paths trail through gorse, heather and the wild flowers of the maquis.

The spectacular drive westward from Portoferraio to Marciana Marina passes a number of popular beaches including Le Ghiaie, noted for its multicoloured pebbles, and **La Biodola**, considered the chicest sandy beach on the island. There, serried lines of deckchairs contain bronzed Florentine villa owners dressed in Valentino swimwear.

At La Biodola and **Procchio**, a more egalitarian paradise, the rocky ocean bottom means clear, sediment free water. Between Procchio and Marciana Marina is "La Paolina", a rock named after Napoleon's sister whose passion for nude sunbathing still scandalises the natives today.

Marciana Marina has made a smooth transition from fishing village to elegant resort. Set amidst magnolias, palms and oleanders at the end of a long valley, the resort narrowly avoids picture-postcard beauty. The thin, pastel-coloured houses in the old quarter are reminiscent of those on the Ligurian coast. On August 12 the port explodes in a firework display in honour of Santa Chiara, the patron saint.

Marciana Alta, perched above, is the island's best preserved medieval town. The chestnut woods frame the red-tiled rooftops, narrow alleys and crumbling Pisan fortress. The local "Antiquarium" displays Etruscan sacred objects as well as Roman oil lamps and ivory statues found in wrecks off the coast.

From Marciana, a cable car lurches over crags and chasms to the summit of **Monte Capanne**. Even in the height of summer this wooded mountain area is quiet and breezy. Hot springs and old hermit caves often come in sociable pairs. Depending on the season, patches of orchids, snapdragons and helianthemums are as common as the cedars and chestnuts above. Even the coastal vegetation is more exotic than in the east; eucalyptus and magnolia rather than

Herbs, flowers and sun-dried tomatoes overlook the woods of the Maremma.

vines or rough maquis.

From Marciana to **Marina di Campo** in the south, the high road winds past the neglected village of **Poggio** to **Monte Perone** nature reserve, vineyards and the plains behind Marina. With its expanse of golden sands, Marina is a loud, rather tacky resort near the airport.

However, two dusty medieval villages nestle in the hills behind. Fortified by the Pisans in the 12th century, **San Ilario** and **San Piero in Campo** conceal Romanesque churches and hermitages. A tangy *panzanella* or crisp *crostone* blows the cobwebs away.

Capoliveri is a traditional inland village with a Roman and Medieval past as dramatic as its location high on the southern promonotory. Carved into the iron mountain of **Monte Calamita**, Capoliveri is also an old mining village. The black, iron-bearing loadstone still plays havoc with the compasses of passing ships but is ideal for the production of sweet red Aleatico, Napoleon's favourite wine.

Often independent, Capoliveri was the only village to reject Napoleon in 1814. Legend has it that only the intercession of a local beauty saved the village. It soon became part of Napoleon's hunting estate and is still noted for its game dishes starring woodcock, pheasant and hare.

The hills are covered with heath, fern and juniper; the scent of thyme and rosemary are never far away. Roads from the hills to the sea often turn into cart tracks but are worth pursuing unless specifically marked *strada privata*; this is often the only access to the loveliest beaches.

Innamorata is a sandy inlet linked to the romance between a nymph and a fisherman. Believing her lover drowned in a shipwreck, the nymph drowned herself; he survived and asked the gods to turn him into a seagull so he could seek her out.

From the village there are views of **Pianosa**, **Montecristo**, **Gorgona** and **Capraia** islands. Inaccessible Pianosa and Gorgona are now prisons, while Montecristo is a nature reserve. Capraia is a miniature Elba without its history or architecture.

Capoliveri also surveys fashionable **Porto Azzurro**, the main town on the east coast and once part of the Spanish protectorate. The vast Forte Longone, built in 1603 as a Spanish naval base, is now a top security prison. Visitors can buy crafts from the prison shop, the scene of a mass break-out in 1987. Forte Focardo, its sister fortress across the bay, has uninviting ramparts running down a sheer cliff.

By day, the port is an uninspired seafront with slightly tacky side streets. In the evening, it is a place for a leisurely *passeggiata*, designer shopping and people watching. It is also the place for seafood specialities: a *cacciucco* of octopus, scorpion, dogfish and prawns; *riso nero*, "black rice" with cuttlefish or squid—perhaps followed by *schiaccia briaca* ("drunken cake"), made with hazelnuts and Aleatico wine.

Alternatively, there is dry Elba Bianco, sweet Moscato, a heady white or Elba Rosso, similar to Chianti. The distinct flavour is due to the iron, phosphorous, arsenic and natural radioactivity in the fertile soil. After enough Elban wine, one's impressions of Porto Azzurro are of harbour lights, cheerful bustle and gently bobbing boats.

Behind Porto Azzurro is the most mystical spot on the island, the remote sanctuary of **Madonna di Monserrato**. It was built in the Toledan style by a Spanish Governor, Ponce de Leon in 1606. A steep, rocky track leads high up the mountain to the tiny red-domed church balanced among the crags. Despite mountain goats cavorting on impossible ledges, the place has great solemnity. There are few visitors and the only sound is of the water running down a conduit in the mountains.

The Spanish facade and belltower find echoes in the Black Madonna inside, which is a copy of an early Spanish painting. Every September, an Elban pilgrimage celebrates the *Festa della Madonna* with a walk past ravines and isolated grottoes to the church. At the foot of the hills is a rustic restaurant with service as leisurely as an Elban Sunday.

GROSSETO

Grosseto is the largest and least known of the provinces of Tuscany, yet it has some of the most beautiful coastline in the entire region. The landscape is varied, passing from the flat plains around Grosseto, now drained, to the thickly wooded peak of Monte Amiata, capped with snow in wintertime, to the smooth hills bordering the province of nearby Siena.

The coastline has a unique mix of Mediterranean flora and fauna along its wide sandy beaches, or on promontories descending to the sea and lagoons. Three different areas (Monti dell'Uccellina, Monte Argentario and Monte Amiata) have been converted into nature parks, perfect for trekking, birdwatching, canoeing and horse-riding.

The region is dominated by the marshy plain of the **Maremma**, "the swamp by the sea", described by Salvatore Battaglia in the *Grande Dizionario*

della Lingua Italiana, as "a generally flat coastal zone, a swampy and insalubrious plain adjacent to the sea, formed following the stagnation of watercourses blocked at the mouth by the existence of coastal sand-bars". Until quite recently travel books tended to warn visitors away from the area, but the marshes have now been successfully reclaimed and it has become a popular tourist spot, especially for nature lovers.

Etruscan influence: Evidence of Roman and Etruscan settlements in the area is considerable. One of the most important Etruscan cities, Vetulonia, is close to Grosseto, as are the once-prosperous Roman and Etruscan settlements of Cosa and Roselle.

By medieval times the coastal plain had become quite unsafe and unhealthy, partly due to the plundering of Saracens from the sea, partly because of the malarial swamps. In the early 14th century the whole area fell under the power of Siena. Towards the end of the 16th century, Grosseto became part of the Grand-duchy of Tuscany, until the formation of Italy in 1860.

Rapid expansion: The capital of the province is a relatively recent city by Tuscan standards. **Grosseto** was built as a fortified citadel only around A.D. 950, when the Saracens looted the former capital, Roselle, less than 10 miles away. The city has expanded beyond its walls only in the last part of this century, to provide housing for its 50,000 inhabitants. Mainly because of its unhealthy climate, Grosseto was for a long time no more than a military citadel, and was never as big as Massa Marittima or Pitigliano. Only during this century has it become the largest city in the area, but it is still primarily an administrative centre with practically no industry.

The old town of Grosseto is quite small, contained within an ancient six-sided citadel created by the Aldobrandeschi family in the 11th century, and surrounded by brick walls added by the Medici in the 15th century.

There is a 14th-century Duomo on the main square, at the end of the traditional *corso*, where all the best shops and a

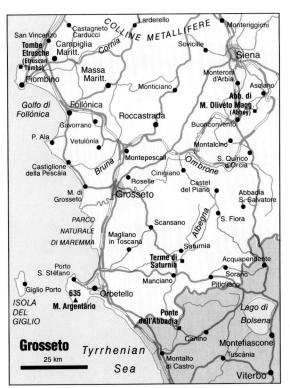

caffé are to be found for the pleasure of late afternoon strollers.

The Duomo, dedicated to S. Lorenzo, was built towards the end of the 13th century on a pre-Gothic church dating back to 100 years before; it is a mixture of Romanesque and Gothic styles, with a rose window and three magnificent doors with Romanesque arches in the main facade. There is an adjoining 15th-century campanile in *cotto* bricks, and also a museum displaying a *Madonna dell' Uccellino* of the Pietro Lorenzetti School, and a *Madonna delle Ciliege*, considered a Sassetta masterpiece.

Next to the duomo in the Palazzo del Licio is the Museo Archeologico, one of the richest museums in the area; it has an excellent collection of pre-Etruscan, Etruscan and Roman artifacts. There is an important Roman site at nearby Roselle, with a nearly intact circuit of Romano-Etruscan walls, a Roman forum, paved streets, basilicas, villas and baths. And Vetulonia, which was originally the Etruscan city of Vatluna, has remains of Roman houses and a Mithraeum.

Grosseto is in the middle of a flat plain formed by the Ombrone river and is about 10 miles away from the sea. Many Grossetans have a second home along the nearby coast, either in modern and congested **Marina di Grosseto** or in the more snobbish and quieter **Principina** hidden in a beautiful forest of maritime pines. Some prefer Castiglione della Pescaia, an old fisherman's village where they can keep a sailing boat, ideally located at the foot of rocky mountains north of Grosseto.

Castiglione della Pescaia is a famous coastal resort. The harbour, crowded with both fishermen's and tourists' boats, is believed to be the Etruscan *Hasta*, or *Portus Traianus* in Roman times. Overlooking the port is the Rocca Aragonese with its mighty walls and towers dating back to the 14th century.

Slightly north of the same promontory lies exclusive **Punta Ala**, an almost private resort situated between maritime pines and the finest sand; it

The marshy plain of the Maremma.

has good hotels, golf clubs (among the few in Tuscany), horse-riding and polo facilities. The water here is nearly always calm, thanks to its sheltered position. A little further along the coast, before Follonica, is a lovely quiet bay, **Cala Violino**, so-called because of its squeaky musical sand!

Massa Marittima is about 15 miles (24 km) inland, despite its maritime name. It is one of the most astounding Tuscan cities, perched on top of a high hill on the edge of the Colline Metallifere, or "ore-bearing mountains", which divide the province of Grosseto from Siena. It was the most important town in the Maremma until the 17th century when the land silted up, and was originally called Massa; but the name of Massa Maremma or Massa Marittima has been introduced to distinguish it from Massa in Massa-Carrara.

Massa Marittima was built around the 10th century, after the decline of ancient Populonia, which was too exposed to plundering from the nearby sea. It was known for its copper and silver mines even in Etruscan times, and the rich variety of metals available nearby was a major factor in the economic development of the city.

The affluence of medieval Massa Marittima is apparent in its rigorous town planning, and in the concentration of the public buildings (Palazzi) around the Cathedral. In the main piazza are Palazzo Vescovile (seat of the bishop), Palazzo Pretorio (seat of the governor, now also an interesting museum), Palazzo del Commune (seat of the city council), Zecca Cittadina (the mint), Fonte Pubblica (public fountain) and Palazzo dell'Abbondanza (the public granary).

The Cathedral (Duomo) is an example of Pisan Romanesque architecture with marvellous reliefs of *Madonna delle Grazie*, ascribed to Duccio Di Buoninsegna (1316) and the *Arca di S. Cerbone* (St Cerbone's ark), a masterpiece of the Sienese school of sculpture, dating back to 1324. There is a fourth-century sarcophagus in the cathedral and St Cerbone (d. 380) is buried

Cathedral of Massa Marittima.

in the crypt.

A memorable experience—and a lot easier to see than Siena's *Palio*—is the traditional *Balestro del Girfalco*, every last Sunday in May and every second Sunday in August. Here the three *terzieri* of Massa (old city, new city and the outer *Borgo*) struggle for victory in a contest which consists of shooting at mechanical falcons with ancient crossbows.

There is a mining museum, located in the Palazzetto delle Armi, and it is also possible to visit a real mine, a network of underground tunnels very near the city.

The **Colline Metallifere** is rich in metal ores, and was the focus of the Industrial Revolution in the area, but by the end of the 19th century mining and related industries were in decline and now these mountains are a remote and lonely region. The ancient mines and factories now in ruins present a surreal picture, hidden away in thick forests littered with strange heaps of coloured metals.

The South: Beyond the river Ombrone, the **Monti dell'Uccellina** nature park covers about 12 miles (20 km) of the coastal mountains and the marshland around the mouth of the river Ombrone. Its most noticeable peculiarity is the tradition of *butteri*—the only Italian cowboys. They actually won a challenge with Buffalo Bill at the end of the last century; to commemorate the event, an annual rodeo is held in August, which brings American cowboys to **Alberese**, a small village in the heart of the wild coastal prairie.

Other local festivals include the *Torneo del Buttero*, in Alberese, the *Sagra del Cinghiale* (boar fair) in Montepescali, the *Sagra del Gnocco* (a culinary speciality) in Batignano, the *Sagra della Gastronomia* (gastronomic fair) in Manciano, the *Sagra della Trippa* (tripe fair) in Montemerano.

Activities within the nature park include canoeing along the Ombrone river, sailing along the coast, trekking or riding across the mountains, visiting the noble ruins of S. Rabano and the

One of the famous *butteri* (cowboys) of the Maremma.

many towers on top of the mountains overlooking the sea, each with its story of pirates and hidden treasures going back to the times of the Saracens and Spanish galleons.

South of Monti dell'Uccellina is **Monte Argentario**. This promontory was once an island, the Insula Matidiae, named by the Emperor Trajan after his granddaughter Matidia. The name of Argentario probably comes from *Argentarius* (money-lender), since it had become a possession of a rich family of Roman money-lenders in the fourth century. The island became attached to the mainland by two long sandbanks, containing a lagoon; a peninsula projects itself into the lagoon from the mainland, on which is the main city of the area, Orbetello.

From 1556 until the Congress of Vienna in 1815, Monte Argentario was politically detached from the Grand-duchy of Tuscany, being a separate state, the "Stato dei Presidii", under Spanish rule. It encompassed the whole promontory and the existing ports of Orbetello, Porto S. Stefano, Porto Ercole, Talamone and Porto Azzurro, in the island of Elba, and many Spanish fortifications still remain.

This complex landscape is a beautiful region for walking, with a wide variety of flora and fauna, and you can see magnificent sunsets and views as far as Corsica from the peak of Argentario.

Among the fortunate permanent dwellers of these hills are the *Passionisti* monks. Following in the tradition of many convents in central Italy, they reserve some cells for pious guests, and even on a short visit to their newly refurbished chapel the traveller may leave with a precious relic: *Amaro dei frati dell'Argentario* (a special bitters produced by the monks).

The coastline is rocky and precipitous with breathtaking descents to the sea beneath. The most easily accessible beach is the Feniglia, but it is also very popular. (It was also where the riotous genius Caravaggio died on his way back to Rome in 1610.) There are many other hidden coves and beaches, but a boat is

Walls of Massa Marittima.

needed to reach them; it is an ideal location for scuba diving and underwater photography.

Porto S. Stefano is now the most important harbour in the area, and little fishing boats nestle against huge yachts in the crowded harbour. Although scarred by World War II bombing, it is still a picturesque town with many boutiques, bars and excellent *gelaterie*. For many years, the mayoress of Porto S.Stefano has been Susanna Agnelli, of Fiat's Agnelli family. One of her main achievements has been to slow down the rapid tourist development of the area.

Orbetello, the State capital, stretches along a very narrow peninsula, surrounded by Spanish walls built over the previous Etruscan fortifications. The city still has a maritime atmosphere, in spite of being now almost three miles (five km) from the sea. The uniqueness of Orbetello is reflected in its cuisine, with a mixture of three traditions: seafood, freshwater fish from the lagoon, like the exquisite *anguilla fumata*

(smoked eel), and game such as wild boar from the hillside and marshes surrounding the town.

The Islands: On the southern side of Monte Argentario, **Porto Ercole** has a 16th-century Spanish fortress on the hill overlooking the harbour. From Porto Ercole, a small ferry-boat sails regularly to **Giannutri**, a tiny uninhabited island 14 miles (22km) away where one can imagine pirates finding refuge long ago. On the island there are the ruins of a Roman villa which belonged to the Domizii Enobarbi family during the first century. The villa, with its columns and mosaics, its baths and private pier, is well worth a visit.

S. Stefano has a ferry connection with the fascinating island of **Giglio**, half an hour's sail off the coast. The island, the second largest in Tuscany after Elba, has an impenetrable coastline with only one easy port, Giglio Porto. Heading up into the hills, among vineyards producing a very strong and unique local wine, *Ansonaco*, Giglio Castello dominates the landscape. It is a fortified settlement, with arches, dark passages and stairs carved from the rock.

Giglio has a number of sandy beaches and is covered in typical Mediterranean vegetation: aromatic plants and orange and lemon groves. It is ideal for sailing, swimming and all water sports, but it is very popular, being close to Rome, and pleasanter visited out of season.

Returning to the coast, there are the important Roman remains of **Cosa**, built on top of what was originally an Etruscan settlement. The city has been excavated and the site contains a main street, forum, a walled acropolis and capitolium from which there are magnificent views out to sea; the site is somewhat overgrown with a melancholy air about it.

Below the rocky promontory is the silted up Roman port and the "Tagliata Etrusca", the Etruscan Cut—which is in fact Roman, built as a canal to drain Lake Burano.

Heading inland from Monte Argentario, one of the first towns on the hills bordering Latium (Rome's region), is **Capalbio**. It is the heart of the Mar-

Skiing on Monte Amiata.

emma and famous for its brigands. A famous *bandito*, Domenico Tiburzi, a local Robin Hood, was sentenced to death and executed in 1896. There was disagreement over whether he could be buried in consecrated land and eventually a typical Italian compromise was reached: he was buried at the edge of the cemetery with his head in sacred ground, the rest of his body out.

Capalbio is much appreciated by Roman intelligentsia, who have bought up every corner of the village as a fashionable summer refuge from the capital. Nearby is the magical **Tarot Garden** created by French sculptor Niki de Saint Phalle, in collaboration with Jean Tinguely. Driving along the Via Aurelia from Rome, you get occasional glimpses of fantastic, brightly coloured figures covered in mirror and mosaic, glinting in the sun.

Capalbio Scalo is a few hundred metres from Lake Burano, where there is a lake and small nature park, a favourite stop for thousands of birds migrating from Yugoslavia to North Africa. Bird-watching (seagulls, coots, pheasants, blackbirds, among others) is the main attraction for a visit, but the flora is also very varied, with cork-oaks, holm-oaks, lake reeds and juniper.

Across the densely wooded hills north of Capalbio is the flat plain of the River Albegna, now completely drained, which leads to the castle of Marsiliana, once an Etruscan town and now the only property left to the Corsini family, who originally owned the entire area. Most of these swamps were expropriated by the state, drained and then distributed to small landowners.

Not far from the coast, **Magliano in Toscana** (to distinguish it from Magliano in Sabina, in Latium) still has intact city walls, built in the 15th century. Both civil and religious architecture show a strong Romanesque influence, with Gothic and Renaissance additions. A perfect example is S. Giovanni Battista, built as a Romanesque church, with Gothic side windows and a Renaissance facade.

A few miles inland, **Scansano**, now a

Church and farmhouse, Monte Amiata.

quiet town with a separate fortified section (*Oppido*) on top of a modest hill, used to be the summer capital of the province, when all administrative powers were moved from malarial Grosseto during the hot season.

Travelling eastwards across hills and moors inhabited by *butteri* and their cattle you arrive at **Saturnia**, about 20 miles (32 km) from the coast. Saturnia is a quiet little town drowsing under the immense weight of its past. It was the Etruscan Aurinia, and then came under Roman control in 280 B.C.

The atmosphere here is so attractive that a number of northern Italians have settled in the area and run speciality shops in the village, which is centred around a large oak-ringed piazza. Saturnia and surrounding villages have some good *trattorie*, ranked among the best in the province.

Through the old Porta Romana, half hidden by vegetation, you can walk two miles down the hill along the old Roman road to **Terme di Saturnia,** a modern spa, where you can experience the heal-ing waters coming from the earth beneath the distant Monte Amiata. There are warm sulphuric pools for swimming, and a wide range of thermal treatments available all year round.

This southern part of Tuscany is in the process of gentrification and many Romans and foreigners living in Rome buy property here. One reason why the area is so attractive is that for centuries it has been neglected by the main traffic routes, one on the coast along the Roman Via Aurelia, and one inland along Roman Via Cassia, both going north from Rome. The old Via Clodia, between the coast and Via Cassia, almost disappeared, cutting out important Saturnia and other towns like Sovana, Sorano and Pitigliano—all of which are well worth including on the traveller's itinerary.

The most important town is **Pitigliano**, which in the mid-18th century was one of the main cities in southern Tuscany. After a drive along a particularly tortuous road, Pitigliano rises up before you, a spectacular sight. It has the dis-

Pitigliano with its wine and oil cellars cut out of caves below.

tinct shape of a crib, built on a hill of volcanic tufa with wine and oil cellars cut out of caves in the hillside.

The main town is centred round a magnificent fortified Palazzo, built by the Orsini family during the 16th century. The Palazzo Orsini is actually a separate citadel, architecturally linked to the town by a vast arched aqueduct, visible for miles.

Pitigliano used to be called "little Jerusalem" because it was a refuge for Jews fleeing from religious persecution in the Papal states. Even today the Jewish section of the city—60 narrow streets crossing two main ones—is still quite distinct. Tiny streets and winding alleys intersect and the backs of the houses form a sheer drop to the valley below. It is one of the few places in Catholic Italy where you can find kosher wine; turkey "ham" (*billo*) is a another Jewish speciality. *Bianco di Pitigliano* from the tufa wine cellars is also a well-known speciality.

Sovana, a few miles away, is a tiny village rich in history. There is an im-portant Etruscan necropolis as well as Roman ruins in the surrounding woods, but a local guide is recommended.

No visit to this area would be complete without a walk in the old streets of **Sorano,** which is also built on a tufa outcrop. Unfortunately some of the buildings have begun to collapse into the steep valleys around the city, but the great majority of Sorano can be seen without danger.

Visible from every corner of the province on a clear day, particularly in a snowy winter, is **Monte Amiata**, the highest peak in Tuscany south of Florence. It is a sleeping volcano, with hot geysers on its slopes and underground waters that supply the spa at Saturnia. Monte Amiata is a paradise for mountain trekkers, and a refreshing alternative to the plains during the hot summer months.

Of the the three main towns, **Santa Fiora** is particularly delightful, and has exceptional works of art in the 12th-century Santa Fiora and Santa Lucilla churches, including ceramics by Andrea and Luca della Robbia.

Arcidosso was the birthplace of David Lazzaretti, "The Prophet of the Amiata". In the 19th century Lazzaretti created a revolutionary social and religous movement with its headquarters on Mount Labro, a lonely peak which forms part of a nature reserve with deer, chamois, wolves, and protected trees, shrubs and wildflowers. The very best time to visit this region is in autumn, when the crowds have left and the wild mushrooms appear.

Local dishes: Maremmana cuisine is not particularly sophisticated but it is unique and dishes peculiar to the region include *prosciutto di cinghiale*, (boar ham); *acquacotta*, a celery and tomato soup, served on top of a slice of stale bread scented with garlic and garnished with a poached egg; *scottiglia*, a mixture of various meats, boar and *capriolo* prevailing, cooked with fresh olives; local *pecorino* cheeses, Monte Amiata chestnuts, *anice* biscuits and *ricotta*. Good local wines include *Morellino di Scansano, Bianco di Pitigliano*, and *Ansonaco di Argentario*.

Narrow streets of Pitigliano.

SIENA

Set on the old Lombardy-Rome pilgrim route, the approach to **San Gimignano** is justly famous. The Siena road curves around Monterrigioni's perfect walls. After speeding through sprawling Poggibonsi, the loveliness of the road to San Gimignano is even more marked. The seasons lie in wait: emerald green wheat and yellow rape seed are only a prelude to golden summer corn, parched olives and autumnal burnt sienna.

The local poet Folgore, nicknamed "Lightning" for his speed of thought, celebrated much the same landscape in the 14th century. The famous San Gimignano towers come into view behind olives, cypresses and the Vernaccia vines.

Apart from the fact that only 13 of the original 76 *belli torri* are left, Folgore would feel at home. Not that "home" conjures up the atmosphere of daily terror, the hazards of rocks and scalding pitch tossed from great heights.

The 12th and 13th-century towers were designed as keeps by the *magnati*, or nobles, during the internecine Guelf-Ghibelline feuds. The original conflict between the town's Ghibelline Salvucci family and the Guelf Ardinghelli family degenerated into more localised disputes between rival factions. Since height meant prestige, power and status, towers were as big as the nobles' egos.

Earthy pleasures: Folgore was lucky enough to be writing in a period of relative wealth and peace. He has left sensuous descriptions of the city's earthy pleasures. In winter, "The silk sheets, sugared nuts, sweets and sparkling wine, clothes from Douai" all helped fortify citizens "should the *sirocco* blow". As for wealth and foreign influence, there were "*ambiente palafren, destier di Spagna e gente costumata alla Francesca*" ("nimble horses, chargers from Spain and persons dressed in the French vein").

Unfortunately the arrival of the Black Death in 1348 put an end to silk sheets in San Gimignano until this century. The decimated population fell under Florentine control and this important city became an economic backwater, bypassed by the Renaissance.

While more advanced cities were exchanging towers for palazzi as feudal lords became civilised by communal life, San Gimignano destroyed nothing and built nothing. The city's misfortune has made it the best preserved medieval city in Tuscany.

The Romanesque **Collegiata**, framed by towers and fortified palazzi, does not have the status of a cathedral because there is no longer a bishop. Inside, Benozzo Gozzoli's fresco of a plump St Sebastian in agony deserves a glance. The radiant aisles are dedicated to two cycles of Biblical frescoes painted concurrently by two 15th-century artists.

Bartolo di Fredi's Old Testament frescoes on the north aisle are vivid, intimate and full of careless violence. *The Parting of the Red Sea* is an animated jumble of flying and floating bodies, like a happy Hieronymus

Preceding pages: Vincenzo Rustici, (1557-1632); *contrada* procession in the Piazza del Campo, Siena; Towers of San Gimignano. Left, *Palio* banners in the Piazza del Campo.

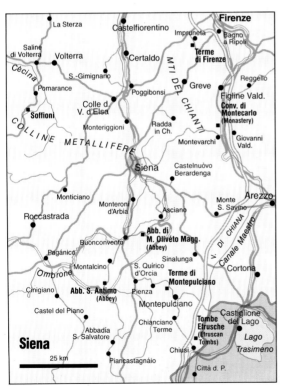

Bosch. There is a childlike but lively narrative in all the frescoes. For people raised on too many words and too little religion, it is fun trying to work out the significance of the Biblical stories through a pictorial narrative. Among Barna di Siena's New Testament frescoes, one odd section depicts an underwater Christ with two angels; and in *The Last Supper* the disciples appear to be eating a baby seal. The New Testament looks a more civilised world since no one except Jesus suffers.

The variety of Biblical animals is astonishing: expressive camels, dogs and sheep often have more emotional resonance than the human subjects. As in Siena Cathedral there is a ceiling of faded stars to complete the magic. This was perhaps Barna di Siena's last view as he fell off his scaffolding and died.

In **Santa Fina's Chapel** off the south aisle, Ghirlandaio's frescoes of the local Saint are rather too flowery. Legend has it that when the Saint died in March 1253, violets sprang up on her coffin and on the towers.

In *Where Angels Fear to Tread*, E.M. Forster, writing of a thinly disguised San Gimignano, described Santa Fina's starvation and death at the age of 15 as a feat "which shows how much is within the reach of any school girl." As the violets still flower on the tower every March, perhaps Santa Fina has the last word. In the Baptistry loggia is an *Annunciation* by Ghirlandaio, as always an admirable colourist.

Also in the **Piazza del Duomo** is the crenellated Palazzo del Popolo, housing the Museo Civico with its countless Sienese "masters" and "schools of". On the second floor, the "Camera del Podesta" contains domestic and profane scenes by Filippuccio. Amongst the gentle erotica is a picture of a semi-nude couple wearing wooden nightcaps and similar expressions. The Piazza della Cisterna is a lovely triangular square with a 13th-century well and medieval palazzi.

If many of San Gimignano's palaces are elegant and architecturally diverse it is because "any immigrant who behaved well for a decade could build within its walls." James Bentley's explanation accounts for the profusion of Florentine, Sienese, Lucchese, Pisan and even Moorish styles.

The final visit should be a short walk along the city walls to the 14th-century fortress. This semi-derelict Rocca has views over tiered gardens and olive groves winding down to the "Vernaccia" vineyards. As you leave, do not be surprised by the smell of sulphur—it is only Monte Amiata doing her stuff again.

Siena City: Siena is a *chiaroscuro* city, from its striped marble Cathedral to its tunnelled alleys, brilliant Campo and black-and-white city emblem. In its surging towers it is a true Gothic city.

Where Florence is boldly horizontal, Siena is soaringly vertical; where Florence has large squares and masculine statues, Siena has hidden gardens and romantic wells. Florentine art is perspective and innovation while Sienese art is sensitivity and conservatism. Siena is often considered the feminine foil to Florentine masculinity.

Siena Cathedral.

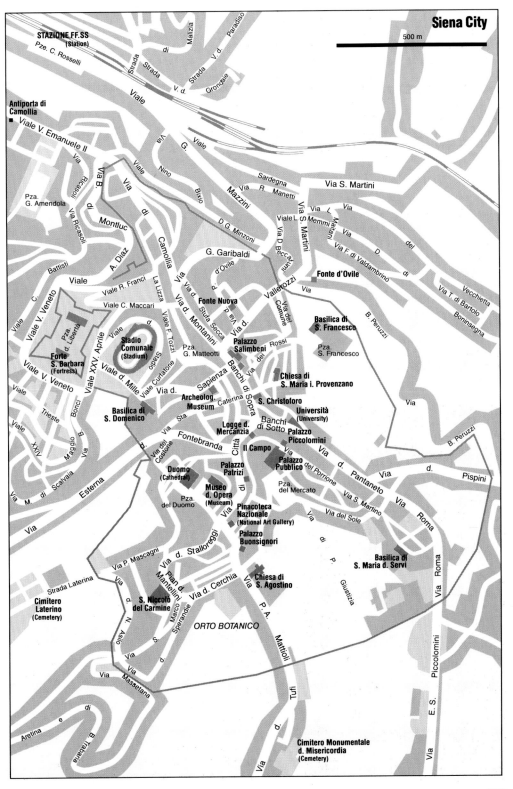

Siena City

500 m

STAZIONE FF.SS
(Station)
Pze. C. Rosselli

Antiporta di
Camollia

Viale V. Emanuele II

Via B.

Pza.
G. Amendola

Montluc

A. Diaz

Viale

Viale R. Franci

Viale C. Maccari

Battisti

Strada

Strada

V. d.

di

Malizia

V. d. Paradiso

Grondaie

Viale

Via G.

Nino

Viale

Camollia

La Lizza

d'Ovile

Via d.

Via d. Montanini

Bixio

Mazzini

D.G. Minzoni

G. Garibaldi

Sardegna

Via R. Manetti

Via S. Martini

Viale L S. Memmiani

Via Z.

Via S. Martini

Via

Via F. di Valdambrino

del

di

Vecchietta

Via T. di Bartolo

Boninsegna

Fonte d'Ovile

B. Peruzzi

Vallerozzi

Via d. Comune

Via

Fonte Nuova

Via d. Stura Secca

Fonte Nuova

Pza.
G. Matteotti

Palazzo
Salimbeni

Rossi

Via dei

Basilica di
S. Francesco

Pza.
S. Francesco

Forte
S. Barbara
(Fortress)

Pza.
d. Liberta

Stadio
Comunale
(Stadium)

Viale XXV. Aprile

Viale d. Mille

Viale Curtatone

Viale d. Stadio

Via d.

Sapienza

Banchi di Sopra

Chiesa di
S. Maria i. Provenzano

Viale V. Veneto

Viale V. Veneto

Viale

Trieste

Viale

XXIV

Maggio

Bonci

B.

Scalvaia

Esterna

Via M. di

Via

Basilica di
S. Domenico

Via Sta.

Via d. Costone

Fontebranda

Archeolog.
Museum

Caterina

Città

Logge d.
Mercanzia

Il Campo

Duomo
(Cathedral)

Palazzo
Patrizi

Pza.
del Duomo

Museo
d. Opera
(Museum)

di

S. Christoforo

Università
(University)

Banchi
di Sotto

Palazzo
Piccolomini

Palazzo
Pubblico

Pza.
del Mercato

Via d. Porrione

Via S. Martino

Via d. Pantaneto

Via

d.

Via Roma

Pispini

B. Peruzzi

Pinacoteca
Nazionale
(National Art Gallery)

Palazzo
Buonsignori

Via del Sole

di

P.

Giustizia

Via del Sole

Via d. Stalloreggi

Via P. Mascagni

Pian d.
Mantellini

Via d. Cerchia

Via P. A.

Chiesa di
S. Agostino

Basilica di
S. Maria d. Servi

Via Roma

Strada Laterina

Cimitero
Laterino
(Cemetery)

S. Niccolò
del Carmine

Via N.

S. d.

Via

Via

Marco
Sperandie

ORTO BOTANICO

Mattioli

Tufi

Via E. S. Piccolomini

di

e

Aretina

B. Tolomei

Via Masselana

Via d.

Via

Cimitero Monumentale
d. Misericordia
(Cemetery)

Via E. S.

Via Piccolomini

Approached by night, Siena's towers resemble "firebrands that are the last to die in the ashes of the night." Federigo Tozzi, the most Sienese of authors, also praised the city's radiant femininity. Even by day, the glow of rose-coloured brick warms the narrow passageways and stone arches. The poetic motto of the Shell Contrada could refer to the Campo, the centre of Sienese life, "It's the red of the coral that burns in my heart."

For such a feminine city, Siena has a warlike reputation nourished by sieges, city state rivalry and *Palio* battles. The average Sienese is no ethereal Botticelli nymph but dark, stocky and swarthy. Only in Sienese painting is pale theatricality the norm.

In keeping with Sienese mystique, the city's origins are shrouded in myths of wolves and martyred saints. According to legend, the city was founded by Senius, son of Remus; hence the she-wolf symbols in the oldest part of the city. Saint Ansano brought Christianity to Roman Siena and, although he was promptly tossed into a vat of hot tar and beheaded, he has left a legacy of mysticism traced through Saints Catherine and Bernardino to the present-day cult of the Madonna.

The power of the church came to a dramatic end when the populace rose against the Ecclesiastical Council and established a Republic in 1147. The 12th century was marked by emerging Sienese-Florentine rivalry in which the Florentine Guelfs usually triumphed over the Sienese Ghibellines.

In 1260 the glorious battle of Montaperti routed the Florentines and won the Sienese 10 years of cultural supremacy which saw the foundation of the University and the charitable "fraternities". The enlightened Council of the Twenty-Four, a form of power-sharing between the nobles and the working class, was followed by the Council of the Nine, an oligarchy of merchants which ruled until 1335.

Although modern historians judge the "Nine" self-seeking and profligate, under their rule the finest works of art

Campo surrounded by rose-coloured roof-tops of Siena.

were commissioned or completed, including the Campo, the Palazzo Pubblico and Duccio's *Maestà*.

The ancient Republic survived until 1529 when the reconciliation between the Pope and the Emperor ended the Guelf-Ghibelline feud. The occupying Spanish demolished the city towers, symbols of freedom and fratricide, and used the masonry to build the present fortress. The final blow to the Republic was the long Siege of Siena by Charles V and Cosimo I in 1554.

Three companies of women fought alongside men and caused the Emperor's General to exclaim, "I would rather have defeated Rome with Sienese women than with Roman soldiers." The Sienese lost despite melting down bronze bells to make cannon balls and expelling *bocche inutili* ("useless mouths") to certain death.

After the Sienese defeat, the Government-in-Exile survived in Montalcino until 1559, but Siena became absorbed into the Tuscan dukedom. As an untrusted member of the Tuscan empire, impoverished Siena turned in on itself until this century. As recently as 1909, Henry James called it "cracking, peeling, fading, crumbling, rotting".

Soon after, the city, unlike the countryside, challenged Fascist appointees. In July 1944 American and French troops surrounded Siena and forced the city to surrender unharmed. General Monsambert instructed troops not to "let any shells fall on Siena, otherwise you'll be shot". The State Archives in Palazzo Piccolomini provide a pictorial history of Siena through illuminated manuscripts and paintings.An inscription on the City gates reads, "Siena opens her heart to you wider than this door." But such openness is illusory: Siena offers hospitality but not intimacy. Its cultural and spiritual aloofness owes much to the *contrade*, the 17 city wards who represent self-sustaining cities within the Sienese empire.

Immune to influence and praise, the city takes care of its own from birth to death. The Sienese prefer to work for paternalistic local employers such as

Palazzo Pubblico and Torre del Mangia, Piazza del Campo.

Monte dei Paschi, known as "the oldest bank in the world" and "the city father".

Change is anathema to the city: traditional landowning, financial speculation, trade and tourism are more appealing than new technology or industry. The city has made a virtue of conservatism; stringent medieval building regulations protect the fabric of the city; tourism is low-key and the city is reluctant to build new hotels; old family firms such as *Nannini*'s cake shop do a roaring trade with locals. It is a city with the psychology of a village and the grandeur of a nation.

All roads lead to the **Campo**, Siena's shell-like piazza. It is at its most theatrical in the late afternoon, after a day spent in the shadows of the city walls and inner courtyards. After so much dark, the huge pool of light draws even the most modest visitor to blunder centre stage.

One's eyes adjust to the redbrick piazza, a fountain depicting the Sienese wolf, and to the **Palazzo Pubblico**, the dignified Town Hall surmounted by the slender Torre del Mangia. The Town Hall, built in 1310, is a Gothic masterpiece of rose-coloured brick and silver-grey travertine. Each ogival arch is crowned by the *balzana*, Siena's black-and-white emblem representing the mystery and purity of the Madonna's life. The tower is named after the first bellringer, Mangiaguadagni, the "spendthrift" and is flanked by a chapel built as a thanksgiving after the Plague.

Inside the Palazzo Pubblico is the **Museo Civico** where Simone Martini, Duccio's successor, had to create his masterpiece twice since he painted it on a wall backing on to a damp salt warehouse. His *Maestà* is a poetic evocation of the Madonna on a filigree throne.

It has a rich tapestry-like quality, not unlike the French arras, *The Lady and the Unicorn*. The muted blues, reds and ivory add a gauzy softness. Martini echoes Giotto's conception of perspective yet clothes his ethereal Madonna in diaphanous robes, concealing her spirituality in dazzling decoration.

Opposite is Martini's famous

Interior of Santa Maria dei Servi, Siena.

Giudoriccio, the haughty diamond-spangled *condottiero* reproduced on calendars and *panforte* boxes. But despite Sienese denials, this famous *Trecento* work is probably a *Quattrocento* painting concealing Martini's original. Since the Sienese Republic feared a military takeover in 1318, it would have been odd to commission a portrait of a captain for the Town Hall.

In the next room is a genuine civic masterpiece, Ambrogio Lorenzetti's *Effects of Good and Bad Government*, painted in 1338 as an idealised tribute to the Council of the Nine. The narrative realism and vivid facial expressions give the allegory emotional resonance. A wise old man symbolises the Common Good while a patchwork of neat fields, tame boar and busy hoers suggests order and prosperity. Bad Government is a desolate place, razed to the ground by a diabolical tyrant, the Sienese wolf at his feet. Since much of Bad Government is erased, Good Government triumphs—posthumously at least.

From above, the fishbone design of the Campo forms nine different shades of pink, recalling the Noveschior "Nine". Below, the Sienese awaited news of Montaperti, the Spanish siege, and the German deportation of local Jews. In 1980 Pope John Paul II preached on the same spot where Saint Bernardino denounced witchcraft, superstition and the power of the Sienese Republic. Church and State are well matched: the Mangia Tower and the Cathedral belltower face each other from the same height.

The **Cathedral** is in Castelvecchio, the oldest part of the city. The Duomo is Siena's most controversial monument, either a symphony in black and white marble or a tasteless iced cake. It began in 1220 as a round-arched Romanesque church but soon acquired a Gothic facade festooned with pinnacles. Bands of black, white and green marble were inlaid with pink stone and topped by Giovanni Pisano's naturalistic statues.

Ruskin dismissed it as "over-striped, over-crocketed, over-gabled, a piece of costly confectionery and faithless vanity." Wagner, more attuned to its operatic intensity, burst into tears at its alien, restless beauty.

The interior is creativity run riot—Oriental abstraction, Byzantine formality, Gothic flight and pockets of Romanesque austerity. A giddy *chiaroscuro* effect is created by the black-and-white walls reaching up to the starry blue vaults.

The floor is even more inspiring: major Sienese craftsmen worked on the marble *pavimentazione* between 1372 and 1562. Although the oldest are marble engravings, the finest are Matteo di Giovanni's pensive Sibyls and marble mosaics by Beccafumi.

Nicola Pisano's octagonal marble pulpit is a Gothic masterpiece: built in 1226, it is a dramatic and fluid progression from his solemn pulpit in Pisa Cathedral. Within the Duomo is the frescoed Libreria Piccolomini, the most ornate Renaissance room in Tuscany. Amazingly, Sienese consider the dazzling interior subtle and refined.

The present Duomo would have been the transept of the new one, a scheme devised in the Golden Age and abandoned after the 1348 plague. Beside the Gothic Baptistry, the skeletal remains of the **Duomo Nuovo** are home to the **Cathedral Museum** and Pisano's original statues for the facade. In a dramatically lit room above is Duccio's *Maestà*, which was escorted from the artist's workshop to the Duomo in a torchlit procession; the largest known medieval panel painting graced the High Altar until 1506. Duccio chose Madonna blue for the Virgin's cloak to match the blue stained glass windows in the Duomo. He was inspired by French Gothic and perhaps by the Rose Windows at Chartres Cathedral.

The largest panel depicts the Madonna enthroned among saints and angels, and, since the separation of the painting, faces scenes from the Passion. Although Byzantine Gothic in style, the Maestà is suffused with melancholy charm. The delicate gold and red colouring is matched by Duccio's grace of line which influenced Sienese painting for the next two centuries.

THE PALIO

It is strange how a race lasting 90 seconds can require a year's planning, a lifetime's patience and the involvement of an entire city. In the Campo, Siena's shell-shaped square, the grey stonework is sanded over and the crenellated *palazzi* float with flags. The slender tower on the Town Hall casts a mobile shadow over the sea of exuberant Sienese and the *Palio* itself, the hand-painted silk banner which is the focus for their spiralling hysteria.

As the horses career round the San Martino bend, a few rebound off the padded walls, a jockey hits the hard track and a riderless horse wins. In just over a minute, the Campo is filled with unbearable happiness and irrational despair.

The *Palio* has raced through war, famine and plague. In the 14th century, criminals were released from prison to celebrate the festival. When the Fascists were gaining ground in 1919, Siena postponed the election of a new Council until after the *Palio*. In 1943, British soldiers in a Tunisian Prisoner of War camp feared a riot when they banned Sienese prisoners from staging a *Palio*: Sienese fervour triumphed and the prisoners sang the ancient Republic's praises all night.

The *Palio* is alive and kicking: the July 1988 *Palio* was attended by Italian Cabinet Ministers, the Luxembourg Royal Family and various European Heads of State. Despite frequent injuries and occasional deaths, the Sienese resist attempts to modify their ritual.

The August *Palio*, dating from the 13th century, originally took the form of a *Palio Lungo*, a bareback race the length of the city. Later Roman and Venetian bullfights and buffalo races were adapted by the city.

The first July *Palio*, introduced after a 17th-century miracle, became known as *Palio della Tonda* since it was the first horse race held in the "round" Campo.

A Sienese adage says, "*Il Palio corre tutto l'anno*" (The *Palio* runs all year). Each *contrada* (city ward) appoints a *Capitano* and two lieutenants to run the campaign. In the *Palio*, the illegal becomes legal: bribery of rival jockeys and plots with other *Contrade* are commonplace. Skulduggery is motivated by traditional duty rather than by financial gain. But luck outweighs the significance of the *Contrada*'s tactics, jockey or horse.

Ten out of the 17 *Contrade* take part in each *Palio*, the seven who did not run in the previous *Palio* and three by lot. The horses are also chosen by lot and *Contradaioli* are exultant if they have won a *bono* and desolate to be saddled with a *brocco*, literally "a sprout". Although each horse is guarded in the *Contrada* stable until the race, horses are sometimes drugged or die during the six practice runs.

Efforts intensify when the Campo is covered with soil in readiness for the race. The words, "*C'e terra in piazza*" ("There's earth in the Campo") are a signal to remove the costumes from the museums and to finalise tactics. Superstition plays a great part: nervous *Contradaioli* look for portents in shooting stars, the direction of the wind and the flight of birds. Marriages between Sienese from rival *Contrade* come under great strain and "real life" is suspended. Many citizens cannot bear to watch the race in the Campo and cluster around the television in the *Contrada* square or pray in the local church.

On the eve of the race, a tense "propitiatory" dinner is held in the *Contrada*. On the day, the "Blessing of the Jockey" is followed by the *Provaccia*, the dress rehearsal. Then, in a moving church ceremony the *Contrada* priest holds the horse's head and commands it, "*Vai e torni vincitore*" ("Go and return victorious"). As the procession leads into the Campo, the *Sunto* bell tolls and the flags unfurl.

After a flag-waving display, the bells are silent and the violent race lurches around the Campo three times. If a riderless horse wins, the animal is almost deified, is given the place of honour in the banquet and has its hooves painted gold.

In the victory celebrations, the winning *Contrada* holds a thanksgiving service in the Cathedral and supporters kiss the floor. Ask a Sienese where he is from and he will say, "*Ma sono della Lupa*" ("But I'm from the Wolf Contrada"). The first loyalty is to the city in the head, not to the city on the map.

The Sienese fondly believe that Giotto copied Duccio but sacrificed beauty to naturalism. The small panels around the walls do, however, reveal some of Giotto's truthfulness and sense of perspective. The modest status of the *Trecento* painter was that of a master craftsman whose only reward was the devotion of the populace. As Siena's best-loved work, the *Maestà* achieves just that.

If it didn't sound too smug, the Sienese would admit to spiritual superiority. Apart from producing two major saints and fine religious art, the city still venerates the Virgin. Siena is too inter-bred for its own good: local feuds span generations; secrets cannot be kept; outsiders are disparaged; *contrade* passions outweigh individual loyalty.

Pride is often indistinguishable from smugness: Sienese art and the Chigi Musical Academy are culture enough; the Sienese accent is naturally the "purest" in Tuscany. One of Siena's leading aristocrats even refuses to set foot in Florence.

The **Pinocateca Nazionale** houses the finest collection of Sienese "Primitives" in the suitably Gothic Palazzo Buonsignori. The early rooms are full of Madonnas, apple-cheeked, pale, remote or warmly human. The beautiful repetition of Siena's favourite theme focuses attention on the style and vivid colouring.

Matteo di Giovanni's stylised Madonnas shift to Lorenzetti's affectionate *Annunciation* and to Ugolino di Nerio's radiant *Madonna*. Neroccio di Bartolomeo's *Madonna* is as truthful as a Masaccio.

As a variant, the grisly deaths of obscure saints compete with a huge medieval crucifix with a naturalistic spurt of blood.

The famous landscapes and surreal Persian city attributed to Lorenzetti were probably painted by Sassetta a century later. But his *Madonna dei Carmelitani* is a sweeping cavalcade of Sienese life, as is the entire gallery.

The Sienese claim that Siena is three cities: "illustrious", "homely" and

Left, full *contrada* regalia for the *Palio*. Below, the *Palio* race lurches round the Campo three times.

"dreamlike". Illustrious Siena is public knowledge but homely Siena belongs to the *contrade* churches, fountains and tabernacles. Fontebranda, Saint Catherine's fountain, is the oldest and most impressive of the enclosed fountains.

Despite its public grandeur, much of Siena is resolutely working class. In Brucco *contrada* pockets of narrow housing, friendly shops and dignified poverty are disguised by old world charm and wishful thinking. The tiny tabernacles reflect spontaneous affection for the Madonna. Sodoma's Madonna del Corvo marks the spot where a crow dropped dead with the Plague, thus infecting the entire city.

Dreamlike Siena embraces the cult of the Madonna and the mystique of the Palio. It can be sensed in the box-like *contrade* churches and in Saint Catherine's sanctuary rather than in the grander churches of San Francesco and San Domenico. The Duomo and the Campo are broad enough to accommodate all Sienas.

But the Sienese are not borne down by the weight of the past. Siena is a sensuous city. On a drowsy summer's afternoon near the Campo, the flapping pigeons perch on a rushing fountain; the air smells of roasted chestnuts; a child eats a piece of sweet, spicy *panforte* and the Chigi choir can be heard practising. Siena is Italy's last surviving city state, provincial and universal, a fitting capital.

The Sienese Chianti: The **Chianti** is a spiritual rather than a geographical location. Its shifting borders reflect the fluctuations in Florentine and Sienese power but its soul remains where it has always been: on Florentine soil. The Sienese countryside is a bit wilder, the valleys deeper and the hills higher, but it is essentially sleepy, overly civilised Florentine Chianti.

Unlike the southern part of the province, the Chianti is not an area for artistic or architectural set-pieces. Instead, it is a place whose turbulent history has shaped a scene of utter tranquillity, a harmony of tame hills and gentle people.

Palio **pride.**

262

In a place where nothing is essential viewing, everywhere is a glorious detour. **Castellina in Chianti** is conveniently sited on the Chiantigiana, the winding route linking Florence and Siena. Castellina surveys symmetrical vineyards and wooded groves, a landscape dotted with low stone houses and late Renaissance villas.

New wine estates have been built from the ransacked remains of medieval castles. Villas have lazily domesticated the original castle or tower, but names like "La Rocca" or "La Torre" reveal the original function.

Castellina's name also reveals its medieval function as a Florentine outpost. In the late 13th century it was the first site of the Chianti League, a group of three Florentine feudal castles, each responsible for a third of the territory. The castle is now a fortified Town Hall hiding a small Etruscan museum and a warren of atmospheric back streets with half glimpsed views of the Chianti hills.

The other attraction is the *Bottega del Chianti Classico*, the wine-tasting centre which gives advice on wine tours and *vendita diretta*, direct sales.

Radda in Chianti became the headquarters of the Chianti League in 1415 and retains its medieval street plan and imposing Town Hall. As in Castellina, the spontaneous rural architecture is more rewarding. Classical Medici villas with 16th-century windows and wells compete with romantic villas, constructed magpie fashion from castles or Etruscan ruins. One 17th-century masterpiece is Vistarenni, a white beacon of sophistication unimaginable in the countryside south of Siena.

The elegant loggias, the openness of the architecture, symbolise the increasing safety of the countryside and its proximity to urban Florence. In the tranquil Chianti, the country is richer and more civilised than the town. The reverse is true of the urban-inspired communes south of Siena.

Outside Radda is **Volpaia**, the most picturesque village in the Chianti. A tortuous road climbs to the medieval village with its towers, ruined castle and

Flag waving display at the *Palio*.

Brunelleschi-style church. If Chianti villages and towns have little sense of identity and few artistic treasures today, it is because they came into being with fully-fledged Florentine and Sienese identities. While villages lacked artistic patronage and volition, military outposts like Radda had no time to develop artistically. Only the Chianti abbeys, endowed separately, had the independence to shape their own culture.

Between Radda and Gaiole is the aptly-named **Badia a Coltibuono**, Abbey of the Good Harvest, set among pines, oaks, chestnuts and vines. Since the Dissolution of the Monasteries in 1810, this medieval abbey has belonged to one family.

Although the lovely 15th-century cloisters, chapel and frescoed ceilings are only visible to guests enrolled on a Tuscan cooking course, the 12th-century walls and belltower are harmonious enough. Below the abbey are cellars filled with Chianti Classico, the abbey's traditional living.

No less famous is the aromatic chestnut blossom honey or the *vergine* olive oil, "a product of grass, flowers, pine trees, sea air, altitude, climate and soil." The owner forebore to mention that much of the produce can be bought on the premises or savoured in the abbey restaurant.

Gaiole in Chianti, the baby baron of the Chianti League, is a newer riverside development in a wooded valley. It is a popular *villeggiatura*, a summer escape for hot Florentines in search of family-run hotels, home cooking and the familiar *gallo nero* wine symbol.

History lies in wait at Meleto and Vertine, unusual castles, and Barbischio, a medieval village, is a short walk away. Tempting footpaths marked *Sentieri del Chianti* lead all the way to Siena. With vineyards rising up gentle slopes, tranquil Gaiole and sleepy Greve are traditional Chianti.

The countryside from Gaiole south to Siena and east to Arezzo is higher, wilder and wetter. The wooded peaks of the Chianti Sienese are vibrantly green and fresh with scents of thyme, rosemary and pine kernels. Deep chestnut woods provide ideal cover for wild boar, recently reintroduced.

Of the many Florentine castles in the woods, **Brolio** is the most impressive—not least because of its views over the original Chianti vineyards to Siena and Monte Amiata. On the medieval chessboard, every Florentine castle faced its Sienese shadow.

If the surviving castles are Florentine, it is because Siena lost the match and all its pieces. While Sienese Cereto and Cettamura are small heaps, Florentine Brolio and Meleto are resplendent.

As a Florentine outpost, Brolio's past spans Guelf-Ghibelline conflicts, sacking by the Sienese in 1529 and even German occupation and Allied bombing in 1944. The medieval walls are the most striking feature, along with the 14th-century chapel set amid lush grounds.

Brolio has long been controlled by the Ricasolis, Chianti landowners since the eighth century. Baron Bettino Ricasoli, Italian Premier in 1861, founded the modern Chianti wine industry, a

'Burnt sienna' of the city walls.

264

business continued by the present family. The common saying, "When Brolio stirs, Siena shakes" is still true today, not least in the wine trade.

The Chianti is a place for pottering and chance encounters, one of which is tiny **Campi di San Gusme**, just south of Brolio. A short climb leads to a small tower, Romanesque church and views of tumbledown castles, villas and vineyards. The tower was designed to be higher than the tallest cypresses encircling it, but the trees grew and the tower did not.

Even on a hot day there is a breeze, occasionally shared with locals. In the late summer, *feste* are held to celebrate the grape harvest, the Chianti, everything and nothing. Quintessential Tuscany.

A Renaissance theme park: In contrast to the Chianti, towns south of Siena were never dependent on powerful Sienese and Florentine masters for their identity. The southern towns developed independently around local noblemen or industries and expressed their differences artistically. Shifting allegiances and even political domination did not mean an acceptance of new, extraneous values but only an entrenchment in local culture and traditions.

Pienza is an exquisite Renaissance dolls' house. Although created by a humanist Pope, Pius II, Pienza is too perfect to be human and too precious to be spiritual. Every fountain, piazza and painting is harmonious. Model citizens walk through streets as romantic as their names: Via dell'Amore, Via del Bacio, Via della Fortuna.

Pienza's origins go back to 1458. When E.S. Piccolomini was elected Pope, he could not resist playing God in his home village, Corsignano. He chose the noted Florentine architect, Bernardo Rossellino, to ennoble the hamlet in accordance with humanist principles.

Pius's vision knew no bounds—in that sense it was a true Renaissance vision. He held that, "In our change-loving Italy, where no ancient dynasty exists, a servant can become king." As one of 18 children from an impover-

The red earth of the Sienese landscape.

ished but noble Sienese family, the future Pope also showed Renaissance aspirations.

When the first masterpiece in modern town planning emerged late and over budget, the Pope reduced his fraudulent architect to tears with his words, "You did well, Bernardo, in lying to us about the expense involved in the work…Your deceit has built these glorious structures; which are praised by all except the few consumed with envy." Bernardo was rewarded with a scarlet robe, 100 ducats and new commissions.The decision to build a cathedral enabled the Pope to rechristen Corsignano the village as Pienza the city, named after himself. The result is what locals call a *citta d'autore*, a city inspired by one vision. After Pienza, other cities look cluttered and confused.

Much of the symmetry lies in the cathedral square, Piazza Pio II, and the slightly listing cathedral only adds to the charm. Despite a Renaissance facade, the interior is late Gothic and decorated with mystical paintings from the Sienese school. In one central alcove is an odd *Assumption* by Vecchietta in which Saint Agatha holds a cup containing her breasts, torn off by the executioner.

The Cathedral's facade, the gracious arches, the well and Palazzo Piccolomini, the Pope's home, are just as Pius left them when he set off to fight the crusades and never returned. At night, impromptu concerts are often held in the ill-lit square: the tilted church, the ghostly musicians and the solidity of Pius's presence can have an unnerving effect.

Palazzo Piccolomini, now a museum, is based on the Palazzo Ruccellai in Florence. The ancient custodian is the soul of indiscretion: "Listen, he was the only one of them to die a natural death." The Palace is lined with grand and homely treasures,including a library and arms collection.

Still, an image of domestic clutter prevails. In the Pope's bedroom, the intriguing book-holder, as cumbersome as a church lecturn, is proof that the Pope did not read in bed. The library opens onto a tranquil loggia with Etruscan urns, hanging gardens and a panorama across the Orcia valley to Monte Amiata. It was here that the aesthetic concept of a view was first introduced to boringly functional Europe.

Critics call Pienza a Renaissance theme park; admirers liken it to an absent friend's drawing room. The "look, don't touch" element makes Pienza a precious city in both senses of the word. If overwhelmed by beauty or hunger, one can retreat to the restaurants behind the main square.

Pienza is famous for its homemade cheeses, especially *pecorino* and *ricotta*. "Lucrezia Borgia" biscuits provide a suitable antidote to a surfeit of piety.

Just outside Pienza is the Pieve di Corsignano, a simple but coherent Romanesque church where the Pope was baptised.

Cinquecento pearls: The winding road from Pienza up to **Montepulciano** is lined with *vendita diretta* signs, offering pecorino, wine and even leather

Pienza: a Renaissance theme-park.

goods. If Pienza belongs to Rossellino, Montepulciano is Antonio da Sangallo's masterpiece.

Just outside the city walls, at the end of a long line of cypresses lies San Biagio, the Renaissance building most at ease with its setting. The isolation focuses attention on the honey-coloured *travertine*, the Greek Cross design, the dome and the purity of the line. Sangallo's design skills rival Bramante's, not just in the church, the elegant well, the porticoed Canon's House but elsewhere in the city. The airy interior has a deeply classical feel, more akin to the Roman Pantheon than to a small Tuscan church.

From San Biagio there is a short walk to S. Maria delle Grazie, a 16th-century church whose Renaissance organ is still played at summer concerts. Although Montepulciano is also a "Pearl of the *Cinquecento*", it is no museum piece. After Pienza, its assymetrical design and spontaneous development give it the architectural tension the earlier city lacks.

Renaissance church of San Biagio, Montepulciano.

Pienza's reverence of Pope Pius is surpassed by Montepulciano's devotion to Poliziano. The renowned scholar, poet and resident tutor to Lorenzo de' Medici's children was named after the Latin term for the town. The tradition of scholarship is upheld in the city's annual Renaissance Convention. Likewise, early morning buses are filled with 2,000 young Poliziano coming to receive a "humanistic education".

As a humanist, Poliziano was "bent on doing over the whole house of Italian civilisation from top to bottom." But McCarthy's view of him as a querulous interior designer does not reflect Poliziano's deep love of the Montepulciano countryside. The spring landscape inspired Botticelli's painting *Primavera* and Poliziano's *Stanzas*. Both friends portrayed gardens of female delight in which "*Ogni bella e sicura fra tanti damigelli.*"

Poliziano's claims that maidens would be "safe in the shady arbours among so many young men" were probably correct. Poliziano himself is

rumoured to have died in ecstasy while playing a love song on the lute to a favourite "beardless youth".

Poliziano's house is just off the main square, Piazza Grande, the highest part of town and the highest spot culturally. In the summer, the square becomes a stage for concerts and traditional Bruscello plays, originally performed by peasants on the threshing floor.

On the last Sunday in August the route is filled with sturdy Poliziani pushing heavy barrels uphill. The barrel race, *Bravio delle botti*, started out as a Sienese *Palio* but after numerous accidents the horserace was transformed into a pageant and an equally violent barrel race.

Florentine design has shaped the grand facades on Piazza Grande but earlier Sienese Gothic touches are present in the interiors, double arches and doorways. Both styles reflect the city's buffeting between the two city states and the eventual supremacy of Florence. The Palazzo Comunale has a Florentine Michelozzo facade adorning Sienese

turrets.

The tower, modelled on Florence's Palazzo Vecchio's, surveys the whole province: from Monte Amiata to Siena and even Lake Trasimeno. Once in the Palazzo, do not be deterred by the presence of a police station and the absence of a custodian: the view is legally yours in the morning.

Sangallo's **Palazzo Contucci**, on the other side of the square, is a secret. Ring the concealed bell and an elderly housekeeper or the Contessa herself will point to palatial 18th-century ceilings before alluding to the vast Contucci cellars below.

In the Cantina, Adamo, the wine master, will be delighted to expand on the entire noble history of the Contucci family and on his essential role on the Vino Nobile Wine Tasting Committee. Vino Nobile, a smooth red wine with a hint of violets, was "ennobled" in 1549 when Pope Paul III's sommelier proclaimed it "a most perfect wine, a wine for lords". In Montepulciano today, naive or noble-looking purchasers are

Sant' Agnese, Montepulciano.

often recommended the 1887 vintage. Vino Nobile is excellent with two local peasant dishes: *bruschetta*, a toasted garlic bread drenched in olive oil, or *panzanella*, a bread salad with herbs.

The Renaissance Palazzo Bucelli is for those with more sober tastes. It is a reminder of the city's Etruscan origins, dating back to Lars Porsena, the mythical King of the Etruscans. The Palazzo, decorated with a mosaic of Etruscan urns and pots, is a sign of what civilised Tuscans call "urban decoration" and unenlightened foreigners call theft. The Poliziani are not alone in rifling tombs for useful garden furniture.

This palace was one of the many delights Henry James missed when, after quaffing Vino Nobile "too constantly", he declared Montepulciano dirty, "parched and brown and queer and crooked". For those without a "crooked" alcoholic vision, there is a drive or walk to Montefollonico, a medieval village with one of the best restaurants in Italy, *La Chiusa*.

As well as its "*Cinquecento* Pearls",

Siena province glories in its hidden villages, each with a separate identity and artistic treasures espied almost incidentally over the brow of a hill. The following route is just one in which every village becomes more itself as time goes by.

Near Montepulciano a circular itinerary unites tiny villages once ruled by the Cacciaconti barons. Otherwise, the only link is that each tiny village considers itself civilised and the others feudal.

Petroio, set on a rocky, wooded promontory, is a grand fortified village on an old pilgrim route. It is now undergoing a revival thanks to its terracotta, examples of which adorn the city walls, Palazzo Pretorio and medieval towers. The Canon's House contains a remarkable *Madonna and Child* by Taddio di Bartolo.

Near the village is the intact Abbadia a Sicille, built by the Knights Templar as a refuge for knights on the way to the Holy Land. The adjoining Romanesque church is decorated with two Maltese crosses but an Olivetan coat of arms

Palazzo del Comune, Montepulciano.

marks the abolition of the Templars.

The high road to **Castelmuzio** is dotted with *Divieto di Caccia* warnings to Sienese businessmen out to hunt boar at weekends. Quite seriously, it is advisable to wear bright clothes for walking across country in the hunting season.

Castelmuzio, set among farmland and woods, is a medieval village wrapped up in itself, its museum of Sacred Art and its direct line to San Bernardo. Narrow shops in winding streets sell honey, salami and cheese made by an ageing population of church-goers.

Once a Cacciaconti fortress, aristocratic **Montisi** commands a view over two valleys. Montisi is a feudal and feuding village, sure of its superiority over "*primitivo*" San Giovanni d'Asso in the valley. Dwellers in the Castello, or "high town", have survived attempts to tame them in the Communal period and also German bombing in World War II.

Although the "low town" has a few young families and newer attitudes, the "high town" is a relic of medieval Italy. While some peasants still sell eggs individually, the distinguished Colonello rattles around in his one hundred-roomed castle and sells the noble local wine, Vino Rosso dei Cacciaconti through his housekeeper.

The village offers intriguing alleys, views, two tiny Romanesque churches, one decorated with a Scuola di Duccio crucifix. A few apparently stark, uninviting farmhouses conceal wonderful frescoes and the occasional private chapel.

One can return to Montepulciano via **Sinalunga**, a schizophrenic Tuscan town with a hideous "low town" but a pleasant "old town". The town's original name, Asinalunga, echoes its shape, "the long donkey". But in the lively market, pigs not donkeys are in evidence: the entire population can be seen devouring *porchetta*, the local speciality.

The mysterious craters: Siena Province's strangest area lies to the west of these villages. From Buonconvento to

The Abbey of Monte Oliveto Maggiore.

Rapolano Terme is a primeval landscape. Appropriately called **Crete**, this area is a moonscape of interlocking pale clay hummocks and treeless gullies. In winter it is cold, bleak and even more crater-like. Locals speak of these infertile furrows as *maligne crete*, in the same vein as the American "Badlands". Sienese city dwellers love this barren landscape but desperate farmers are increasingly accepting European Community funds to flatten the land and grow wheat.

There is an extraordinary range of ill-concealed wildlife in the area: by day, wild deer roam by the Ombrone river; by night, porcupines and foxes are about in the woods. If intrepid walkers venture out in the late autumn evening they may meet a strange character with a couple of dogs, a torch and a harness. He is a truffle hunter, sniffing out truffles in the dampest ditches.

More legal are the Sardinian peasants selling cheese. Unlike many Tuscans, Sardinians are prepared to live in remote, infertile places. Sadly, the local population associate the "Sardi" with only three things: *pecorino*, horseriding and kidnapping.

Buonconvento, situated on a plain in the heart of the Crete, is a place for hunting and eating. It is also a quiet historical town, known for its *muraria*, the imposing red 14th-century walls and grand wooden gates. In 1366 Siena rebuilt the walls because, as a Sienese outpost, Buonconvento had been devastated. Sadly, few visit the Palazzo Pretorio or Pinacoteca with its pictures from the Duccio school.

The town is essentially a place for a leisurely introduction to truffles or game; or for a summer picnic in the peaceful gardens beside the town walls. Tobias Smollett, the "choleric philistine", hated Buonconvento. But then his horses had just run off, he was hungry, and he knew nothing of truffles.

From Buonconvento to **Monte Oliveto Maggiore**, the rugged landscape is dotted with striking hill-top farmhouses. It is an empty road along which pheasants may appear at any moment. Called the Accona Desert in medieval times, it retains its spiritual remoteness.

After so much pale, undulating land, the red abbey of Monte Oliveto is glimpsed through a wood of pines, oaks and olives. If the land appears to fall away from the abbey, it is not far from the truth: land erosion and frequent landslides provide a natural defence to the mystical centre.

In 1313 Tolomei, a wealthy Sienese, abandoned the law for a life of prayer in the wilderness with two fellow hermits. After a vision of white-robed monks, Tolomei established an Olivetan Order under Benedictine rule. The monks followed Saint Benedict's precept that "a real monk is one who lives by his own labour".

Fortunately, a meagre diet, fervent prayer and lack of conversation stimulated the monks to artistic endeavour in the form of wood carving, sculpture and manuscript design. As a noted artistic centre, the abbey invited Luca Signorelli and Il Sodoma to decorate the Renaissance style cloisters with scenes from St Benedict's life.

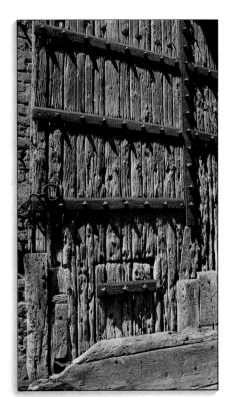

14th-century walls and grand wooden gates of Buonconvento.

The moated gateway, adorned with della Robbia terracottas, leads through cypresses and meaningful "*Silenzio!*" signs to the monks' domain. To see the wonderful if over-restored frescoes is more difficult than it looks. Today's no doubt religious but very grumpy monks are still puritanical about female attire: even bare wrists need to be covered by one of the monks' stock of headscarves. Once inside the Chiostro Grande, St Benedict's life unfolds in surprisingly profane ways.

Of the two contemporaries, Signorelli had the more spiritual approach. But his loveliest is a domestic scene portraying two monks being served food and wine by girls at an inn. St Benedict guessed that the monks had broken the monastic rule by eating outside the monastery. The fresco's expressive grace lies in the monks' absorption and in the sculptural sensuousness of one woman's neck.

However, in 1497, after only nine frescoes, Signorelli left the rest to Sodoma. The Olivetan monks' interfering ways were no match for the freedom, novelty and financial rewards dangled by Orvieto Cathedral.

Vasari adored Signorelli's spirituality as much as he loathed Sodoma's exuberance, hedonistic lifestyle and, "licentious" fondness for "boys and beardless youths" which earned him his nickname in the first place. Sodoma's confident homosexuality helped him to flout the conventions of religious art.

One fresco originally depicted naked courtesans out to seduce the monks but the livid Abbot insisted on Sodoma "dressing" the courtesans. In his self-portrait, Sodoma has an actor's sense of his audience, a complicity shared by the pets at his feet.

Sodoma's love of what Vasari called his Noah's Ark of "badgers, squirrels, apes, dwarf asses and Elba ponies" is often present but his landscapes only come to life with the temptations of the flesh. His gaze rarely focuses on the main subject but is deflected by the turn of an attractive leg, a mischievous smile, a perky badger or a soldier's

Fortified village of Rocca d'Orcia.

buttocks. Needless to say, the inhibited monks preferred Signorelli's work to that of the man they labelled "*Il Mataccio*", imbecile or madman.

The excitement of Sodoma aside, Monte Oliveto is a spiritual retreat. The austere refectory, the library cluttered with ancient manuscripts, the marquetry work of the choir stalls are as peaceful as the hidden walks deep into the woods. A restaurant and cells are also available for overnight visitors unafraid of the monks or Sodoma's ghost.

The watery valley: The **Val d'Orcia** is a poor but beautiful rural area bordering the southern Crete. The villages have suffered from the desertion of the countryside in the 1950s and 1960s. The abandoned farmhouses used to be green oases near the barren Crete. Since the peasants had to be self-sufficient under the Mezzadria system, every patch of land was cultivated, from the rosemary and camomile by the house to the enclosed orchard.

Conservationists plead for *Agriturismo* and developers plan leisure centres. As local politician Fabio Pellegrini said: "Beware of linking the beauty of the countryside with the living conditions of the peasants—such a harmony has never existed."

San Quirico d'Orcia is a dignified little valley town still waiting for its heyday. It survived an attack by Cesare Borgia's troops in 1502 and 1944 war shelling to its formal Collegiata and city walls.

Its Romanesque Collegiata, made from sandstone and local travertine, has three remarkable portals. The finest is the South portal, decorated with lions and caryatids by the Giovanni Pisano school. Inside, a Sano di Pietro tryptich incorporates the town's red-and-gold coat of arms.

From San Quirico, an exciting rough walk leads to Ripa d'Orcia, Rocca d'Orcia and Castiglione d'Orcia, three medieval fortresses.

After the turning to the shabby medieval town of Bagno Vignoni, **Ripa d'Orcia**, an enchanted castle set in cypress groves, comes into view. Although pheasants and goats are common here, locals make claims for wolves. After failing to see a wolf, the intrepid traveller clambers on to **Rocca d'Orcia**, a fortified village once owned by the warring Salimbeni clan.

The energetic can press on to **Castiglione d'Orcia** for more of the same. Wonderful views and exhaustion can be assumed. On a winter visit in 1332, Saint Catherine of Siena felt God had abandoned her to the howling winds; a sensation still true today.

Just beyond San Quirico is **Bagno Vignoni**, a tiny but energetic spa station. In the middle of a severe medieval piazza, bubbling warm water gushes into an enclosed stone pool. The hot springs were used by Romans and became public baths in medieval times. Saint Catherine perhaps bathed here on her day off between miracles or saving the Papacy.

The new baths down the hill are open at night on summer weekends. From the pool, all senses are fulfilled at once: the imposing Rocca D'Orcia looms above; outside the pool of light, the sound of

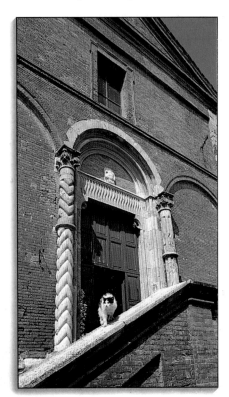

14th-century church of San Francesco, Chiusi.

sheep and crickets reverberate; the softness of the hot chalky water dissolves tiredness; and the lingering smell of sulphur evaporates into the night air. The locals add the bizarre touch: while formation swimmers "dance" in time to Big Band music, spectators stare upwards for shooting stars, a feature on dark nights in mid-August. After a swim, a short *passeggiata* around the old baths shows the well-restored square at its most romantic.

The Etruscan towns: Although set among attractive low hills, **Chiusi** is an unprepossessing town, devoid of Renaissance charm. The "low town" is a commercial centre and the shabby "high town" is endearing, but overwhelmed by its glorious Etruscan past.

Then as now, the Chiusini were farmers, merchants and craftsmen, a spirit which predominates over artistry. Yet with a little Etruscan knowledge and much curiosity, the town is as fascinating as any in Tuscany. It boasts a complete underground city; an unrivalled collection of female cinerary urns; and the only tomb paintings in their original setting in Tuscany.

As one of the greatest city states in the Etruscan League, Chuisi or "Kamars", controlled the area from Lago di Trasimeno to Monte Amiata. After reaching its zenith as a trading centre in 7 B.C., Etruscan Kamars became submerged by Roman Clusium and then by medieval Chiusi.

The old city survives on three levels of civilisation: the huge Etruscan necropolis under the city hills; the Roman street grid system below the Cathedral; and the medieval city above. If locals seem unimpressed by modern Chiusi, it is simply because they remember that their King, Lars Porsena, conquered Rome in 508 B.C.

The city's decline was hastened by its proximity to malaria-ridden marshes. Drainage works started by Cosimo de' Medici and continued today, have created a healthier commercial climate within the grand Etruscan walls.

The **National Etruscan Museum** is a wonderfully confusing experience,

Chiusi Cathedral built from Etruscan and Roman fragments.

concealing one of Italy's finest collections. Still, the collection as it stands attests to the vitality of Kamars and shows a distinctly female bias in the outstanding female canopic jars, cinerary urns and rounded *cippi* tombstones. The containers have Egyptian style lids resembling human or animal heads.

The Etruscans borrowed freely from the Greeks and Egyptians. The imitation Greek vases are less rational but more vigorous than the originals.

Unique to Chuisi is *bucchero*, glossy black earthenware, often in the form of vases with figures in relief. This pottery has a sophisticated metallic finish which cannot be reproduced by modern craftsmen. Although much of the domestic pottery has a naturalness verging on the commonplace, the sarcophagi, the cinerary urns and the crouching sphynx reveal an underlying obsession with death and the appeasement of shadowy spirits.

In Chiusi Cathedral three civilisations are visible at once: the "barbaric" Romanesque Cathedral is built from Etruscan and Roman fragments; and the antique cistern beneath the belltower is from 1 B.C. After fanciful speculation on the Etruscan galleries running underneath the town, a visit to the tombs can be arranged with the curator.

Before this, it is well to look out for signs of "urban decoration": genuine Etruscan urns and sculptures in local gardens. The Etruscan physiognomy can also be spotted in the ironic smile or oblique glance of the bartender.

The tombs contain sarcophagi, cinerary urns and, in the case of the Monkey Tomb, rare wall paintings depicting athletic games and domestic scenes. Outside the town, ignore the two unremarkable towers, Beccati Questo and Beccati Quello, translated in Chiusi's tourist brochures as the "Get an Eyeful of This One" and "Get an Eyeful of That One" towers. Get a mouthful of the local fish instead. After underground Chiusi, **Chianciano Terme** is literally a breath of fresh air. It boasts the healthiest and wealthiest climate in Tuscany: hills, spas, pine forests; and more doctors and

The hot springs at Bagno Vignoni.

fur coats per square metre than elsewhere in Italy. "Chianciano for a Healthy Liver," the signs into town invite, exhort or cajole.

The medieval "low town" with its small Etruscan museum and Signorelli fresco is studiously ignored by Italian visitors. The "high" spa town is where Italians have flocked since Roman times to enjoy the unique powers of *Acqua Santa*: as one of the world's top spas, Chianciano is a seriously rich town.

This is the place to spot Italian "August evacuees" relaxing in hotels, pools, parks, bars, outdoor concerts and designer shops. Alternatively, it is the place for a spot of elderly matchmaking, plastic surgery or both.

Near Chianciano are some of the loveliest walks and drives in Tuscany. Many walks start from **La Foce**, a 15th-century farmhouse which overlooks the fertile Valdichiana and the desolate craters of the Val D'Orcia. There are views across an Etruscan site to Monte Amiata and Monte Cetona. Its excellent strategic position meant that its owners, the Anglo-Italian Origos, used it as the partisans' refuge during World War II.

From there, a rough track leads to Petraporciana, the partisans' hidden headquarters and to a primeval forest. This *faggeta* is full of giant oaks, cyclamens, wild orchids or snowdrops: a perfect short spring or autumn walk.

Beside La Foce is **Castelluccio**, a castle which commands the best-loved view in the province: a sinuous line of cypresses plotting an Etruscan route across the craters. When Britain's Prince Charles stayed at La Foce, proud locals were not surprised to see him painting this very view.

A short walk leads to Pocce Lattaie and prehistoric caves with dripping stalagtites shaped like teats or nipples. These pagan caves were used in fertility rites and propitiatory offerings made to the gods. To tread where no prince has ever trod, be prepared to hire a guide and a torch.

Routes to Monte Amiata: From Chianciano, an idyllic rural drive leads

Romanesque abbey of Sant' Antimo.

through Castelluccio to Sarteano and Cetona, two small medieval and Etruscan towns. These views of desolate *crete*, fortified farmhouses and hazy Monte Amiata are captured by Paolo Busato in his celebrated photographs. It is worth sacrificing a hired car to the dirt roads but the nervous can take the more direct route to Sarteano.

Castiglioncello di Trionoro is a tiny village with a Castello, and a church containing a *Trecento* Madonna. The village is set amid vast expanses of abandoned countryside in which Etruscan remains are uncovered by chance every few years.

Spilling over its double ring of city walls, **Sarteano** is a popular thermal centre that has retained its traditional identity. The town offers Etruscan remains, a grandiose 13th-century Rocca and crumbling Renaissance palazzi built into the city walls. Prehistoric caves can be explored at the Villa Contucci. The thermal centre contains two excellent swimming pools heated by radioactive water. In August, Sarteano holds a famous *Giostra* or tournament.

Cetona clings onto a richly wooded hill and, with the lowest incomes in the province, is struggling to survive. The grand 18th-century houses on the plains are a relic of past prosperity. The town's star attractions are a medieval fortress, set among oleanders, and a villa owned by the fashion designer Valentino.

Although Cetona is noted for its textiles and copies of Etruscan vases, it now relies on *Agriturismo* to keep its population from leaving. A short stay in a local farm with mountain walks and *bruschetti* drenched in olive oil has much to recommend it.

The varied approaches to **Monte Amiata**, southern Tuscany's highest peak, are at least as good as arrival. The fast Pienza to Abbadia San Salvatore route allows for a detour to Siena's loveliest thermal baths, **Bagni San Filippo**. A turning to the right shortly before Abbadia leads to a cluster of houses and orchards and the sulphurous smell indicates the thermal centre.

The winding walk down to the pool

passes a pediluvium before reaching a magnificent rocky waterfall and a modern pool. Mud and massage treatments are available for those not already coated in chalky white masks. Although Italians are quite happy swimming in hot baths in the height of summer, visitors tend to collapse with exhaustion after two lengths.

The alternative route via Sarteano and **Radicofani** was the one taken by both Dickens and Montaigne to a location second only to Volterra for natural drama. While the mountain villages have sports and leisure industries to thank for their revival, the villages on the edge of Amiata are in limbo, trapped rather than enhanced by a medieval identity—and, in Radicofani's case, a medieval economy.

Dickens found Radicofani "as barren, as stony, and as wild as Cornwall, in England". Perched on a craggy basalt rock 2,513 ft (766 metres) above sea level, it is the only place in Italy to possess a triple Medicea wall. The town overlooks an area rightly called *Il Mare di Sassi*, the "sea of stones" suitable for only very hardy sheep.

The town is linked to the exploits of Ghino di Tacco, the "gentle outlaw" immortalised by Dante and Boccaccio. Exiled Ghino controlled the town from Radicofani Castle, built by Hadrian IV, the only English Pope. A fierce basalt sculpture of Ghino stands in this forbidding town of low stone houses with external stairways, blind alleys and severe facades. Although an 18th-century earthquake destroyed much of the town, quite enough atmosphere remains.

The drive from Radicofani to **Abbadia San Salvatore** is via Le Conie, a tortuous road known as "Amiata's sentry". For those not interested in skiing, mountain walks and disused mercury mines, Abbadia is best known for its much overrated **Abbazia** and its medieval "high town".

The Romanesque San Salvatore is all that remains of a once magnificent abbey. Unfortunately it has been heavily restored twice, once in 16th-century

Interior of the abbey of Sant'Antimo.

Baroque and again in 1925. A 12th-century crucifix and the crypt with its 36 different columns remain relatively unspoilt, however. Geometric symbols, grapes, palm leaves, animals, and gordian knots decorate the pillars in this sober place.

From Abbadia, a winding road with sharp bends and sheer drops leads to the summit of **Monte Amiata**, 5,700 ft (1,738 metres) high. The wooded area around the extinct volcano has attractive walks and, since hunting is banned, there is plenty of opportunity for animal spotting. The Fosso della Cocca, a leafy tunnel, is the best place for unusual widlife and vegetation.

Although **Castel del Piano**, set among pine forests and wild raspberries, is the oldest settlement in the area, **Piancastagnato** is a better base. Perched among chestnut groves, the town offers a newly-restored Rocca, Franciscan monastery and odd villages.

Pope Pius II, on a visit to Amiata from Pienza in 1462 wrote: "The soft spring waters run through mountain spots more beautiful than nymphs or fauns could have found". Given the sulphurous odour, the nymphs must have had a cold at the time.

Quintessential Sienese town: In both temperament and identity, **Montalcino** is certainly the most Sienese town in the province. Its history is a microcosm of all Sienese history. From a distance Montalcino even looks like a Sienese *Trecento* painting: the landscape could be a background to a Saint's life; in the foreground would be the fortress and scenes of rejoicing after an historic victory.

Montalcino has been known as "the last rock of Communal freedom" since its time as the Sienese capital in exile between 1555 and 1559. After the fall of Siena, exiles gathered around Piero Strozzi and the Sienese flag. As a reward, Montalcinesi standard bearers traditionally have the place of honour in the procession preceding the *Palio* in Siena.

The magnificent 14th-century Rocca is the key to Montalcino's pride. The approach is through olive groves and the slopes famous for Brunello wine. But the assymetrical fortress, astride a spur of land, dominates the open landscape. From the fortress gardens, there is a sense of boundless space and absolute freedom.

In winter, the wind howls over the massive walls and drives visitors to a different type of fortification in the *Enoteca* bar inside. This "National Wine Library" naturally serves Brunello, the first wine in Italy to be given the DOCG *Denominazione* for excellence.

The fortress still contains the tattered flag of the old Sienese Republic. Depicting the Virgin and Child, it represents the Republic's struggle for liberty. Visiting Sienese have been known to weep on seeing the *standardo*.

Visiting Montalcino is not a trip, it is a pilgrimage. Oddly enough, Montalcino's history has come full circle: after countless changes to its boundaries, it is now in possession of exactly the same land as in medieval times. Its liberal and left-wing traditions have also survived:

The *fortezza* at Montalcino dominates the landscape. Following page, the craggy *Rocca* of Radicofani, approaching Monte Amiata.

in the 1920s the town had a proud anti-Fascist record and held out against the Germans until 1945. Today it is equally proud of its tiny "nuclear-free zone".

Architecturally, Montalcino offers a neo-classical Cathedral, a Gothic loggia, a Romanesque church and a myriad of intriguing alleys. The Duccio and della Robbia schools are well-served by the Civic and Sacred Museums. Sano di Pietro's Byzantine-style *Madonna dell' Umilita* is particularly moving. Most significant is the Palazzo Comunale, a mass of Fiorentinita finished off by a Sienese tower to prove that the Sienese always surpass the Florentines.

In spring, the area is incredibly green but yellow rape seed, poppies, sunflowers and grapes soon retaliate. Before leaving, *pici*, home made spaghetti, and sweet *sospiri* ("sighs") are available in a French-style *fin de siècle* bar.

Nearby is **Sant' Antimo**, the remains of a Romanesque abbey founded by Charlemagne. If the church is closed, try the sacristan in **Castelnuove Abate**, the village up the hill. Designed in the style of the French and Lombard models, the abbey is built from local *travertine* which closely resembles alabaster or onyx.

But what sets Sant'Antimo apart is the interior. It has a translucent quality and, as the light changes, turns luminously golden, white and brown. Its setting, amidst cypresses in a peaceful valley, inspired Charles Tomlinson to write of the wind in the cypresses as "a continual breathing, an underwater floating of foliage" chasing its shadowy reflection against the stone tower.

Not far away, **Sant'Angelo in Colle**, a fortified hill-top village, once cast a dramatic shadow over Grosseto and other enemies. Until 1265 it was a Sienese outpost, but the tower is all that remains. Today it is a quiet medieval village with time and consideration for peaceful visitors.

Modern Siena province ends just there. As a frontier castle, Sant'Angelo looked down onto the plain which falls into Grosseto. After Siena province, Grosseto can look deceptively flat.

AREZZO

The landscape of the province of Arezzo is rugged with steep valleys that form a kind of backwoods hiding its towns and villages from public view. The north is a remote area of chestnut woods, vineyards and monasteries; to the south are the prosperous farms of the Valdichiana—an area which was once mainly swamps and lakes. Arezzo, the Roman Arretium, was originally an Etruscan city but in 294 B.C. it became a military rest station on the Via Cassia between Rome and Florence. The principal Roman site is the amphitheatre off the Via Margaritone, built in the 1st century B.C. It could hold between 8,000-10,000 people but was unfortunately much plundered to build the city walls, churches and other buildings.

The view of the town from the south is quite unremarkable. The buildings run down the side of a low hill and are absorbed into the landscape while from the north and the west Arezzo looks the classic hill town, surrounded by a high wall and crowned by the **Duomo**.

The Duomo's construction, mainly from the late 13th to the the early 16th centuries, was aimed at re-asserting the authority of the Church over the Commune, and it has been described as one of the most perfect expressions of Gothic architecture in Italy. The Gothic facade however is fake and dates from 1914.

Internally the effect is very similar to the North European Gothic style. There are clustered columns, pointed arches and 15th-century stained glass windows. There are also local interpretations of the Gothic style in the nave; the 14th-century marble tomb of Arezzo's patron saint, Donatus, for example. Other great works here are the 14th-century cenotaph of Guido Tarlati, which flanks the St Mary Magdalen fresco by Piero della Francesca.

On the first Sunday of every month Arezzo holds an antique fair which is one of the largest and oldest in Italy. Stalls run around the base of the Duomo, down the cobbled main street in the old quarter, the **Corso Italia**, and into the Piazza Grande beneath the arches of Vasari's Palazzo delle Loggie.

A visit that coincides with this event is recommended because if you get overwhelmed with the huge range of artifacts on sale there are many distractions. You can visit the **church of San Francesco** in Piazza San Francesco and see Piero della Francesca's fresco cycle *The Story of the True Cross* or the Church of San Domenico and see Cimabue's Crucifix.

The **Museo Archeologico** is stacked with some of the best examples anywhere of the red-glazed Coralline ware for which Arezzo has long been famous. In the **Museum of Medieval and Modern Art** is evidence of the goldsmith's work which has been much sought after since the Renaissance.

In fact, the town itself still sports a large number of jewellers, though not as many as the even bigger range of antique shops and furniture restorers. The

antique dealers benefit from the success of the Sunday market but the restorers' tradition is sadly on the wane. Both are to be found in the vicinity of the **Piazza Grande** behind the church of Santa Maria della Pieve, in streets like the Via Seteria and the Via di Pescaja.

The Piazza Grande is essentially medieval. Built around 1200 as the centre of the old city, its sloping space is flanked on two sides by 13th and 14th-century houses and small palaces while on the third side is the apse of the *pieve* with the Palazzo Tribunale and the Palazzo della Fraternita dei Laici next to it.

On the fourth and higher side of the Piazza is Vasari's **Palazzo delle Loggie** which, when it was built in 1573, changed the entire appearance of the medieval square. The simplicity of Vasari's design creates a balance in the square which the frenetic designs of the earlier buildings could never give it.

All this is very diverting. You could, of course sit quietly in the Biblioteca della Citta di Arezzo in the Via dei Pileati and read about the great intellec-tuals who lived in Arezzo—Maecenas, the rich friend and patron of Virgil and Horace; Petrarch; Guido d'Arezzo, the inventor of musical notation; Pietro Aretino; and Giorgio Vasari, the 16th-century documenter of the lives of Italian painters.

Petrarch's house can be visited (though it was hit by a bomb during World War II and what remains is only a reconstruction). So can Vasari's house, which contains some of his own frescoes and family documents.

Arezzo can be seen in one day; the hotels here are not of a very high standard, so it would be better to commute from Monte San Savino or from Cortona.

A dream town: The Upper Tiber Valley is tightly enclosed at its northern end by Alpe di Catenaia and the Alpe della Luna. According to tradition, **Sansepolcro** was built in the foothills of these Appennine peaks, near the Tiber, on the whim of two 10th-century pilgrims, Arcano and Giles, who had been inspired in a dream. Having just arrived

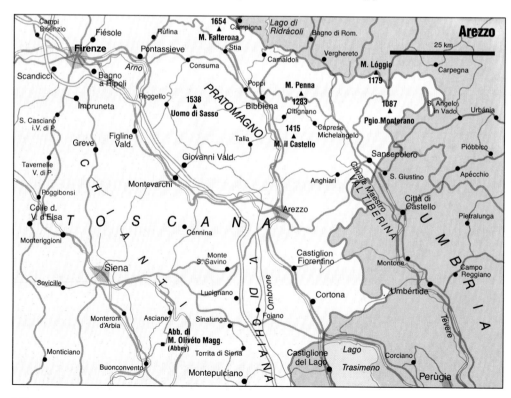

back from Palestine with relics of the Holy Sepulchre, they built a chapel on the site of the present Duomo and dedicated it to the Holy Sepulchre; the Borgo of Sansepolcro is the progeny of this.

Sansepolcro is famous for two things. It was the birthplace of Piero della Francesca, one of the greatest painters of the 15th century, and it is the source of much of Italy's pasta. Buitoni factories on the outskirts of the town produce miles of spaghetti and macaroni, carrying the name of Sansepolcro all over the world.

The old town huddled behind crumbling ramparts is an important artistic centre. The narrow quiet streets are linked by four ancient gates, the best preserved of which is the Porta Fiorentina—though the most important was, once, the Bastione del Nord, designed in the 15th century by Buontalenti.

At the town centre, at the junction of Piazza Torre di Berta and the Via Matteotti, is the Duomo dedicated to St John the Evangelist. Begun in the 11th century as a monastic abbey, it was tampered with in virtually every succeeding century and today bits of it are medieval, Renaissance or Baroque.

A wide range of excellent and indifferent artworks cover the walls of the interior including, beside the Sacristy door, a tabernacle by the della Robbia School. Perugino's *Ascension of Jesus* is also here. The Torre di Berta itself was a 12th-century tower, built at the most ancient point of the city. This was blown up by the retreating Germans in 1944.

Luckily this ruthless vandalism failed to destroy the other important buildings of this part of the town—the 16th-century Palazzo delle Laudi (the Town Hall) and the Palazzo Gherardi, begun in 1300, both in the Via Matteotti and the Palazzo Pretorio opposite the Piazza Garibaldi where in the Middle Ages the citizens would gather to discuss problems affecting the community.

The survival of Piero della Francesca's greatest work, the *Resurrection*

Antiques market in Piazza Grande, Arezzo.

(according to Aldous Huxley, the greatest painting in the World), was under threat from destruction by the Allies during World War II as they bombarded Sansepolcro, believing that the Germans were still in town.

Today this fresco is in the **Museo Civico** in Via degli Aggiunti, saved by citizens placing sandbags against it. It is an early contribution to the search for a solution to the problem of how best to define space within a painting and to achieve the greatest harmony of its elements.

It stands opposite della Francesca's polyptych of the *Madonna della Misericordia*, another of della Francesca's most important works. In the *Resurrection* Christ and the soldiers are as rough and as rustic as della Francesca's *Madonna* in the tiny chapel of the Madonna del Parto outside Monterchi, a few miles south of Sansepolcro.

The Madonna, heavily pregnant, and obviously aching after nearly nine months of carrying a child, has unbuttoned the front of her dress, while above two angels hold up the entrance to the tent in which she stands. A double row of cypresses lines the avenue from the main road to the chapel up which pregnant locals have trudged for years in order to ask the Madonna for an easy delivery. The chapel is closed on the dot of midday, so try to get there early.

Birthplace of Michelangelo: Northwest of Sansepolcro, on a steep slope above the Tiber, is the hamlet of **Caprese**, birthplace of Michelangelo. Protected by an almost complete set of walls, this clutter of rustic buildings—which includes the Buonarotti house, the old town hall where Michelangelo's father was the Florentine governor, and the tiny chapel in which Michelangelo was baptised—are interesting more for their connections than for their contents.

The town hall contains full-size reproductions of Michelangelo's works and an assortment of Michelangelo memorabilia. Outside in the garden is a sculpture park of very questionable tributes to the master from other, more recent artists.

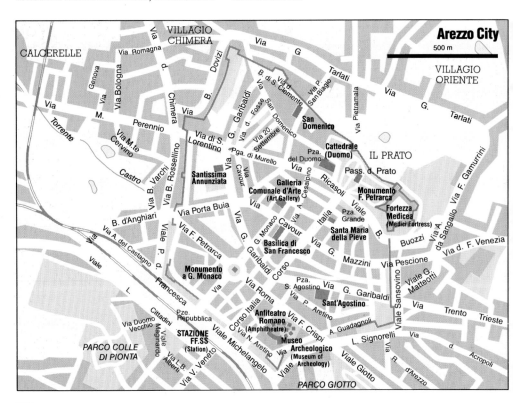

The countryside in this region is characterised by steep rocky gorges, forests and very rich pastureland. Many of the villages and hamlets here are almost inaccessible and the countryside has for a large part remained unimproved and unspoilt.

At its remoter edges it cannot be much different from the day St Francis took to a lonely, desolate crag crowned with beeches on the wooded slopes of Monte Penna at La Verna, using a niche between two huge boulders as a hermitage. The mountain was given to the Franciscans as a free gift by a local devotee, Count Orlando da Chuisi di Casentino, who had been inspired by one of St Francis's sermons.

On this spot in 1224 St Francis is supposed to have received the stigmata while he was praying. Today a Franciscan sanctuary still occupies the rock and an air of solitude remains. Around a tiny piazza is a collection of monastic buildings, including one large church containing yet more terracotta sculptures by the della Robbia family, the *Annunciation* and the *Adoration of the Child*, several chapels and the conventual buildings.

On the mountain above La Verna is the spot where the saint was assailed by Satan and another where the Wolf became a Lamb. The journey to La Verna today from the town of Chiusi La Verna down below is as much of a pilgrimage as it was in the Middle Ages. A crazy twisting road drives higher up through the birch and fir forest providing a cool retreat in the summer for Florentines escaping the summer heat.

Intimations of mortality: The Casentino is the upper most stretch of the Arno Valley. It is shut in by high mountains and so most access routes are tiny winding roads and distances have to be traversed in second gear and extremely slowly.

Ten miles (16 km) north-east of La Verna, high in the mountains of the Casentino, is another more ancient monastery called **Camaldoli**. It was founded in 1012 by St Romuald, a former Benedictine, as a reaction to what

Caprese, birthplace of Michelangelo.

he felt was the lax and luxurious life lead by most Benedictines in their monasteries.

St Romuald and his followers lived here in silence and solitude. The monastery has a pharmacy in which very little has altered since the Middle Ages. An alligator hangs from the rafters and rows of dusty pots, pestles and mortars nestle up to an upright coffin with a glass lid in which is a skeleton. On the glass face of the coffin is an inscription: "In this glass you see yourself foolish mortal. Any other glass is not telling the truth."

Another 1,000 feet (300 metres) up the mountain above the monastery is the Eremo di Camaldoli, a hermitage consisting of nothing more than a small baroque church and eight cells, each surrounded by a high wall and a tiny garden. Here the hermits are still obeying the rules their founder laid down for them in the Dark Ages. One or two of the hermits have been incarcerated in solitude for up to 15 years. At specified times a walk around these walls is permitted though a view of the hermits is not.

A brief sojourn in the loneliness of Camaldoli would easily be balanced by a visit to noisy **Bibbiena**, a typical Tuscan hill town, and one of the more important centres in the area which, unlike most other hill towns these days, is still prey to insane traffic jams.

In the church of S. Maria del Sasso are two richly decorated panels by Giovanni della Robbia and in the church of S. Ipolito and S. Donato there is a triptych by Bicci di Lorenzo. In Via Dovizi is a rustic palace, Palazzo Dovizi, home of Cardinal Dovizi who, as Cardinal Bibbiena, became the famous secretary of Pope Leo X.

Today Bibbiena is best known for its own particular brand of salami and a lively variety of shops and bars. From the main piazza there are distant views to Camaldoli and to Poppi, the latter the gateway to an interesting district of castles and fortified towns, all of which retain traces of the barbarous quality of life lead by the inhabitants of this part of

Main square of Bibbiena.

292

Tuscany in the late Middle Ages.

The region was continually fought over by the Guelf Florentines and the Ghibelline Aretines and a decisive battle in 1289 which firmly established the dominance of the former over the latter is marked by a column on a site called Campaldino, just between Castel San Niccolo and Poppi.

From the latter today the views over Campaldino are of green fields, vineyards and cornfields. In 1289 the bloody battle that took place here decimated the population of the area and Dante who was in the ranks of the Florentine army introduced an episode from it into his *Purgatorio*. Here he describes in meticulous detail the scene and the tragic death of Buonconte da Montefeltro, a fellow young Florentine.

Poppi glowers over the surrounding countryside from its hilltop. At its highest point is the particularly brutal-looking and now decaying Palazzo Pretorio, formerly a castle of the Counts Guidi, designed for them by Arnolfo di Cambio. It is not unlike the Palazzo Vecchio in Florence.

The streets of the town are lined with arcades joined by steep steps and decorated with finely carved capitals and cut stone seats. The silence of Poppi today is a reminder of the fact that young people born in remote country hill towns are constantly being drawn to the bright lights of the cities. At Poppi only old men sit about in the cafés and there is none of the ebullience and noise of Bibbiena and Arezzo.

In the distance on a hill above the village of Pratovecchio is the 11th-century **Castello di Romena**, surrounded by thickets of oak, once again a former possession of the Guidi family to whom most of the Casentino belonged. The Guidi sheltered Dante here after his expulsion from Florence at the beginning of the 14th century.

Of the 14 towers that Dante would have seen at the castle, only three now remain. **Pieve di Romena**, a stone's throw from the castle and standing on a lonely slope below the castle, is one of the most important Romanesque

Poppi glowering over the surrounding countryside.

churches in Tuscany.

Beneath its apse, excavations have revealed the remains of an Etruscan building as well as two earlier churches. Finely executed Romanesque capitals on the top of the gigantic granite columns of the nave make references to the four Evangelists and to St Peter. Most notable is the present apse of this building which dates from 1152. The key to the church is kept by the farmer's wife, in the house directly over the road.

At **Stia** is the Castello di Porciano, which looks down over the valley to the Castello di Romena and further on to Poppi, also in the possession of the Guidi.Whereas these monuments are all easily accessible, the fortified remains at Castel Castagnaia with the nearby ruined Roman temple, both to the west of Stia, are not. The road peters out and a walk through rough stony countryside is necessary to get to them.

Another of the Guidi castles was in the tiny village of Montemignaio. Today only the remains of this exist but in the village church is Ghirlandaio's *Virgin and Child with the four church Elders*.

South of Bibbiena is yet another important castle at Focognano on the southwestern slope of the Pratomagno. One of the few castles in the region to have been restored is at Chitignano, just a few miles to the east of Focognano. The medieval remains were rebuilt in the 18th century. There are other ruined castles at Talla and Subbiano—at the latter Castelnuovo with its 15th-century tower which overlooks the main road, is of particular interest.

Warlike bishops: The Valdarno region was the other much fought-over battle ground of the Ghibellines and the Guelfs in the Middle Ages. At the close of the 13th century, in an effort to resist pressure exerted on them by the warlike Aretine bishops who controlled powerful and well fortified castles in the Arno valley, as at Cennina, for example, the Florentines built three fortresses, in reality fortified towns, at San Giovanni Valdarno, Terranuovo and Castelfranco di Sopra.

San Giovanni was fortified as a bulwark against the Aretines. Today it is a lively industrial centre with a prominent display of architectural and artistic wealth. The central piazza was designed by Arnolfo di Cambio while the church of Santa Maria della Grazia, in this piazza, contains Massacio's *Virgin and Child with the Four Saints*.

Arnolfo was also responsible for the Palazzo Comunale in the middle of the piazza, and facing Santa Maria della Grazia. Just outside the town is the Renaissance monastery of Montecarlo in which is preserved the *Annunciation* by Fra Angelico.

Castelfranco di Sopra, in contrast to San Giovanni Valdarno, still retains its military character; the fortified Porta Fiorentina is as forbidding as it ever was, but these days the only thing the walls protect is an antique atmosphere. Little change has taken place here and most of the 14th-century streets and buildings have survived.

Castiglion Fibocchi defended the ancient road from the Valdarno to the Casentino and all that remains from this

A farm worker's house.

period is a tower and some castellated walls. The medieval nucleus spawned a village, little altered, which is still largely residential and the fine Renaissance residences here are as varied as those of Castelfranco di Sopra.

Etruscan heritage: Under scrutiny, the Valdarno reveals an even more ancient heritage than the comparatively recent warring of the Middle Ages. The villages of Loro Ciuffenna and Cennina bear names derived from Etruscan dialect. A more medieval rusticity is evident in their village alleyways and ruined castle fortifications. The far-distant past feels closest early in the morning when the mist covers the floor of the valley, looking like water from the height of the surrounding hills.

In prehistoric times the Arno basin was a lake and from it farmers frequently dig up fossil remains and bones of long extinct animals. At **Montevarchi**, south of San Giovanni Valdarno, is the important **Accademia Valdarnese**, a museum of prehistory which houses an impressive collection of fossilized remains from the Pliocene period, discovered in this stretch of the Arno valley.

The town itself contains a bizarre relic. This is a phial of the milk of the Virgin and it is kept on the altar of the Madonna del Latte. Apart from the museum and the church, there is not much to detain the traveller here, though at tiny Galatrona in the hills to the south of the town, above Bucine, is a beautiful hexagonal font in the parish church. It is covered with reliefs of the life of St John the Baptist.

The Val di Chiana is the most extensive of all the valleys in the Appenine range. The entire valley between the towns of Monte San Savino and Cortona was once covered in water.It was drained by the Etruscans and all that remains is Lake Trasimeno, just across the Tuscan border in Umbria.

By the late Middle Ages the area had become a swamp, and for refuge from malaria, as well as from marauding hostile armies, the people took to the hills, shutting themselves on outcrops

View from Castello Conte Guidi, Poppi.

of rock behind high defensive walls.

Monte San Savino has been a citadel since Etruscan times, though the fortifications that survive today are medieval. In 1325 the inhabitants were unable to fend off a ruthless Aretine mob who razed the town to the ground for displaying Guelf tendencies. It was subsequently rebuilt and not much happened there until its formerly strong Jewish community was wiped out, many burnt at the stake, for resisting the French army in 1799.

Progress has hardly touched Monte San Savino; it retains a large number of medieval and Renaissance upper class houses of which the Palazzo Comunale, with a facade by Antonio da Sangallo the Elder, is the most important.

The other important edifice is the Loggia del Mercato by Sansovino and the churches of Santa Chiara and Sant'Agostino. The wild hills of the country to the northwest of this town shelters a feudal retreat, the Castello di Gargonza, on the western slope of Monte Palazzuolo.

This 13th-century castle, in fact a *borgo* or walled village, dominates the Chiana valley and is the centre of a vast wooded estate producing oil and wine. For nearly 400 years from 1385 a varied history shunted this castle about from one ownership to another. Dante is known to have been here in 1304 when the castle was used as a gathering point for Ghibellines from Arezzo and Florence.

Still privately owned the walled precinct contains a number of small cell-like peasant houses which have been well-restored as self-catering establishments, now run (and owned) by the Guicciardini family. Tiny stone streets, a chapel dedicated to Santi Tiburzio and Susanna, a massive baronial tower, gardens and a magnificent view down to the Chiana, make Gargonza a very pleasant retreat.

English mercenary: Another castle, originally a *borgo* as well and at one time not unlike Gargonza in character, is the **Castello di Montecchio Vesponi**, crowning a peak above the

Monte San Savino.

main road from Castiglion Fiorentino to Cortona, just south of Arezzo. Although seriously dilapidated in parts, the owners of this gargantuan castellated building won an award for the restoration of the eighth-century tower within the enclosure.

This castle was once the property of the English *condottiere* Sir John Hawkwood, who had been hired by Florence to capture Arezzo in 1384. Montecchio was his reward. Nowadays it is only occasionally open to the public but you can drive up to the walls and walk around the outside.

From here you can see in the distance **Castiglion Fiorentino** with its medieval girdle of walls dominated by the Cassero fortress.In this village there is an unusually high number of churches, of which no less than five are worth a visit. The most important is Pieve San Giuliana, which contains Signorelli's *Deposition of Christ*, and San Francesco which is part Romanesque and part Gothic, with a 17th-century cloister attached to one side.

Just outside the village is a strange but very fine octagonal church called Santa Maria della Consolazione. The Palazzo Comunale within the walls contains works which have been taken from all the surrounding churches—paintings, sculpture and goldsmiths work—an unbelievable quantity for such a small place.

Southeast Arezzo: The southeastern part of the province of Arezzo contains three other interesting little towns: Foiano di Chiana, Marciano di Chiana and Lucignano. **Foiana** clings to the side of the hill and from afar is very picturesque. Much of it is 15th and 16th century, though traces of medieval defences can be seen around the edge of the town.

The etymology of the town's name reveals a Roman origin, and two miles to the northeast of the centre are the remains of what is believed to have been a Roman bath house, at Cisternella. **Lucignano**, just south of Monte San Savino, was originally an Etruscan stronghold, though today its overriding char-

The last golden rays of the sun.

acteristic is a very peculiar medieval town plan which arranged the streets concentrically around a castle that was rebuilt in the 15th century.

With only a few exceptions the town's buildings, predominantly 13th to 18th-century, are perfectly preserved, as is its Gothic church of San Francesco. In the 14th century Palazzo Comunale are frescoes from the Sienese and Aretine schools as well as examples of finely worked gold ornaments—evidence of the fact that the province was once particularly famous for its goldsmiths' work.

Marciano, a tiny village of great character, was also fortified in the Middle Ages and most of these fortifications still survive unchanged. Much of the castle remains and so do the walls and a gateway with a clock tower built into it. Two miles (three km) to the southeast is the octagonal chapel of San Vittorio, designed by Vasari in 1572 to mark the spot where the Florentines defeated the Sienese in 1554.

The most important town in the province of Arezzo is **Cortona**. It sits at a height of 2,130 ft (650 metres) above the Val di Chiana, perched on a ridge on the side of Monte Sant'Egidio. Cortona is really a massive fortress, accessible only via a dizzy road of hairpin bends and loops.

The town is so high that it is perceptibly cooler here than in the plain below and in the evenings it is always subjected to a gentle breeze. Although the town is characteristically medieval, it was at one time a fortress belonging to the Umbrian tribe, predating even the Etruscans whose considerable relics are scattered around the Porta Colonia at the end of Via Dardano the northend of the town.

The Romans colonised it, the Aretines sacked it in 1258 and in 1409 it was sold to the Florentines, linking it from then onwards to the fortunes of the Grand Duchy of Tuscany.

The road from the plain to the city winds up through terraced olive groves scattered about with villas and farms surrounded by ilexes and cypresses,

monasteries and churches. The first church on the way is the domed **Santa Maria della Grazia**, on the slopes beneath the town.

Beyond it is the **Porta Sant' Agostino** from which Via Guelfa leads to the Piazza Repubblica at the heart of the town. Here the 13th-century Palazzo Comunale adjoins the Palazzo Pretorio, a 13th-century mansion rebuilt in the 17th century, facing the **Piazza Signorelli**, which houses the museum of Etruscan antiquities.

It also houses some of the paintings from local churches, works by Luca Signorelli and Neri di Bicci; but it is the **Museo Diocesano** in the Piazza Duomo that houses the greatest masterpieces— a work by Duccio, and others by Fra Angelico, Pietro Lorenzetti and Luca Signorelli.

Signorelli was born in Cortona and the Chiesa di San Niccolo in a tiny courtyard below the Medici fortress appropriately still contains one of his greatest works, *The Deposition*. The Church of San Francesco contains the body of St Francis of Assisi's follower and disciple, Brother Elia Coppi of Cortona, (who, after the death of St Francis, swept away the ideal of poverty, bringing the Franciscan Order into line with the materialistic world).

Pilgrimages: The Basilica of Santa Margherita, which towers over Cortona from above, contains the near perfectly preserved body of the mystic Santa Margherita who died in 1297. She was eventually received into the Third Order of St Francis. The local citizens still make pilgrimages up the winding stone-flagged streets of the town to her tomb to pray during hard times.

Cortona is predominantly medieval. Narrow streets turn into steep flights of shallow steps down which it is easy to drive a small car. The overhanging houses of the Via del Gesu are quaint, even rustic, while scattered around are some fine medieval palaces—the 18th-century **Palazzo Ferreti** in particular (Via Nazionale) and Brunelleschi's **Palazzi Lovari** and **Mancini** (Via Guelfa).

The narrow steps of many villages are frequently negotiated by small cars. Following pages: Tuscan villa; the cloudy heights of Monte Senario.

TRAVEL TIPS

GETTING THERE

BY AIR

Alitalia (AZ) is the international state airline, with routes all over the world. British Airways (BA), British Caledonian (BR) and Aer Lingus (EI) also operate daily between the UK/Ireland and Pisa. There is a duty-free shop at the airport.

Fares available on scheduled services are:

(1) Normal fares – the most expensive but no restrictions.

(2) Eurobudget – tickets are issued on payment. Return reservations may be left open.

(3) Pex Fares – return only. Reservations made and tickets issued at the same time. The stay in Italy must include a Saturday night.

(4) Superpex – the least expensive; return only. Reservations must be made at least 14 days before departure; tickets are issued at the same time. The stay in Italy must include one Saturday night.

BY RAIL

Tickets: A return ticket from London to Pisa costs £135, which allows for a break of journey at any intermediate station en route. It may be bought from any branch of Thomas Cook at least a week in advance or from London Victoria Station.

Tickets for Italian railways are issued by the Italian State Railways, CIT, 50 Conduit Street, London W1 (Tel: 01-434-3844).

In addition to first and second class, special tickets include:

– The "Travel-at-Will" ticket (*Biglietto turistico libera circolazione*). Most suitable for tourists who intend to travel extensively on Italian railways, they allow unlimited travel on any Italian train, including Rapido, without payment of the supplement. They are only sold in London and main Italian stations to non-residents of Italy.

– The Kilometric Ticket (*Biglietto chilometrico*) allows for up to 20 trips totalling not more than 3,000 km. This can be used for two months by as many as five people together or separately.

– An Inter Rail ticket (Tessera Inter Rail) is for people under 26. It allows them to travel freely for one month in the 22 countries of Europe, with a reduction of 50 percent in Italy. (The ticket gives free travel in European countries, with 50 percent discount in the country of purchase.)

BY ROAD

Channel Crossing by car: To cross the Channel to Italy, the most convenient car ferries for direct routes are from Dover and Folkstone to Calais and Boulogne; others leave from Portsmouth to Le Havre and Southampton to Cherbourg.

The AA or RAC will give up-to-date advice on Channel crossings with or without a car. The Channel Tunnel is due to open in 1993.

COACH

European Coach Service: A regular coach service is operated by National Express for a European journey from London (Victoria Coach Station, Buckingham Palace Road) via Dover-Paris-Mont Blanc-Aosta-Turin-Genoa-Milan-Venice-Bologna-Florence (via Santa Caterina da Siena) to Rome. Return fare London-Florence is about £135. Details of bookings from National Express, Victoria Coach Station, London, SW1 (Tel: 01-730-0202).

Long-Distance Coach Services: Europabus and other companies operate long-distance coach trips in the summer from 1 June to 30 September. They are escorted by a guide and include visits to the main places en route. Examples of routes are:

Florence-Padua-Venice (255 km, 1 day; daily in each direction).

Florence-Siena-Perugia-Assisi-Spoleto-Rome (380 km, 1 day; daily).

TRAVEL ESSENTIALS

VISAS & PASSPORTS

Subjects from Common Market countries require either a passport or a Visitor's Identification Card to enter Italy. A visa is not required.

Holders of passports from most other countries do not require visas for a period not exceeding three months, except for nationals of Eastern bloc countries, who need to obtain visas from the Italian Embassy in their own country.

The Italian Consulate at 38 Eaton Place, London, SWl (Tel: 01-235-9371), can issue and advise on passport and visa regulations.

POLICE REGISTRATION

A person may stay in Italy for three months as a tourist, but police registration is required within three days of entering Italy. If staying at a hotel, the management will attend to the formality. Although this regulation seems to be rarely observed, it is advisable that you carry a set of passport photos in case you need them for registration.

MONEY MATTERS

The monetary unit is the Italian Lira (plural Lire), abbreviated to Lit. Notes are issued for 500, 1000, 2000, 5000, 10,000, 20,000, 50,000 and 100,000 lire. Coins are in denominations of 5, 10, 20, 50, 100, 200 and 500 lire. As small denominations are in short supply, sweets are offered as change in shops. The 200 lire telephone token (*gettone*) is often used as currency in place of the 200 lire coin.

TRAVELLER'S CHEQUES

The use of dollar or sterling travellers' cheques is advised and all major companies' cheques are accepted. Travellers' cheques are gradually being replaced by credit cards. Both can be used to obtain cash in any commercial bank and in exchange for goods and services in shops and hotels.

CREDIT CARDS

Most of the main credit cards including Visa, Access and American Express are accepted in hotels, restaurants and shops and for air and train tickets and cash in any bank. The American Express office in Florence is c/o Universalturismo, Via degli Speziali, 7r (Tel: 217-241).

EXCHANGE RATES

Exchange rates are displayed outside banks and Exchange Offices. They are also printed in daily newspapers. It is customary to get more lire for other currencies in the summer months, but the rate fluctuates according to world markets. There is one rate to buy lire and one to sell. For quick approximations, £1 is equivalent to about L.2,000.

BANKS

Working hours: 8.20 a.m.-1.30 p.m. and at varied times between 2.35-4.30 p.m. Closed on Saturday and Sunday.

IN FLORENCE

American Service Bank, Via della Vigna Nuova, 2r. Tel: 218-141.

Banca Commerciale Italiana, Via Strozzi, 8. Tel: 27851.

Banca d'America e d'Italia, Via Strozzi, 16. Tel: 278-721.

Banca d'Italia, Via dell'Oriuolo, 37/39. Tel: 218-741.

Credito Italiano, Via Vecchietti, 11. Tel: 27971.

IN SIENA

Banca Nazionale dell'Agricoltura, Banchi di Sopra 56-58.

Banca Nazionale del Lavoro, Piazza Tolomei 1.

Banco di Roma, Via dei Termini 37.

Cassa di Risparmio di Firenze, Piazza Tolomei.

• Exchange Offices
(only allowed to change from foreign currency into Italian lire)

Viaggi Seti (Piazza del Campo 56) – changes notes and travellers' cheques.

Coop "Siena Hotels Promotion" (Piazza S. Domenico) – changes notes, travellers' cheques and Eurocheques.

Biglietteria Stazione Ferro Viaria (Railway station ticket office, Piazza Rosselli) – open day and night, including holidays. Changes notes and travellers' cheques.

IMPORT & EXPORT OF CURRENCY

The amount of Italian cash allowed in and out of Italy is 400,000 lire per person (including children), but check with a bank before departure. Foreign currency up to the value of 1 million lire may be taken out of the country. To export more than this amount, a declaration form V2 must be obtained from the customs police when entering the country, stating the amount brought in.

HEALTH

With Form E111 from the Department of Health and Social Security, UK visitors are entitled to reciprocal medical treatment in Italy. As few Italians have faith in their own state health service, it may be advisable to take out insurance for private treatment in case of accident.

Holiday insurance policies and Private Patients Schemes (BUPA etc.) give full cover during your stay abroad.

In high summer, the weather can be very hot; sunscreen, shady hats and mosquito repellent are recommended.

WHAT TO BRING/WEAR

Towns like Florence, Lucca and Siena are sophisticated, so take something smart for shopping or dining out, although jackets and ties are rarely required for men. It does tend to rain unexpectedly so an essential piece of clothing is a plastic raincoat with an attached hood, large enough to cover anything worn, and light enough to be folded and carried.

Decent dress is required when visiting religious buildings; men and women are expected to have their arms covered and shorts are frowned upon. Women often carry a headscarf as a simple headcovering. Sun hats are also recommended as protection.

Shoes need to be sturdy and comfortable, suitable for walking – especially climbing steps – if sightseeing.

Binoculars are a good idea both for nature studies and architectural details.

ANIMAL QUARANTINE

Two certificates have to be produced for dogs and cats accompanied by travellers:

(1) A bilingual (English/Italian) Certificate of Health from a Veterinary Inspector of the Ministry of Agriculture, Fisheries and Food stating that the animal is free of any clinical signs of disease and

(2) That the animal had been vaccinated against rabies not less than 20 days and not more than 11 months prior to the date of issue of the health certificate.

CUSTOMS

Examination of luggage, passports, currency and hand baggage takes place on both entering and leaving Italy at airports, ports and frontiers. Formalities are also carried out on trains.

ENTERING ITALY

Registered luggage may be sent to Italian towns where Customs Offices exist and examination takes place on arrival at the destination.

The following may be imported duty-free for personal use: clothing, books, camping equipment, fishing tackle, two cameras with ten rolls of film each or twenty-four plates, one cine-camera with ten rolls of film (photographic material is expensive in Italy), one canoe or similar boat less than 5½ metres in length, sports equipment (skis, rackets etc.). One portable typewriter, one record-player with a reasonable number of records, one pram, one musical instrument, one tape recorder with a portable radio and portable television set (subject to a license fee to be paid at the Customs), and personal jewellery (it is advisable to have jewels listed and kept with the passport to avoid any problems on exit).

Items other than those listed above can be imported duty-free on condition that the owner can prove they are essential for his profession or trade (medical equipment, art material, samples etc.). All items listed must be for personal use only and must not be sold or traded.

Professional photographers must carry an A.T.A Carnet (issued through the London Chamber of Commerce, 69 Cannon Street, London EC4) for temporary importation of equipment. For further information, you may contact Customs, Via Valfonda, 25 (Tel: 214-316).

GETTING ACQUAINTED

GOVERNMENT

Italy is a Republic headed by a president who holds office for seven years. There are two houses of Parliament, the Chamber of Deputies, and the Senate. Power is distributed regionally among 20 regions of which Tuscany is one. Tuscany itself is divided into 9 provinces: Florence, Pistoia, Lucca, Massa-Carrara, Pisa, Livorno, Grosseto, Siena and Arezzo. The regional capital is Florence and the population is about 3½ million.

GEOGRAPHY & ECONOMY

The typical image of Tuscany is of a gentle agricultural landscape, but there are also rugged mountains in the North which encompass the marble quarries of the Apuan Alps, the valleys of the Garfagnana and the ski resorts of the Apennines. To the South are the flat alluvial plains of Grosseto as well as metal mining and power stations. Agriculture however remains the mainstay of the economy with world famous production of wine and olive oil. Tourism also plays a vital part in the local economy as visitors flock to an unrivalled centre of art and architecture.

TIME

Italy is always one hour ahead of Greenwich Mean Time (GMT), with an extra hour added in the summer from late April to the end of September.

CLIMATE

The Tuscan climate is pleasantly mild in the Spring and Autumn; cool and wet in the winter, and very hot near the sea and on low-lying land in the summer with a pleasant warmth in the hills. There is very little wind except for the Tyrrhenian coastline around Marina di Pisa and Tirrenia, but surprise storms can be very heavy at any time of the year, and flooding in a number of places has caused severe damage in the past. The rainfall in Tuscany is generally higher than most other parts of Italy. The temperature is slightly lower than other areas, making it more agreeable in the summer though somewhat colder in winter.

CULTURE & CUSTOMS

Italy is the world's sixth economic power on the basis of purchasing power but a report on social trends notes that since Italy became prosperous, manners and morals are changing for the worse. Still, Tuscans are generally friendly and will appreciate efforts to speak the language. Any attempt to rush or pressure them, however, will be regarded as the height of bad taste, and whatever you want will only take longer. Almost everything is done on the basis of personal favours or contacts so any personal recommendations you can muster will always come in useful.

TIPPING

Allowances should be made for tipping. These are some general guidelines:

Small tips of L.50-L.100 for coffee or drinks at an ordinary bar; L.500 for sitting at a table and L.1,000 at hotel bars. In hotels, tip doormen about L.500 for getting a taxi; chambermaids L.1,000 per day or L.3-4,000 per week; the concierge L.5,000 or more according to the help given and length of stay. Other staff who carry luggage, give room service, or give help with parking or cleaning a car, L.1,000 minimum.

Tip cloakroom attendants and usherettes in a cinema or theatre L.500 each. Give hairdressers L.3-5,000 depending on the cutting, styling or treatment given. Add 10 percent to a taxi fare.

In restaurants, the service charge of normally 15 percent is added to the bill which, according to law, you must have and keep until at least 100 metres from the restaurant. An extra tip is not necessary, though it is customary in cities to give about 5 percent to the waiter who may not receive the service charge.

BUSINESS HOURS

Shops in the main Tuscan cities open from 8.30 a.m.-1 p.m. and 3.30-7.30 p.m., Monday to Friday. Some open on Saturday, but all shops are closed on Sunday except for a few in coastal resorts and tourist centres which open on Sundays in the summer.

Banks open from Monday to Friday, 9 a.m.-1.30 p.m. and most of them for a short period in the afternoon.

HOLIDAYS

On Italian national holidays, all shops, banks, offices and schools are closed. Some cities celebrate their own Saints Day, but shops and offices usually stay open.

January 1	Capodanno (New Year's Day)
January 6	Epiphany Lunedi dell' Angelo (Easter Monday)
April 25	Anniversario della Liberazione (Liberation Day)
May 1	Festa del Lavoro (Labour Day)
24 June	Saint John the Baptist – in Florence only
August 15	Ferr'Agosto (Assumption of the Blessed Virgin Mary)
November 1	Ognissanti (All Saints' Day)
December 8	Immacolata Concezione (Immaculate Conception)
December 25	Christmas Day
December 26	S. Stefano (Boxing Day)

RELIGION

The state religion is Roman Catholicism, and even the smallest village has its church. Other denominations also hold their own services.

COMMUNICATIONS

MEDIA & TELEVISION

Each large Italian town has its own newspaper. *La Stampa*, *Corriere della Sera*, and *La Repubblica* also have a national following. *La Nazione* is the paper favoured by most Tuscans.

Television is deregulated in Italy. In addition to the state network, RAI, there are about 1,000 channels.

POSTAL SERVICES

Main post offices in major towns are open all day, otherwise the hours are 8 a.m. to 1.30 p.m. Stamps are sold at post offices and tobacconists. There are letter boxes in most main streets, at post offices and railway stations. The postage rates are:

• **Inside Italy and within the EC**
Letters: L.650 for the first 20 g; L.900 for

next 50 g.

Postcards: L.500 (small); L.550 (larger)

Express letters (up to 20 g): supplement L.3,000 plus the relevant postage

Registered letters: L.2,800 plus the relevant postage

• **To countries outside the EC**

Letters: L.800

Cards: L.600

CAI post is a service for sending important documents world-wide in 24/48 hours.

POSTE RESTANTE

Correspondence addressed c/o Post Office with FERMO POSTA added to the name of the locality will be held for collection. Letters will be held at the local Central Post Office and will be handed over from the Fermo Posta counter on proof of identification – usually a passport – and a fee.

TELEPHONE

Italy has plenty of public telephones and almost every bar has a public phone, but not all can be used for long-distance calls. The phone kiosks at railway stations take coins, *gettone* (token) and cards. The minimum amount of money for a call is L.200, the price of one *gettone*. Telephone cards may be purchased from a machine, which also sells *gettone*, and the PTP (*posto telefonico pubblico*) offices.

In bars and telephone centres at stations, payment is *by scatti* (units) – talk first, then pay at the end of the call.

There is direct dialling to most countries in the world from Italy. Within the country, use a three-number code which is different for each city; when calling from outside the country, use the international code.

From London, dial 010-39 then the area code number, dropping the 0.

From Italy, dial 0044 then the area code number, again dropping the 0.

Directories are easy to understand and give comprehensive information, or call 12 for Information from a private telephone.

TELEGRAM, TELEX & FAX

Most large hotels have a full communications service, though the more traditional have yet to install facsimile machines. Telegrams and telexes may be sent from any SIP office, post office or railway station. Only main offices and stations have FAX, but they will be introduced everywhere shortly.

ITALCABLE operates telegram services abroad, transmitting messages by cable or radio. Both internal and overseas telegrams may be dictated over the telephone.

There are photocopying machines at main railway stations such as Florence and Pisa.

Telegrams from trains: To send an internal telegram from TEE, Rapido, Expresso or Diretto trains, ask the guard for a special form. The telegram cannot exceed ten words.

Telegrams can also be received on trains between 6 a.m. and 10 p.m. by indicating the name of the passenger, the number of the train, and the name of the station at which the telegram is to be received.

EMERGENCIES

SECURITY & CRIME

Petty crime is a problem in Italy, particularly the snatching of handbag and jewellery. Always carry valuables securely either in a money belt or handbag which can be worn strapped across the body. Cars are also vulnerable, so avoid leaving personal belongings in view and always lock your car. Do report any thefts to the police since you will need evidence of the crime to claim insurance.

MEDICAL SERVICES

Chemists/Pharmacies: Chemists (*Farmacia*) are very knowledgeable about common illnesses and sell far more medicines without prescription than in other Western countries. There is a list in every *Farmacia* of those open at night and on Sundays. Chemists open 24 hours (*Farmacie aperte 24 ore su 24*) in Florence are:

Farmacia Comunale 13 – in the station. Tel: 263-435.

Farmacia Molteni, Via Calzaiuoli 7r. Tel: 263-490.

Farmacia Taverna, Piazza S. Giovanni 20r. Tel: 284-013.

First Aid Service (*Pronto Soccorso*): A First Aid service with a doctor is found at airports, railway stations and in all hospitals. *Pronto Soccorso* (Misericordia) in Siena can be found at Via del Porrione 49 (Tel: 0577-280-028). In Florence, the *Pronto Soccorso* are:

Pubblica Assistenza, Via Paisiello, 18. Tel: 356-535.

Croce Rossa Italiana, Lungarno Soderini, 11. Tel: 215-381.

Fratellanza Militare, Piazza S. M. Novella, 17. Tel: 215-555.

Radio Soccorso Misericordia, Piazza Duomo, 20. Tel: 212-222.

EMERGENCY NUMBERS

Medical Aid/Ambulances   116

Public Emergency Assistance
(Ambulance, Fire, Police)   113
(Replies in foreign language in main cities.)

Police Immediate Action   112

IN FLORENCE

Heart Emergency
(Mobile Coronary Unit)   214-444

Night-time and Holiday
Medical Assistance   477-891

Ambulances (Misericordia)   212-222

Fire Brigade   222-222

IN SIENA

Casualty Ward
Policlinico, Viale Bracci, Loc Le Scotte. Tel: 0577-290-807.

Ambulance Service
Pubblica Assistenza, Via del Paradiso, 17. Tel: 0577-280-110.

Lost Property
Commune di Siena, Casato di Sotto, 23. Open: Monday-Saturday 9 a.m.-1 p.m.

LEFT LUGGAGE

The main railway stations are open 24 hours and provide numerous services including telecommunications and left luggage. The fee for luggage service is usually L.1,500 per item although the price increases every September.

GETTING AROUND

MAPS

Touring Club Italiano does a good foldout map of the Tuscany region showing major and minor roads.

FROM THE AIRPORT

The international airport, Galileo Gallilei (Tel: 050-28088 or 48219) in Pisa has its own railway station. Trains take ten minutes into Pisa Centrale and 25 minutes for the 64 km (40 miles) to Florence. Car hire is available from the airport, and so are taxis.

BY AIR

ATI is the internal airline with routes to 26 Italian cities. By leaving on a Saturday and returning by the following Sunday, there is a 30 percent discount on all Alitalia and ATI domestic services. Infants under two years, accompanied by an adult, get a 90 percent discount; over two and under 12, 50 percent discount; and from 12 to 21, a 30 percent discount. There are also discounts up to 30 percent if you travel at night.

Flights cost from £160 return and although there are cheaper rates, the routes are not specifically geared to low-cost charter flights.

BY RAIL

The State-subsidised railway network is a cheap and convenient means of transport, with first and second class fares. Trains run on the main tourist routes and timetables are planned with bus, ferry and air connections. Categories of trains include:
– Locale: Very slow, stops at every station.
– Diretto: A little faster; stops at most stations.
– Expresso: Reasonably fast, missing out the small stations.
– Rapido: Fast trains running between main towns. On some trains, seat reservation is obligatory and a special supplement must be paid.
– Super Rapido Inter City: Luxurious, first class only trains between main Italian cities. Special supplement charged and reservations essential.
– TEE (Trans Europe Express): These have first class only and booking is obligatory.

There are also sleeping cars between Continental ports or towns to Italian towns, in coaches of the International Sleeping Car Company. Reservations essential.

Dining Facilities: Most rapido and expresso trains have buffet trolleys with bread rolls, canned drinks and coffee. Dining cars have retained the Italian respect for freshly cooked three course meals with wine, pasta, meat and vegetables followed by cake, fruit and cheese. Expensive (about £20) but available to all fare-payers, irrespective of class.

Special Deals: A Family Card (Carta Famiglia) for at least three people costs L.5,000 and lasts for three years. It entitles the holders to 30 percent reduction, and for children between 4 and 12, it gives 50 percent off their tickets, which are already discounted. (Children under 4 not occupying a seat travel free. From 4 to 12, tickets are at half price.)

A Silver Card (Carta d'Argento) for those over 60 gives a 30 percent discount. Each card costs L.5,000 for one year; L.15,000 for five years; and L.20,000 for life.

There are many other deductions for groups and children. For those between 26 and 60 travelling alone, the only reduction is 15 percent to travel no more than 250 km between the chief town in a province (*capoluogo di provincia*) to the chief town of the region (*capoluogo di regione*), eg. between Pisa and Florence.

RAILWAY STATIONS

The main railway stations are open 24 hours and are integrated with road and sea transport. They provide numerous services including telecommunications, left luggage, food and drink, tourist information and porters (average charge of L.2,000 per case). Most large stations have *Alberghi Diurni* (day hotels) that provide restrooms, dressing rooms, baths, showers and hairdressers for the convenience of travellers.

Florence

Train information office at the ends of tracks 9 and 10. Train reservation office and a money exchange office inside the main station hall. Both open daily from 8.20 a.m. to 7 p.m. except on holidays. The left luggage counter is usually very busy. Each piece of luggage is left at your own risk, and badly packed or awkwardly shaped packages are likely to be damaged by the uncooperative staff.

Siena

The railway station is the centre for most communications. There is an information office, a 24-hour telephone bureau, telex, left luggage (and bicycles), photo-copier, and restaurant. Immediately outside the station is a bus ticket office and a tourist office.

BY ROAD

Coaches: They are very comfortable and often quicker, though usually more expensive, than trains. There are numerous sightseeing tours in all the main cities. Morning tours usually start at 9 a.m. and finish at 12.30 p.m., while afternoon tours start at 2.30 p.m. and finish at 6.30 p.m. Details are available locally.

Addresses of bus/coach companies are:

ACIT – Piazza S Santonio, Pisa. Tel: 501-038. (For travel in Pisa Province.)

LAZZI – Via Mercadante 2, Florence. Tel: 363041. (For travel in Tuscany.)
– Piazza V Emanuele II, Pisa. Tel: 46288.

SITA – Viale dei Cadorna 105, Florence. Tel: 278-611. (For travel in Tuscany and other parts of Italy.)

WATER TRANSPORT

Sea transport from Italian ports has decreased in recent years, but occasional passenger liners dock at Livorno and it is still a busy commercial port.

Yachts and small cruisers moor at Marina di Pisa, a few miles from Pisa.

FERRY SERVICES TO ELBA

Car-ferry services operate to the Island of Elba by:
– **Narvarma** whose main offices are at Portoferraio, Viale Elba 4 (Tel: 916-743).
– **Toremar** have offices in Livorno, Via Calafati, 6 (Tel: 22772).

Together they offer services (up to 20 a day in high season) in each direction. The first departure in the morning from Piombino is 6.15 a.m. and the last back from Portoferraio is 6.50 p.m. Fares range from L.15,000 to L.44,000.

In the summer, additional services run from Livorno plus hydrofoil services between Piombino and Elba (Piombino-Cavo, 20 minutes; Piombino-Portoferraio, 40 minutes).

PUBLIC TRANSPORT

CITY BUSES

Buses within each province are cheap and plentiful. A set amount, L.500 to L.700, is payable for one journey, each province setting its own fare level. Tickets are purchased in booklets of 10 and have to be clipped by a machine on the bus at the start of a journey. Failure to do so risks a fine of 10 times the price of the ticket, either on the spot or within a month. Only monthly season tickets are available.

BUSES IN PISA

All the times of buses within the Province are clearly displayed on a board in the APT office in Garibaldi Square, Pisa. The yellow figures indicate daily services, red means services on festivals only and white shows services on weekdays (Monday-Friday). There are buses every half an hour to Livorno and every hour to Pontedera, to change for Volterra.

Just outside Pisa Centrale Station on the left is a ticket window where they sell bus tickets. Each costs L.500 for one journey.

All provincial buses are routed past the railway station in every town.

TAXIS

Taxis are plentiful in all towns and tourist resorts. They wait in special taxi-ranks at railway stations and main parts of the city but can always be called by telephone. (In Florence, dial 4390 or 4798 for Radio Taxi.) Meters display the fares. A fixed starting charge varies from L.1,500 to L.4,000 and each subsequent kilometre, L.500.

There are extra charges for night service, Sunday and Public Holidays, luggage and journeys outside the town area.

PRIVATE TRANSPORT

Italy holds the worst record in Europe for road accidents. Drivers in the North tend to drive very fast, regardless of the number of cars on the road or the conditions. The high level of traffic in city centres means many areas, particularly round historic sights, are closed to most vehicles.

The state highways in Tuscany are the No 1 "Aurelia", west of Pisa, and national motorways (autostrade), the A.11, the "Firenze-mare" and the A.12, the "Sestri Levante-Livorno".

DRIVING LICENCE

The driver must possess a Driving Licence issued by countries with reciprocal agreements. Although the new EC licence does not officially require an Italian translation, it is advisable to take one. All other licences need a translation, obtainable (free) from motoring organisations and Italian Tourist Offices.

INSURANCE

It is strongly advised to obtain a Green Card (international motor insurance certificate) from your own insurance company at least 10 days before travelling. For minimum cover, they may be bought at ferry terminals in Britain and at the Customs Office at any border. Further comprehensive cover may be bought for "breakdown insurance" – it offers some compensation for replacement vehicles and transport home if the car breaks down.

PARKING

Outside cities and towns, parking on the right-hand side of the road is always allowed, except on motorways (autostrade), at crossroads, on curves and near hilly ground not having full visibility. If a vehicle has stopped and is blocking the road for any reason, the driver must try to clear the road. If it is impossible, he is required to warn other vehicles by placing a special triangular danger signal at a distance of at least 50 yards behind the vehicle. All vehicles must carry these signs, which can be obtained on hire from all ACI offices at the Frontier by paying a deposit of L.2,000. This deposit will be refunded by the Italian Automobile Club, less the L.500 hiring fee, when leaving the country upon presentation of the receipt obtained at the point of entry.

In Florence, there is free parking outside the city with shuttle services to the centre. The Florentines consider parking metres unsightly but there are a few. Illegally parked vehicles will be fined and towed away.

THE ITALIAN HIGHWAY CODE

The Italian traffic rules are aligned to the Geneva Convention and Italy uses International Road signs. Some slight differences from the UK are as follows:

Road Signs: ALT is a stop line painted on the road for road junctions; STOP is for a pedestrian crossing

Right Hand Drive: Vehicles must keep to the right hand side of the road and close to the nearside kerb, even when the road is clear.
On three-lane roads, the middle lane is reserved for overtaking, which must always be signalled in advance.

Speed Limits: In urban areas, the maximum speed for all vehicles is 50 km/h; on country roads, up to 600cc is 80 km/h, up to 900cc is 90 km/h, up to 1300cc is 100 km/h and over 1300cc is 110 km/h. On motorways, the speeds allowed in the same order are 90, 110, 130 and 140 maximum.
Each Province declares speed restrictions: in most, the speed limits are lower at weekends and in the summer months.

Side Mirrors: These are compulsory on the left-hand side of the car, for both right- and left-hand drive vehicles. Drivers may be required to have one fitted in Italy.

Seat Belts: The wearing of seat belts is compulsory.

Precedence: At crossroads, motorists must give precedence to vehicles on their right, except on recently built roundabouts, when those already on the roundabout have priority.
Trams and trains always take precedence from left to right. If a motorist approaching a crossroads finds a precedence sign (triangle with point downwards) or a stop sign, he must give precedence to all vehicles coming both from right and left.

RUSH HOURS

The busiest times in the cities are between 9.30 a.m. and 1 p.m., when most business is done. There is a lull in the afternoon until 3 p.m. then traffic is heavy again between 4 and 8 p.m.

On country roads and motorways, heavy traffic builds up leading into the cities in the mornings and out again in the evenings around seven. In the summer, roads leading to the coast on Saturday mornings are especially busy; and on late Sunday afternoons, enormous queues form on routes going into the cities when people return from a day or weekend away. For traffic news in Florence, you can enquire at 06-4212.

MOTORWAY TOLLS

Charges for driving on motorways in Italy can be considerable. A ticket is taken from a machine on entering and payment is made at the end or at intermediate stages. For small or set amounts, coins may be thrown into a container; otherwise an attendant takes the toll and gives change. It saves time to go prepared with handfuls of coins and L.1,000-L.2,000 notes. Within Tuscany, there is a charge on the A.11 from Florence to Pisa of L.3,000 for motorcycles and small cars (Class 1); from Florence to Lucca, between L.2,300 and L.5,800.

Access signs to the motorways, unlike those of other European countries, are in green, not blue.

ITALIAN AUTOMOBILE CLUB (ACI)

The Automobile Club d'Italia, whose head office in Via Marsala, 8, 00185 Roma (Tel: 06-4998), is the equivalent of the British RAC or AA. Addresses in Tuscany, where drivers may obtain useful maps and road information, are:

Arezzo
Via le L. Signorelli 24a. Tel: 0575-23253.

Florence
Via le Amendola, 36. Tel: 055-24861.

Grosseto
Via Mazzini, 105. Tel: 0564-21071.

Livorno
Via G. Verdi, 32. Tel: 0586-34651.

Lucca
Via Catalini, 1. Tel: 0583-582-626.

Massa Carrara
Via Europa, 9. Tel: 0585-42122.

Pisa
Via S. Martino, 1. Tel: 050-47333.

Pistoia
Via Racciardetto, 2. Tel: 0573-32101.

Siena
Via le Vittorio Veneto, 47. Tel: 0577-49001.

CAR HIRE

Self-drive hire is available from major rental companies (Hertz, Avis, Europcar) in most cities and resorts with different rates and conditions. Generally the smaller firms offer cheaper rates but cars can only be booked locally. Booking from the UK, perhaps in an air-drive package, is much cheaper than hiring on arrival. Even with four or five people sharing, a self-drive car is fairly expensive. Sample charges are:

4-seater 750 cc – £173 weekly + £26 tax
5-seater 1300 cc – £212 + £32
5-seater luxury car – £404 + £60

Rates generally allow unlimited mileage and include breakdown service, maintenance, oil, seat belts but not petrol. Basic insurance is included but additional cover is available at fixed rates. Most firms require a deposit equal to the estimated cost of the hire. They often hold a credit card payment, which serves as the charge on return of the car. People travelling by air or rail can take advantage of special packages.

Cars may be hired from the airport at Pisa and the railway station at Florence.

Rental firms in Siena:
Self-drive: Autonoleggio ACI, Viale Vittorio Veneto 47. Tel: 49118.
With driver: Autonoleggio Intercar Eurodrive, Via S. Marco 96. Tel: 41148.
With driver: Autonoleggi Perugini Boero, Via R Franci 8. Tel: 286-010.

BREAKDOWNS & ACCIDENTS

In case of a breakdown on an Italian road, dial 116 at the nearest telephone box. Tell the operator where you are, the registration number and the type of car and the nearest ACI office will be informed for immediate assistance. They are usually very efficient.

On motorways, telephones are 2 km apart, with special buttons to call for the police and medical assistance. Both have to be contacted if an accident involves an injury.

BICYCLES

Bicycles can be hired in Lucca at Noleggio Biciclette, Comune di Lucca, Via delle Conce. It is open from 10 a.m. to 7 p.m.; closed from October to April. On leaving an identity card – usually your passport – you may hire by the hour a sturdy, red and white bike with a large number on it. Choose one with good brakes and a stand. Prices are:

1 Bicycle – 1 hour or fraction of an hour, L.1,000; per day, L.6,000
1 Tandem – 1 hour or fraction of an hour, L.3,000; per day, L.20,000

Mopeds can be rented in Florence through "Sabra" at Via Degli Artisti, 8 (Tel: 576-256 or 579-609).

HITCHHIKING

This is illegal in Italy but the **Agenzia Autostop** (Lift Centre for Italy and Europe) in Florence at Corso dei Tirntori 39, 1st Floor (Tel: 247-8626), will, for a small fee, arrange lifts (usually with long-distance lorry drivers) to all parts of Italy and Europe.

WHERE TO STAY

HOTELS

Besides *Alberghi Diurni* (day hotels) at large stations, Tuscany also has a wide range of hotels and other accommodations to suit every budget and taste.

Charges quoted in city guides and at hotels include heating, service and IVA (15 percent tax). Accommodation can be booked in advance through the Italian Tourist Office. Rooms in palaces and castles are available from about £20 a night; farmhouses can cost as little as £6 per night for two.

The following have been recommended by visitors and tourist authorities; a list of local hotels can also be obtained from the regional tourist office.

Note: It is important to keep receipts for hotel and restaurant bills as you may be asked to produce them by a tax inspector checking the establishment.

Safety: Only camp in recognised sites. The murderer, "Cicci, the Monster of Scandicci" is still at large and two of his annual victims in eight years have been foreign couples camping.

ABETONE

Boscolungo, Via Brennero 224. Tel: 60582. *Pensione* with swimming pool from L.80,000.

AREZZO

Hotel Europa, Via Spinello 43. Tel: 357-701. Conveniently near railway station.

Albergo Minerva, Via Fiorentina 6. Tel: 27891. Outskirts; convenient for motorists.

CARRARA

Hotel Michelangelo, Corso Flli. Rosselli, 3. Tel: 70-86163.

CASTAGNETO CARDUCCI

La Torre, 57022 Livorno. Tel: 0565-775268. Cheap, country hotel with separate restaurant offering wild boar dishes.

CASCINAV

Hotel Villa Guelfi, Via Tosco Romagnola, 941 Loc. S. Anna Cascina. Tel: 775-182.

Albergo Vivaldi, Corso Matteotti Cascina. Tel: 050-702-508.

CHIUSI

Centrale Hotel, Tel: 0578-20118. Reasonably priced. Recently renovated and decorated.

CONTIGNANO

Albergo Ristorante "Eni", Tel: 52025.

ISLAND OF ELBA

Associazione Albergatori, Calata Italia, 21. Tel: 92754. Will help find rooms or campsite for no charge. Open: Daily in Summer 8.30 a.m.-12.30 p.m. and 3-7 p.m.; Winter 8.30 a.m.-12.30 p.m. and 3-6 p.m.

Biodola: The Hermitage, Tel: 969-932. Bungalows in pinewoods by beach. Lively.

Hotel Emy, Via G Carducci, 5, Portoferraio. Tel: 917-661. Good views and very popular.

Hotel Il Faro, Via Cairoli, 18, Portoferraio. Tel: 92364. Quiet beach location. Small single rooms from L.22,000.

L'Ape Elbana, Salita Cosimo de Medici, Portoferraio 2. Tel: 92245. Fantastic view of harbour and very comfortable; with restaurant. From L.15,000.

FIESOLE

Villa San Michele, Via Doccia 4, Fiesole. Tel: 59451. One of the most exclusive hotels in Italy. A converted monastery (parts of which were designed by Michelangelo) on a quiet hill in Fiesole. Rooms are discreetly elegant and facilities include heated pool, piano bar and loggia for *al fresco* meals.

FLORENCE

Florence is well provided with expensive hotels. Cheaper accommodation is mostly booked in advance. An accommodation service is offered by the Information Turistiche Alberghiere (ITA) at the railway station. There is usually a long queue, and they charge a commission. Less crowded is the accommodation service by platform 16, open from September to July.

Expensive

Villa Medici, Via Il Prato, 42. Tel: 261-331. Has a swimming pool, gardens, and large airy bedrooms; convenient location near the station.

Excelsior, Piazza Ognissanti 3. Tel: 264-201. The grandest hotel in Florence – a lavishly furnished 19th-century building on the banks of the Arno. Celebrities and business executives stay here. Panoramic rooftop restaurant.

Grand, Piazza Ognissanti 1. Tel: 681-3861. Smaller than its sister hotel (the Excelsior, across the square) but almost as grand. It re-opened in 1986 and rooms are still being added. Queen Victoria and other foreign royalty stayed here in the 19th century.

Savoy, Piazza della Repubblica 7. Tel: 283-313. Old-established hotel in centre of shopping district. Solid, old-fashioned comforts and good service.

Croce di Malta, Via della Scala 7. Tel: 218-351. Curious combination of mock-Renaissance and post-modern, but has the advantage of garden, pool and convenient location for the station.

Hotel de la Ville, Piazza Antinori 1. Tel: 261-805. Plushly furnished first class hotel close to all the fashionable shops. Quiet, very comfortable rooms.

Kraft, Via Solferino 2. Tel: 284-273. Civilised and efficiently run hotel in quiet location 15 minutes' walk from centre. Rooftop restaurant and swimming pool with excellent views. Popular with Americans.

Lungarno, Borgo Sant' Jacopo 14. Tel: 264-211. Delightful modern hotel on south bank of the Arno. Drawings of Cocteau and Picasso feature among the owner's impressive collection of modern art. Good views of river from front rooms.

Mona Lisa, Borgo Pinti 27. Tel: 247-9751. A favourite amongst visitors to Florence. Renaissance palazzo with antiques, drawings and sculpture. Delightful garden.

Plaza Lucchesi, Lungarno della Zecca Vecchia 38. Tel: 264-141. Comfortable, civilised and very efficiently run hotel overlooking the Arno.

Grand Hotel, Villa Cora, Viale Machiavelli, 18. Tel: 229-8541. Quiet, elegant hotel set in a huge park on a hill above Florence.

Hotel Regency Umbria, Piazza Massimo d'Azeglio, 3. Tel: 245-247. A small, charming, central hotel. Gourmet restaurant.

Moderate

Lungarno Hotel, Borgo San Jacopo, 14. Tel: 264-211. A modern hotel overlooking the Arno near the Ponte Vecchio.

Annalena, Via Romana 34. Tel: 222-402. Elegant and spacious palazzo inside although the outside looks an ordinary *pensione*. Very pleasant staff. Near Boboli Gardens.

Pensione Quisisana and **Ponte Vecchio**, Lungarno Archibusieri, 4. Tel: 216-692 or 215-046.

Hotel Porta Rossa, Via Porta Rossa 19. Tel: 287-551.

Hermitage, Vicolo Marzio 1, Piazza del Pesce. Tel: 287-216. Small, intimate and exceptionally popular hotel close to the Ponte Vecchio. Pretty rooftop terrace with views of the Arno. Some rooms very noisy.

Loggiato dei Serviti, Piazza S.S. Annunziata 3. Tel: 219-165. Newly converted from a fine Renaissance building which twins Brunelleschi's Foundling Hospital (Innocenti) on the opposite side of the square. A charming, refined hotel with tiled terracotta floors, original vaulting and old furnishings. Particularly popular with art lovers.

Pitti Palace, Via Barbadori 2. Tel: 282-257. Perennial favourite with English-speaking visitors (the owner's wife is American). Pretty roof terrace and sitting rooms, convenient location just south of the Ponte Vecchio, but some bedrooms are very noisy.

Residenza, Via Tornabuoni 8. Tel: 284-197. Small *pensione* in upper floors of old building on the city's smartest shopping street. Homely public areas with lots of plants and pictures. Bedrooms range from rustic to modern.

Tornabuoni Beacci, Via Tornabuoni 3. Tel: 268-377. Deluxe guest house, very comfortable and very welcoming. Pretty rooftop terrace for breakfast and drinks. Half board terms compulsory. Particularly popular with Americans.

Villa Belvedere, Via Benedetto Castelli 3. Tel: 50124. Exceptionally friendly and modern; south of city. Sunny rooms, pretty garden and lovely views across Florence. Swimming pool and tennis court.

Inexpensive

Pensione La Mia Casa, Piazza Santa Maria Novella 23. Tel: 213-061. One of the cheapest and most attractive 17th-century palazzo. Popular with Americans and musicians. Near the station.

Pensione Adria, Piazza Frescobaldi, 4. Tel: 215-029. Quiet, comfortable, popular with Antipodeans.

Pensione Sorelle Bandini, Santo Spirito 9-10. Tel: 215-308. Elegant top floor *pensione* that belies the rather scruffy entrance. Almost always full, so book at least a week in advance.

Pensione Bretagna, Lungarno Corsini, 6. Tel: 263-618. A favourite with British business travellers.

Beacci Tournabuoni. Via Tornabuoni, 3. Tel: 212-645. Pleasant *pensione* in the centre of town.

Aprile, Via della Scala 6. Tel: 216-237. One of the more appealing hotels near the station. A Medici palace with original frescoes and some painted ceilings. Huge range of bedrooms, some very simple.

Cestelli, Borgo SS Apostoli 25. Tel: 214-213. Tiny, intimate guest house in narrow medieval street. Rock-bottom prices but very simple rooms and only one with private bathroom.

Liana, Via Alfieri 18. Tel: 245-303. Simple hotel north of centre in former British Embassy. Quiet, pleasant but slightly faded.

Porta Rossa, Via Porta Rossa 19. Tel: 287-551. Large and old fashioned, with huge spartan rooms. Favourite amongst the *literati*.

Rigatti, Lungarno Generale Diaz 2. Tel: 213-022. Family-run, typically Florentine *pensione*, occupying two floors of a 15th-century palazzo. Lovely old furnishings and private home atmosphere. Choice of noisy rooms with a river view or quieter ones overlooking courtyard.

Splendor, Via San Gallo 30. Tel: 483-427. Modest hotel close to the Accademia, set in old building with painted ceilings. Antiques and 1960s furnishings somewhat uncoordinated but good-sized rooms and very reasonable prices.

GIOLE IN CHIANTI

Castello di Spaltenna, 53013. Tel: 0577-749-483 SIENA. Small hotel in 12th-century monastery. Typical Tuscan food in popular restaurant.

LIVORNO

Hotel Touring, Via Goldoni, 61, 57100. Tel: 0586-21080 LIVORNO. Efficient chain hotel.

LUCCA

Hotel Cinzia, Via della Dogana, 9. Tel: 41323. Clean and quiet in central location.

Napoleon, Viale Europa. Tel: 531-141. Luxurious hotel outside city walls.

Hotel Celede, Via Ginisti, 27. Tel: 954-106. Good modern hotel inside city walls.

Universo, Piazza Guido. Tel: 43678. Large Victorian hotel where Ruskin always stayed. Expensive.

Ilaria Pensione, Via del Fosso, 20. Tel: 47558. Reasonable bed-and-breakfast, conveniently central.

Diana, Via del Molinetto, 11. Tel: 42202. Central location off Piazza San Martino.

LUNIGIANA

Hotel Ristorante Albergo, "Del Pino" Bastia di Licciana Nardi (Massa-Carrara). Tel: 0187-474-084. Quiet, comfortable modern *pensione* in mountain village, surrounded by pine trees. Full board available. Rooms from L.25,000

Hotel Giardinetto, Via Roma, 5, Fivizzano (Massa-Carrara) 54034. Tel: 0585-92060. Singles from L.18,000.

Albergo-Ristorante Roma, Via Roma, 84, Comano (Massa-Carrara). Tel: 0187-484-216. Singles from L.38,000.

Golf Hotel, Via Pineta, Pontremoli (Massa-Carrara) 54027. Tel: 0187-831-573. Singles from L.45,000.

MARINA DI CARRARA

Hotel Mediterraneo, Via Genova 2h. Tel: 0585-635-222 or 54036 MARINA DA CARRARA. Large modern hotel one block from the waterfront; near marble port so can be noisy at times.

Hotel Miramare, Viale C Colombo 23, Tel: 634-743.

MARINA DI PISA

Albergo Manzi, Lungomare, 25, 58013 Marina di Pisa. Tel: 050-36593. Rooms on the sea front. Moderate.

Pensione Milena, Via Padre Agostino 14. Tel: 36863.

MASSA MARITTIMA

Duca del Mare, Piazza Dante Alighieri 1/2. Tel: 0566-902-284.

Hotel Cris, Via Roma 9/10, Angolo Via Cappellini. Tel: 0556-903-830. In the centre of town (the only hotel in the centre). Very clean and comfortable and reasonably priced.

Il Girofalco, Via Massetana Nord, 25. Tel: 0566-902-177.

MONTECATINI TERME

Florio, Via Montebello 41. Tel: 78632. Moderately priced hotel with own garden.

Torreta, Viale Bustichini, 63. Tel: 70305. Reasonably priced hotel with swimming pool.

Grand Hotel Plaza e Locanda Maggiore, Piazza del Popolo, 7. Tel: 75831. Four-star hotel with wide range of facilities including swimming pool. From L.60,000.

Guhel, Via Torino, 4. Tel: 70010. From L.34,000.

MONSUMMANO TERME

Grotta Giusti, Via Grotta GiuS.ti, 171. Tel: 51165. Luxury hotel with swimming pool and spa facilities.

La Speranza, Via Grotta Giusti, 62. Tel: 51313. Cheap *pensione* with its own garden.

PANZANO IN CHIANTI

Villa Le Barone, 50020 Firenze. Tel: 055-8522. Elegant Englishness. Swimming pool.

PESCIA, Pistoia

Hotel dei Fiori, Via 8 Settembre, Tel: 477-871. From L.34,000.

Azienda AgrituriS.tica Marzalla, Villa de' Rossi, Via S. Moro, 79-51030 Candeglia (PT). Tel: 0573-43748. Quiet converted farmhouse with swimming pool in the grounds of a magnificent 17th century villa near Pescia. Reservations essential.

PESCIA, VELLANO

Fedora, Via G. Matteotti, 168. Tel: 405-517. *Pensione* in delightful mountain village about 24 km (15 miles) from Pescia.

PISA (NEAR THE STATION)

Expensive

Cavalieri (CIGA). Piazza della Stazione 2. Tel: 43290, Fax: 050-502-242.

D'Azeglio, Piazza V Emanuele 18b. Tel: 500-310.

Moderate

Roma, Via Bonanno 111. Tel: 502-532. Pleasant. Overlooking a garden.

La Pace, Galleria B di Viale Gramsci, 4, 56100 Pisa. Tel: 29351 or 502-266. Very clean.

Royal Victoria, Lungarno Pacinotti 12. Tel: 502-130. Has some of the best views of the Arno. Old-fashioned charm.

Inexpensive

Hotel Moderno, Via Corridoni, 103. Tel: 25021 or 598-067. Newly built hotel 100 metres from the station.

Pisa Hotel, Via Manzoni 22. Tel: 44551. Good service and comfort.

Albergho Milano, Via Mascagni. Tel: 23162. To the left of the station exit.

Casa della Giovane, Via Corridoni, 31. Tel: 22732. A ten minute walk to the right of the station. For women only.

PISA (NEAR THE LEANING TOWER)

Expensive

Grand Hotel Duomo, Via Santa Maria 94, 56100 Pisa. Tel: 561-894.

Moderate

Hotel Kinzica, Piazza Arcivescovado 4, Pisa. Tel: 560419. Efficient and welcoming.

Inexpensive

Hotel Giardino, Via C Cammeo. Tel: 562-101. Tucked behind the corner bar and self-service restaurant at the Porta Nuova. English and French speaking.

Albergo "La Torre", Via C Battisti, 17, Pisa. Tel: 050-21558, 25220, 56100 Pisa.

Camping Torre Pendente, Viale delle Cascine, 86. Tel: 561-704. Good facilities, very clean and cheap.

PISTOIA

Hotel Patria, Via Crispi, 8, 51100 Pistoia. Tel: 0573-25187. Charming small hotel in historic centre. Parking permits available.

Il Convento, Via San Quirico 33, 51100. Tel: 0573-452-651. Five km from town. Tranquil and comfortable.

Milano, Viale Pacinotti, 10. Tel: 23061. Newly renovated and very comfortable with the added boon of a parking lot.

Firenze, Via Curtatatone e Montanara 42. Tel: 23141. Good cheap hotel.

PORTA SAN MATTEO, Siena

Hotel La Cisterna. Tel: 0577-940-328. Superb views can be enjoyed from the restaurant "La Terrazze".

PORTO ERCOLE, Grosseto

Hotel Pellicano, Cala Dei Santi, 58018 Porto Ercole, Grosseto. Tel: 0564-833-801. Expensive comfortable hotel with cliff-top restaurant. Meals served on a terrace or in pinewoods. Tuscan delicacies such as wild boar paté and marinated eel.

PUNTA ALA

Piccolo Hotel, Alleluja. Tel: 0584-922-050. Very pretty first class hotel.

RADICOFANI

Albergo Ristorante "La Torre", Tel: 55943.

RIGOLI

Villa Corliano, 56017 Pisa. Tel: 050-818-193. Ten km from Pisa, this is an old and imposing hotel.

SAN GIMIGNANO

Hotel Pescille, 53037. Tel: 0577-940-186. Three km from San Gimignano. Converted farmhouse.

SATURNIA

Terme di Saturnia Hotel, Tel: 0564-601-061. Luxury hotel convenient for spa treatments.

SIENA

Albergo Centrale, Via Calzoleria, 24. Tel: 280-379. Clean and spacious.

Albergo Chiusarelli, Via Curtatone, 9. Tel: 280-562. Palm trees and genteel decay.

Albergo Tre Donzelle, Via delle Donzelle, 5. Tel: 280-358. Good value and position.

Cipriano (Apartment), Strada delle Tolfe, 8. Tel: 44322 or 49796. Serena Via Aretina, 29/A. Tel: 220-431. Minimum stay of seven days.

Nuove Donzelle, Via delle Donzelle, 1/3. Tel: 288-088. Friendly and cheap.

Palazzo Ravizza, Pian dei Mantellini 34. Tel: 280-462. Moderate prices. Traditional.

SINALUNGA

Locanda dell'Amorosa, 53048 Siena. Tel: 0577-679-497. Expensive, but lovely setting with superb restaurant. No single rooms.

THE MAREMMA

Hotel Agnelli, S Quirico di Sorano. Tel: 619-015. Five km from Sorano near Vitozza. A new hotel and pizzeria.

Albergo Ristorante Pizzeria La Botte, Montorio di Sorano. Tel: 638-633.

Albergo Ristorante Taverna Etrusca, Piazza del Pretorio, Sovana. Tel: 616-183.

Albergo Ristorante Scilla, Via del Duomo 5, Sovana. Tel: 616-531.

TIRRENIA

Atlantico Continental Hotel, Viale Belvedere. Tel: 37031. Four-star Luxury class. Swimming pool, private beach and tennis court.

Gran Hotel Golf, Via dell'Edera. Tel: 37545. Four-star hotel with own golf course.

Hotel Medusa, Via degli Oleandri, 37/39, 56018 Tirrenia. Tel: 050-37162 or 37125. Central and quiet.

Garden Hotel, Via dell'Ornello 10/a. Tel: 37578. Inexpensive.

Piccolo Hotel, Via del Tirreno 257. Tel: 37483. Inexpensive.

Vittoria, Viale del Tirreno. Tel: 37451. Rooms and small apartments.

Camping St. Michael, Via Bigattiera, Tirrenia. Tel: 050-33103. Quiet location, 400 metres from the sea.

Mare e Sole, Localita' Calambrone, Viale del Tirreno. Tel: 32757. Near the sea.

Pineta, Loc. Calambrone, Via delle Mimose. Tel: 37623. 100 metres from the sea.

Hotel Medusa, Via degli Oleandri, 37/39, 56018 Tirrenia. Tel: 050-37162 or 37125.

VOLTERRA

Villa Nencini, Borgo Santo Stefano, 55, 56048 Pisa. Tel: 0588-86386. Attractive small hotel in 17th century villa.

CAMPSITES

There are a number of well-run campsites in Tuscany. A list of sites with location map, **Carta d'Italia Parchi di Campeggio**, can be obtained free of charge by writing to: Centro Internazionale Prenotazioni, Federcampeggio, Casella Postale 23, 50041 Calenzano (Firenze). Tel: 055-88239, Telex: 570397.

FLORENCE

Below are some campsites in Florence. For more information on all sites in Florence, write to Federazione Italiana del Campeggia, Casella Postale 649, 50100 Firenze.

Camping Michelangelo, Italiani e Stranieri, Viale Michelangelo, 80, 50125 Firenze. Tel: 681-1977. (500 tents.) Open between April and October. Take No.13 bus from station. Crowded in high season. Good facilities.

Camping Villa Camerata, Viale Righi 2/4, 50137 Firenze. Tel: 610-300. Open: April-October. Take No.17B from station.

SIENA

Campeggio "Siena Colleverde", Strada di Scacciapensieri, 37. Tel: 0577-280-044. Open from end of March to end of October. Two km from city.

CARAVAN & CAMPER HIRE

Addresses of caravan and camper hire firms in Tuscany include:

Central Camping, Via del Termine 22, Firenze. Tel: 055-372-336.

Laika Viaggi, 50028 Tavernelle val di Pesa. Tel: 055-373-608.

ACI Tour Travel, Via Catalani 3 (loc. S Lucia), Lucca. Tel: 0583-588-181.

Arcobeleno, Via Aurelia Nord 64, S Pietro in Palazzi (Livorno). Tel: 0586-660170.

Innocenti Noleggio, Piazza Italia, 25, Montecatini Terme (Pistoia). Tel: 0572-78873.

Getur, Viale Marconi 1/c, San Sepulcro (Arezzo). Tel: 0575-76028.

In the UK, contact: **Eurocamp Independent**, Edmundson House, Tatton Street, Knutsford, Cheshire, WA16 6BG. Eurocamp arranges all transport and have sites at:

Bibbona (La Capanne), open from Easter to Mid-September. In the countryside, it has its own pool, bar and pizzeria.

At Fiesole, **Camping Panoramico**, Via Peramonda, 50014 Fiesole (FI). Tel: 599069. On a terraced site, overlooking the city of Florence. Open throughout the year.

Camping Michelangelo, Viale Michelangelo 80, 50125 Firenze. Tel: 681-1977.

Camping Villa Camerata, Viale Righi 2/4, 50137 Firenze. Tel: 610-300.

Campeggio "Vecchio Ponte", Paliano, Via Costoli 16, 50039 Vicchio (FI). Swimming pool "Le Sorgenti", Via Costoli. Tel: 844-8306.

YOUTH HOSTELS

FLORENCE

Santa Monaca Hostel, Via S. Monaca, 6. Tel: 296-704 or 268-338.

Ostello della Gioventu, Villa Camerata, Viale Righi 2/4. Tel: 601-451.

Villa Favard, Via Rocca Tedalda, Firenze. Tel: 690-847. Six km from town.

SIENA

Ostello della Gioventu, "Guido Riccio", Via Fiorentina, 17, Localita Stellino. Tel: 0577-52212. Excellent, but two km from centre Siena.

FARM HOLIDAYS

Staying on farms (*agriturismo*) in Tuscany is increasingly popular and more organised. The **Head Office of Agriturist**, Corso V Emanuele, 101, Rome (Tel: 06-656-241) will provide full information or obtain details from the regional office, **Agriturist Comitato Regionale**, Piazza S. Firenze, 3, 50122 Firenze (Tel: 055-287-838). To rent a farmhouse in Tuscany, the **Azienda Soggiorno**, Via Banchi di Sotto, Siena, or any other local tourist office has addresses.

VILLA HOLIDAYS

Particularly recommended for Lunigiana region of Northern Tuscany is "Hello Italy", a small company with a good selection of villas and houses of various sizes. The owners live locally and provide a a summer "club house" for visitors, as well as very detailed information about the region. (They can also help with property hunting in the area.)

Italy Office: Hello Italy (Lunigiana Holidays), Piazza degli Archi Antichi, 14, Panicale, 1-54016 Licciana Nardi. Tel: 0187-474-366, Fax: 0187-474013.

UK Office: 71 Busbridge Lane, Godalming, Aurrey GU7 1QQ. Tel: 04868-21218.

CASTLES & MONASTERIES

Accommodation is available in a variety of castles, palaces and monasteries. Standards will vary from very simple (and cheap) to luxurious. A list of places can be obtained from the Italian State Tourist Office in London or enquire at the local tourist offices.

FOOD DIGEST

Breakfast is a minimal affair in Italy; most Italians grab a capuccino or an espresso or two with a pastry at a local bar or cafe, usually consumed standing at the bar. Lunch is a serious business, with antipasto followed by soup or pasta (*primo*), followed by a substantial meat or fish dish (*secondo*) with vegetables (*contorno*) ordered separately. Pasta is not generally eaten as a main course. The evening meal follows a similar pattern.

IVA is VAT; it will be included in your bill. *Pane e coperto* includes bread etc. and will also be included.

WHAT TO EAT

Tuscany is known for its excellent food. Some of the traditional dishes are:

Bistecca alla Fiorentina – a thick, T-bone steak grilled over charcoal, sprinkled with freshly ground black pepper and a trickle of olive oil.

Minestrone alla Fiorentina – a vegetable soup with slices of country bread.

Zuppi di Fagioli all' Fiorentina – vegetable and bean soup with olive oil, flavoured with rosemary, onions, garlic, celery and tomatoes.

Il Lampredotto – boiled tripe eaten in a sandwich with a green sauce.

Schiacciata alla Fiorentina – a simple cake made with flour, sugar, eggs and olive oil.

Stracotto – beef cooked for many hours in red wine.

Pappardelle alla Lepre– pasta with hare sauce.

Trippa – savory tripe cooked in onions and tomatoes.

Cacciucco alla Livornese – a stew of all kinds of fish with a very hot sauce.

Tortino di Carciofi – baked artichoke omelette.

Baccala alla Livornese – salt cod cooked in tomatoes, black olives and black pepper.

Fagioli all' Uccelletto – haricot beans cooked with sausages in a sauce of tomatoes, garlic and sage.

Cinghiale di Maremma – wild boar from the Maremma region near Grosseto.

Cee – pisan dish of young eels with olive oil, garlic and sage.

Crostini – canapes spread with chicken liver or game pate.

Ribollita – bean stew.

Panforte di Siena – a confection made of honey, candied fruits, almonds and cloves.

Castagnaccio – chestnut cake with pine nuts and sultanas.

Ricciarelli – a very delicate biscuit of honey and almonds from Siena.

WHERE TO EAT

Restaurants: The restaurants listed are recommended by tourist authorities and visitors. For more expensive restaurants booking is always advisable especially during the summer months.

ABETONE, Pistoia

La Capannina, Via Brennero, 254. Tel: 60562.

AREZZO

Buca di San Francesco, Piazza San Francesco 1. Tel: 0575-23271. Closed Monday evening. Famous cellar restaurant beside the church of San Francesco. Kings, presidents and nobel prize winners have eaten here. Strong on atmosphere, not so good on cuisine.

Better value food at the modern **Il Torrino**, Superstrada dei Due Mari. Tel: 0575-36264. Closed on Monday.

ARTIMINO, Florence

Ristorante La Delfina, on the road out of Artimino to the Pian di Rosello.

CARRARA

Bar Nuovo Punto, Via Verdi 19, Carrara. Cheap local bar/restaurant with pleasant garden at the back. Good pastas and salads.

Soldaini Via Mazzini, 11. Tel: 71459. Closed on Monday.

Trattoria Cavatore, Piazza Settembre. Smart, with new light versions of Italian staples: salmon carpaccio, baked polenta, vegetable rissotto.

Ristorante Venanzio, Piazza Palestro, 3 Colonnata (Carrara). Tel: 241-070. Regional cooking in a restaurant at the heart of the marble quarries.

MARINA DI CARRARA

Trattoria da Gero, 305 XX Settembre. Tel: 55255.

Loris Pizzeria, Via Muttini, 24. Tel: 786-685. Good pizzas.

CASCINA

Dar Mago, Via Tosco Romagnola, 941, Loc S Anna. Tel: 775-182. (Restaurant at the Hotel Villa Guelfi.)

Baracchina di Antonio. Via Ponte di Cascina. Tel: 702-049.

CETONA

Convento San Francesco, Tel: 238-015. Tuscan food using local produce served in monastery restaurant.

CUTIGLIANO

Fagiolino, Via Carega, 1. Tel: 68014.

Ristorante "Fiorella", Tel: 52000.

FLORENCE

Expensive

Enoteca Pinchiorri, Via Ghibellina, 87. Tel: 242-777. Closed Sunday, Monday lunch, and August. Reservations essential. Occupies a 15th-century palace with delightful courtyard for *al fresco* meals. Rated among the top restaurants of Europe. Excellent *nouvelle cuisine* and an impressive collection of wines.

Il Cestello, Hotel Excelsior, Piazza Ognissanti 3. Tel: 294-301. Very elegant hotel restaurant with top quality Tuscan and international dishes. Popular rendezvous for business executives. Stunning views from the rooftop restaurant.

Regency, Piazza Massimo d' Azeglio 3. Tel: 245-247. Top-notch food in exclusive hotel restaurant, overlooking a garden.

La Capannina di Sante, Piazza Ravenna. Tel: 688-345. Closed Sunday, Monday lunch, one week in August and Christmas. One of the best fish restaurants in town, patronized by the local business community.

La Loggia, Piazzale Michelangelo 1. Tel: 234-2832. Closed Wednesday and two weeks in August. Popular tourist spot with superb panorama over the city.

Reasonable

Cantinetta Antinori, Piazza Antinori 3. Tel: 292-234. In a 15th-century *palazzo* serving typical Tuscan snacks and meals served with wines from the well-known Antinori estates. Good place for a light lunch at the bar or a fuller meal in the elegant dining room.

Bronzino, Via delle Ruote 25r. Tel: 495-220. Closed Sunday and three weeks in August. Spacious restaurant out of the centre and named after the painter who lived and worked here in the 16th century. A favourite haunt for discerning Florentines.

Buca Mario, Piazza OttaViani 16. Tel: 214-179. Closed Wednesday, Thursday lunch, and three weeks in July. Cellar restaurant with good home-made pasta and grilled meats. Very popular with tourists.

Cibrèo, Via dei Macci 118r. Tel: 234-100. Closed Sunday, Monday, six weeks from August to September. One of the most popular restaurants in town amongst new generation Florentines. Mainly nouvelle cuisine grafted on to Tuscan cooking. No pastas. The same food, at half the price, is served in the *Vinaria* section, just around the corner.

Coco Lezzone, Via del Parioncino 26r. Tel: 287-178. Closed Sunday and Wednesday evening; Summer: Saturday and Sunday, but open Wednesday. Crowded, chaotic white-tiled trattoria with good Tuscan cooking. Favourite haunt of locals.

Da Noi, Via Fiesolana 46r. Tel: 242-917. Closed Sunday, Monday and August. Reservations essential. Run by former staff of Enoteca Pinchiorri (see above). Small and intimate with good quality nouvelle cuisine and Italian dishes. No written menus but excellent English spoken.

Le Fonticine, Via Nazionale 79r. Tel: 282-106. Closed Saturday, Sunday and four weeks in July/August. Friendly family-run restaurant near station specializing in Tuscan and Emilian dishes. Excellent home-made pastas.

Inexpensive

Angiolini, Via S. Spirito. Tel: 298-976. Closed Sunday and Monday. Bustling, typically Florentine, in the Oltrarno district.

Belle Donne, Via delle Belle Donne 16. Tel: 262-609. Closed Saturday evening and Sunday. A hole-in-the-wall restaurant near the railway station, worth visiting for simple rustic specialities.

Burde, Via Pistoiese 6. Tel: 317-0206. Closed evenings and two weeks in August. Authentic Tuscan trattoria with home-made soups, pastas and puddings. Tuesdays and Fridays are the best days for fish. No dinner served.

Il Caminetto, Via dello Studio 34r. Tel: 296-274. Closed Tuesday, Wednesday and July. Hearty, simple and filling food.

Il Fagioli, Corso Tintori 47r. Tel: 244-285. Closed August, Sunday and also Saturday in summer. Simple, friendly trattoria with typical Tuscan fare.

Il Latini, Via dei Palchetti 6r. Tel: 210-916. Closed Monday, Tuesday lunch, and three weeks in July and August. Typical Tuscan food at communal tables in noisy cellar restaurant.

Tarocchi, Via dei Renai 12. Tel: 234-3912. Lively and friendly pizzeria.

Vittoria, Via della Fonderia 52r. Tel: 225-657. Closed Wednesday and August. Basic trattoria in the San Frediano district with good simply cooked fish. No meat.

PIZZA RESTAURANTS

Inexpensive

Acqua al Due, Via dell'Acqua 2r. Tel: 284-170. Young people's meeting place.

Borgo Antico, Piazza Santa Spirito 6r. Tel: 210-437.

Pizzeria-Ristorante I Ghibellini, Piazza S Pier Maggiore, 8. Open: Thursday-Tuesday. Quiet square; outstanding food and service.

Yellow, Via Proconsolo, 39r. Tel: 211-766.

La Bussola, Via Porta Rossa 58r. Tel: 293-376.

Trattoria Da Za-Za, Piazza Mercato Centrale, 26r. Open September-July: Monday-Saturday, 12 p.m.-3 p.m. and 7-10 p.m. Excellent food, local clientele.

Trattoria Le Mossacce, Via del Proconsolo, 55r. Between the Cathedral and the Bargello.

FAST FOOD/SELF-SERVICE

Italy & Italy, Piazza Stazione, No. 25. Open: 10 a.m.-midnight.

Giovacchino, Via Tosinghi 34r. Tel: 213-276. Near Cathedral.

Trattoria, Via Palazzuolo, 69r. Open September-July: Sunday-Friday, 11 a.m.-3 p.m. and 7 p.m.-midnight. Popular with tourists and locals.

CAFES AND ICE CREAM

No visit to Florence would be complete without tasting an ice cream made on the premises.

Break, Via delle Terme 17. Simple, fun and a good choice for buffet lunch.

Doney, Piazza Strazzi 16-19. Elegant premises for afternoon tea.

Giacosa, Via Tornabuoni. 83. Closed on Monday. Up-market cafe where the young affluent eat home-made pastries, with the best *cappuccino* in Florence.

Giubbe Rosse, Piazza della Repubblica. Once favoured by writers and poets, and still popular, with an open air café and a dining room serving snacks or full meals.

Rivoire, Piazza Signoria 5. Closed on Monday. Views of the Palazzo Vecchio but prices are high.

Vivoli, Via Isola delle Stiche 7. Closed Sunday afternoon and Monday. Best ice cream in the world. Occasional queues. No seats.

GROSSETO

Enoteca Ombrone, Viale G Matteotti, 71. Tel: 0564-22585. Superb local dishes and a spectacular cellar of olive oil; over 40 varieties to sample at table with bread rubbed with garlic. Highly recommended!

Il Pelicano, Cala Dei Santi, 58018 Porto Ercole, Grosseto. Tel: 0564-833-801. Clifftop hotel restaurant. Meals served on a ter-race or in pinewoods. Tuscan delicacies such as wild boar paté and marinated eel.

LUCCA

The Antica Caffe' della Mura, Piazzale V Emanuele. Tel: 834-7962. Set on the city wall, elegant garden restaurant with white marble tables, extensive menu, with specialities like rabbit in mint sauce and risotto with petals of roses. Expensive.

La Buca di Sant Antonio, Via della CerVia, 3, 5510 Lucca. Tel: 0583-55881. Popular though quite expensive with excellent selection of Tuscan specialties; crostini with pheasant paté, hare dishes, polenta with funghi.

Sergio, Via S. Croce, 44. Tel: 49944. Closed on Tuesday. Adventurous local dishes, and will cater for special diets.

Trattoria Buralli (popularly known as "Leos"), Via Tegrimi, 1. Tel: 42236. Reservations essential. Very friendly and the soups are especially recommended.

Trattoria da Livio, Via del Mora, 8. Tel: 46473. Closed on Sunday. Good home cooking.

Aquilina, 55061 S Leonardo in Treponzio. Tel: 0583-90437. Closed on Wednesday. To the south of Lucca, an attractive, cheap *pensione* and restaurant.

Lucca, Solferino, San Marcario in Piano (6 km/4 miles from Lucca). Tel: 0583-59118. Closed Wednesday, Thursday lunch, and two weeks in August. Rated among the best restaurants of rural Tuscany and not wildly expensive.

MARINA DI PISA

La Foce, Marina di Pisa. Tel: 36723.

Janett, Via Maiorca, 34, Marina di Pisa. Tel: 050-36521. Fish specialities.

Pizzeria da Ivo, Piazza Gorgona, 7, Marina di Pisa. Tel: 050-35902.

MONTECATINI TERME

Da Giovanni, Via Garibaldi, 25. Tel: 71695.

MONTEMERANO, Grosseto

Enoteca Dell'Antico Frantoio, Piazza Solferino 7, 58050 Montemerano (GR). Tel: 0564-602-615. Erik Banti's new restaurant famous for its wine cellar, and superb food; duck breast carpaccio, artichoke tagliatelle, rabbit stuffed with ham.

Caiano Montemerano, Tel: 0564-602-817. New look at traditional regional dishes, pretty restaurant with *al fresco* dining in summer. Specialises in wild mushrooms and truffles. Expensive.

PESCIA

Ristorante Il Delfino, Via Mammianese 171. Vellano, Pescia (PT). Tel: 0572.

Cecco, Viale Forti. Tel: 477-955.

Gambero Rosso (Collodi), Via S. Gennaro. Tel: 429-364. Elegant Tuscan cooking in building designed by architect Giovanni Michelucci.

PISA

Pisa has two Michelin rosetted restaurants:
– the **Sergio**, Lungarno Pacinotti 1 (Tel: 0577-48245). Closed Sunday, Monday lunch, January and the last two weeks in July; and
– the smaller and slightly cheaper **Al Ristoro dei Vecchi Macelli**, Via Volturno 49 (Tel: 0577-20424). Closed Sunday lunch, Wednesday, one week in January and most of August. Reservations advisable.
At the lower end of the market is **Da Bruno**, Via Bianchi 12 (Tel: 0577-560-818). Located outside the walls, it serves typical Tuscan dishes at very reasonable prices. Other restaurants serving at reasonable prices are:

La Grotta, Via S. Francesco 103. Tel: 502-727. Closed on Sunday. Attractive setting and excellent food.

Pizzeria Antonietta, Via Santa Maria, 179. Tel: 050-561-810. Closed on Tuesday. Opposite the tower.

L'Europea, Via Santa Maria, 177. Tel: 22416 or 560-932. Closed on Thursday.

Manfredo, Via Cammeo, 43. Tel: 050-562-315. Closed on Wednesday. Good food, pleasant staff. Meals are served outside in summer.

Trattoria Andrea's, Via Pietrasantina, 35, Madonna dell'Acqua (PI). Tel: 050-890-821.

Da Stelio, Piazza Dante 11. Tel: 26443. Closed on Sunday.

La Scaletta, Via Pietrasantina, 107. Tel: 562-269. Attractive restaurant in a round conservatory. Excellent food and service.

Trattoria Asmara, Via Cammeo 27, 56100 Pisa. Tel: 050-552-711. Closed on Friday. The French proprietor, Jeanne, has made this into a bistro, with pretty pink tablecloths, superb food and walls covered in paintings by artists who make it their regular haunt. At the Porta Nuova.

Pick-a-Flower, Via Serafina, 14. Tel: 42561. Closed on Sunday. Popular bar for quick snacks and meeting place for students.

PIOMBINO

Ristorante Orazio, Via Lombroso 55. Tel: 33297. Closed on Monday.

Ristorante Piave, Piazza Niccolini. Tel: 33050. Closed on Monday.

PISTOIA

Il Ritrovio di Iccio, Via dei Fabbri, 5/7. Tel: 366-935. Friendly restaurant in historic centre, piano music and Tuscan cooking including Roman dishes like *gran faro*, a wheat broth.

Antica Trattoria dell'Arca, Via Gorizia 17, 51100 Pistoia. Tel: 0573-24620.

Chiavi d' oro, Via Pacini 19. Tel: 0573-30226.

Rafanelli, Via S. Agostino, 47. Tel: 532-046. Substantial and delicious Tuscan home cooking.

Cucciolo della Montagna, Via Panciatichi, 4. Tel: 477-043. Elegant and quiet with a good selection of classic Italian and regional dishes.

PITIGLIANO

Trattoria Alla Porta, Piazza Petruccioli 1, 58017 Pitigliano (GR).

PODENZANA, Massa

Ristorante La Gavarina D'Oro, Via Castello Podenzana. Tel: 0187-410-021. Rustic mountain restaurant specialising in *panigacci*, crisp pancakes served with creamy cheese and home cured meats.

PORTE ERCOLE, Grosseto

Il Pelicano, Cala Dei Santi, 58018 Porto Ercole, Grosseto. Tel: 0564-833-801.

Cliff-top hotel restaurant. Meals served on a terrace or in pinewoods. Tuscan delicacies such as wild boar paté and marinated eel.

RADICOFANI

Ristorante "La Grotta" Tel: 0578-55866.

Ristorante "Il Pama" Tel: 55919.

ROSELLE

Ristorante Il Tordaio, Via Batignanese 113.

Canonica, Roselle, Grosseto. Tel: 402-248. Cheap basic food and friendly service.

SAN MINIATO

Ristorante Miravalle, Piazza Castello 3. Tel: 418-075. Superb view. Offers regional cooking.

SIENA

Certosa di Maggiano, Via Certosa 82, 53100 Siena. Tel: 577-288-180. Converted Carthusian monastery; gourmet food served in magical setting in a cloistered courtyard overlooking Siena.

Enoteca Italica Permanente, Fortezza Medicea. Tel: 288-497. Open: daily from 3 p.m.-midnight. The restaurant of the Permanent Wine Exhibition, in the old wine cellars. Expensive.

L'Aquila Ristorante, Via Casato de Sotto 56. Tel: 283-061. Rustic atmosphere, old cellars. Good, simple, medium priced food.

La Grotta del Gallo Nero, Via del Porrione, 66/67. Tel: 220-446. Atmospheric trattoria which offers excellent food and service. Inexpensive.

La Vecchia Taverna di Bacco, Via Beccheria 9/11. Tel: 49331. Closed on Wednesday.

Osteria da "Cice", Via S Pietro 38. Tel: 288-026. Closed on Sunday. Recommended for game and bean dishes.

Ristorante Gambassino, Via della Galluzza 10. Tel: 47554. Closed on Wednesday.

FISH SPECIALITIES

Ristorante Toriddo, Via Diacceto, 1. Tel: 282-121. Closed on Saturday. Not touristy; reasonably-priced.

Il Barbero, Piazza del Campo 80/81. Tel: 40187. Closed on Saturday.

SIENA PROVINCE

Badia a Coltibuono Tel: 0577-749-426. (5 km/3 miles from gaiole) An 11th-century monastic buildings in wine and olive estates. Medium priced, varied menu; excellent ingredients grown on estate.

SINALUNGA

Locanda dell'Amorosa, 53048 Siena. Tel: 0577-679-497. Superb restaurant in restored farmhouse with famous wine cellar.

THE MAREMMA

Ristorante Fidalma, Piazza Busatti 5, Sorano. Tel: 633-056. Birreria Pizzeria Lo Scacciapensieri, Via Roma 22, Sorano. Tel: 633-563. An opening in the old wall of Sorano – an unconventional eating and drinking place.

TIRRENIA

La Bettola, Via delle Rose, 17, Tirrenia. Tel: 050-37657.

VIAREGGIO

Da Renato, Viale Buonarotti, 87. Tel: 0584-32076. Friendly; one block from the sea, tables outside, excellent fish.

VILLAFRANCA in Lunigiana

Albergo Ristorante "Nazionale", Via Baracchini 46, Villafranca Lunigiana (MS). Tel: 0187-493-010. Friendly restaurant catered to the family.

VOLTERRA

The Etruria, Piazza dei Priori 6. Tel: 588-86064. Closed on Saturday. Local cooking.

DRINKING NOTES

Wines: The *Denominazione di Origine Controllata* (DOC) *e Garantita* (DOCG) is a system of controlling Italian wine by EC rules similar to the French Appellation Controlée, but it does not always guarantee top quality. Chianti, the most well-known wine in Italy, and Brunello di Montalcino and Nobile di Montepulciano, all from Tuscany, have been awarded the status of DOCG. Other DOC and Vino di Tavola wines that are often excellent quality, are Vernaccia, Aleatico, Bianco Pisano di San Torp and the red and white wines from Montescudeaio.

THINGS TO DO

Note: The Italian State Tourist Office, 1 Princes St. London W1R 8AY (Tel: 01-408-1254) can supply free maps and brochures on a wide range of holidays and activities, and they produce a useful little booklet, *Italy Traveller's Handbook*, with practical information on travelling, accommodation and activities.

CITY

FLORENCE

Battistero (Baptistry). Open: 9.30 a.m.-12.30 p.m. and 2.30-5.30 p.m.

Brancacci Chapel (Cappella Brancacci), Piazza del Carmine. Tel: 212-331. Open: daily 7 a.m.-12 p.m. and 3.30-7 p.m.

Buonarroti or Michelangelo's House (Casa Buonarroti), Via Ghibellina 70. Tel: 241-752. Open: weekdays 9 a.m.-2 p.m.; holidays 9 a.m.-1 p.m. Closed on Tuesday.

Dante's House (Casa di Dante), Via S. Margherita 1. Tel: 283-343. Open: weekdays 9.30 a.m.-12.30 p.m. and 3.30-6.30 p.m.; holidays 9.30 a.m.-12.30 p.m. Closed on Wednesday.

Dome of the Cathedral (Cupola del Duomo). Open: 9.30 a.m.-12 p.m. and 2.30-5 p.m. Closed on Sunday.

Duomo (Cathedral). Open: 7 a.m.-12 p.m. and 2.30-6 p.m.

Excavation of S. Reparata (Scavi di S. Reparata). Open: 9.30 a.m.-12 p.m. and 2.30-5 p.m.

Giotto's Bell Tower (Campanile di Giotto). Open: daily 9 a.m.-7.30 p.m.

PISA

The main sites may be easily visited on foot or by local bus (L.500 per journey) but taking a horse and carriage is a pleasant introduction to the city. Prices are negotiable (in English), but generally start around L.20,000 for a half-hour ride along the Arno, to the Piazza Cavalieri and the Piazza del Duomo. A recommended time is about two in the afternoon, when the streets are quiet and the tourist crowds are having their mid-day meal.

Battistero (Baptistry), Piazza Duomo. Tel: 050-560-547. Open: Winter 9 a.m.-12.45 p.m., 3-5 p.m.; Summer 9 a.m.-12.45 p.m., 3-7 p.m.. Entrance: free (machines for lights and tourist information, L.300).

Campanile (Leaning Tower), situated in the Field of Miracles. Closed for repairs at present.

Cattedrale or Duomo (Cathedral), Tel: 050-560-547. Open: Winter 7.45 a.m.-12.45 p.m., 3-5 p.m.; Summer 7.45 a.m.-12.45 p.m., 3-7 p.m. Entrance: free (machines for lights and tourist information, L.300).
Visitors may not view the interior while services are being held.

Monumental Cemetery of Pisa (Camposanto Vecchio), Piazza del Duomo. Tel: 050-560-547. Open: Winter 7.45 a.m.-12.45 p.m., 3-5 p.m.; Summer 7.45 a.m.-12.45 p.m., 3-7 p.m. Entrance: L.2,000. A collection of mostly Roman sarcophagi.

SIENA

Archivo di Stato (State Archives), Palazzo Piccolomini Museum, Banchi di Sotto, 52. Open: weekdays 9 a.m.-1 p.m.; Saturday 9 a.m.-12.30 p.m.

Cripta delle Statue Duomo (Crypt with statues Cathedral). Open: 1 April-31 October, 10 a.m.-1 p.m. and 2.30-6 p.m. Entrance fee: L.1,000.

Palazzo Pubblico (Town Hall), Piazza del Campo. Open: 1 January-31 March, 9.30 a.m.-1.30 p.m.; 1 April-31 October, 9.30 a.m.-6.30 p.m.; 1 November-31 December,
9.30 a.m.-1.30 p.m.; Sunday 9.30 a.m.-1 p.m. Entrance fee: L.5,000.

Santuario e Casa di Santa Caterina (Sanctuary and House of Saint Catherine), Costa di S. Antonio. Open: daily 9 a.m.-12.30 p.m. and 3-6 p.m.
Catherine of Siena (1347-1380), a writer who set an example by her good deeds, was proclaimed Patron Saint of Italy by Pope Pius XII in 1939 and a Doctor of the Church by Pope Paul VI in 1970. All the places she visited, from the day of her birth, have been consecrated. The house, garden and her father's dye-works now form the "Sanctuary of St. Catherine".

Torre del Mangia (Tower), Palazzo Communale, Piazza del Campo. Opening hours as for Town Hall. Entrance fee: L.2,500.

Bernardino of the Albizzeschi (1380-1444) became known as a talented preacher. He had the name of Jesus painted or carved, abbreviated to the initials, IHS. In Siena the monogram stands out on the facade of the Town Hall and in the "Mappamondo" hall. Sanctified by Nicholas V in 1450, he was proclaimed the "Patron Saint of Advertising" in 1959 by Pope John XXIII.

The Miracle of the Sacred Hosts: On 14 August 1730, a pyx containing 350 consecrated hosts (bread consecrated in the Eucharist) was stolen from the Chiesa S. Francesco (Church of St. Francis). Three days later they were found in a dusty alms-box in the near-by Sanctuary of St. Mary in Provenzano, and returned in a solemn procession, where they remain today. No signs of decay have ever been seen. Every ten years they are fully examined and as there is no scientific explanation how these Sacred Hosts remain fresh and intact, it is believed to be a miracle.
Nearby, in Camprena, the **Monastery of Sant' Anna** was frescoed by Sodoma in 1503-4.

VOLTERRA

Cattedrale, Piazza del Duomo. Tel: 87654. Open: daily 7 a.m.-12 p.m. and 2.30-6 p.m. Entrance: free.

WAR CEMETERIES

American War Cemetery, near Falciani (about eight km/five miles south of Florence, towards Siena). Tel: 202-0020. Open: weekdays 8 a.m.-5 p.m.; Saturday 9.30 a.m.-5 p.m.

British Commonwealth War Cemetery, road No. 67 near Girone (about seven km/four miles east of Florence, towards Arezzo). Open: daily 9 a.m.-5 p.m.; Sunday 9 a.m.-1 p.m.

German War Cemetery, near Traversa, just beyond the Futa pass. Tel: 815-248. Open: daily 8.30 a.m.-12 p.m. and 2-7 p.m.

NATURE PARKS

Parco Naturelle della Maremma (Maremma Nature Reserve), extending from Principina a Mare to Talamone. Sandy bays, parkland pine forests with wide variety of flora and fauna. Can only be visited on foot. Open: Saturday, Sunday and Wednesday.

World Wildlife Fund Bird Sanctuary, Capalbio Scalo, a few hundred metres from Lake Burano. Visits can be arranged by calling direct (Tel: 0564-898-829) or by writing to the Rome section of World Wildlife Fund. There is a lake and small nature park, a favourite stop for thousands of birds migrating from Yugoslavia to North Africa.

Albatross, 20 Via Cavour, Grosseto (Tel: 0564-616-381), has a wide choice of guided ventures, such as canoeing along the Ombrone river, trekking across the mountains, sailing along the coast, or more typically, riding from one end to the other of the park, visiting the noble ruins of S. Rabano and the many towers on top of the mountains.

VILLAS & GARDENS

FLORENCE

Boboli Gardens (Giardino di Boboli), Piazza Pitti. Open: Summer 9 a.m.-7 p.m., Winter 9 a.m.-4.30 p.m.

Medici Villa at Careggi, Viale Pieraccini 17, Florence. Open: 8 a.m.-5 p.m. Closed Saturday afternoon and holidays. Visits only by appointment (Tel: 43991) or write c/o Segreteria della Presidenza USL 10/D, Viale Pieraccini 17. Remodelled for Cosimo de Medici by Michelozzo in 1430s.

Medici Villa at Castello, Localita Castello, Florence. Gardens open in March, April and October, 9 a.m.-5.30 p.m.; in May, June, July, August and September, 9 a.m.-6.30 p.m. Closed on Monday. Magnificent gardens with grotto by Giambologna.

Medici Villa "La Petraia", Localita Castello, Florence. Open: 8.30 a.m.-2 p.m.; holidays 9 a.m.-1 p.m. Closed on Monday. Gardens open in March, April and October, 9 a.m.-5.30 p.m.; in May, June, July, August and September, 9 a.m.-6.30 p.m. Closed on Monday. 14th-century castle and gardens.

Medici Villa of Poggia a Caiano, Poggio a Caiano (a village). Open: 9 a.m.-1 p.m.; holidays 9 a.m.-12 p.m. Closed on Monday. Magnificent villa built for Lorenzo de Medici in the 15th century, with beautiful gardens. Guided tours only in parties of 15 at fixed times.

LUCCA

Villa Reale, Marlia, Lucca. Tel: 0583-30108. Elegant villa remodelled by Elisa Baciocchi, Napoleon's sister; stunning gardens; grottoes, fountains, lemon groves and the *Teatro di verdura,* and an outdoor theatre carved from yew.

Villa Torrigiani, near Lucca, is a 16th-century villa with Mannerist facade and lovely gardens.

PESCIA

Pinocchio Park, Collodi. Tel: 0572-429-342 Open: daily. A monument to *Pinocchio*, written in nearby Villa Garzoni.

PISA

Giardino Scotto (public garden), Lungarno Fibonacci. Open: daily from 8 a.m. to sunset. Entrance: free.

Orto Botanico (Botanical Garden), Via L Ghini. Tel: 23027. Open: weekdays 8 a.m.-12.30 p.m.

Parco Naturale di Migliarino, S. Rossore-Massaciuccoli (near Pisa). Entrance at Tombolo SS1, Consorzio del Parco, Via Cesare Battisti. Tel: 050-43512. Entrance: free.

PISTOIA

Villa Garzoni. Baroque 18th-century villa where Collodi wrote Pinocchio. Extravagant formal gardens with grottoes, maze, fountains and waterfalls.

SIENA

Orto Botanico Botanical Gardens, Via Pier Andrea Mattioli, 4. Guided tours on weekdays 8 a.m.-1 p.m. and 3-5 p.m..

CERAMIC WORKSHOPS

In Sorano, an ancient medieval village of the Maremma, pottery courses of one or two weeks are held between June and September and during the Easter and Christmas holidays. Various techniques of working and firing including majolica firing, bucchero firing (ancient Etruscan technique), reduction and wood firing. Full information from:

Studio Pandora, Andrea Sola, Via della Fortezza, 13, 58010 Sorano (GR). Tel: 011-877-847 or 041-520-5116.

COOKING CLASSES

Italian Cookery classes, from 12-3 p.m. for three consecutive days, are given by an Italian cook with an interpreter. Lessons can be held in both English and German on request. Contact: Scuola di Arte Culinaria "Cordon Bleu", Via di Mezzo 55 red (near the Duomo), Florence (Tel: 055-290-987).

SPAS

Tuscany has a large number of spas, in a variety of locations, catering for different ailments.

Most spas charge a daily entrance fee of around £6. Extra treatments such as mudbaths cost about £15 each per session.

The cost of a complete cure depends on the number of treatments involved and obviously the standard of accommodation. At Montecatini Terme for example, accommodation ranges from simple pensions to five-star hotels.

You can see a doctor before taking a cure and some treatments such as the mudbath should only be undertaken with medical advice.

The following is a brief list of some of the major spas. A complete list and further information can be obtained from the Italian State Tourist Office.

Bagni di Lucca
Bagni Vignoni
Casciana Terme
Chianciano
Monsummano
Montecatini Terme
San Carlo Terme
Terme di Saturnia

OTHER ACTIVITIES

Walking: Various areas of Tuscany are mapped routes for walkers. An expensive, but highly recommended company that arranges walks is **The Alternative Travel Group Limited**, 1-3 George Street, Oxford, OX1 2AZ. Tel: 0865-251-195/6.

These walking holidays are designed for anyone – not just serious walkers. All transport and hotel accommodation is arranged. Two holidays are offered in Tuscany:
– The Tuscan Trail of nine days including Pisa, Volterra, San Gimignano, Colle Val D'Elsa and Monte Maggio, Siena;
– The Southern Tuscan Trail from Pisa then Montepulciano, Chiusi, Pienza, Montalcino, Buonconvento, Casciano di Murio, finishing at Siena.

Tra cielo e terra, a trekking club based in Viareggio, Via Comparini 36/5 (Tel: 0584-391-607), does a " Medieval wayfarer", a three days' walk through Saturnia, Manciano, Sovana and Pitigliano.

Apuan Alps: The Wind Cave is a series of underground pathways with stalactites and stalagmites, rivers and waterfalls. There are four tours, taking from one to three hours. Open from 1 April to 15 October daily; on Bank Holidays only for the rest of the year.

For group reservations, write to: Head Office, "Grotta del Vento", 55020 Fornovolasco, (Lucca) or telephone, preferably the day before, 0583-763-084 or 763-068. There are long waits on busy days if no reservations are made.

PACKAGE HOLIDAYS

Italiatour is Alitalia's package tour operator, offering holidays through its *Intermezzo* brochure on scheduled Alitalia flights from Heathrow and Manchester to six Italian airports, including Pisa. (For brochures, write to: 21 Fleet Street, London, EC4Y 1AA. Tel: 01-353-9686.)

Citalia covers the whole country in its brochure *Italy Complete* (Tel: 01-686-0677).

Package deals, especially weekend breaks, are reasonable:

Nouvelles Frontières (Tel: 01-629-7772) offers four-night packages to Florence from £165.

Thomson Holidays (Tel: 01-387-9321) has three-night flight inclusive packages to Florence from £210 to £248, depending on the hotel.

Pegasus (Tel: 01-370-6851 or 01-373-6055) offers three-night trips from £185.

Sovereign (Tel: 01-897-4545) has three-night stays from £220.

Jetdrive is the name of an Alitalia flight booking combined with an Avis hire car. The only extra charges are optional Personal Accident insurance and petrol.

STUDY HOLIDAYS

For information, *Study Holidays*, published by Central Bureau (Tel: 01-486-5101), lists language learning holidays. For a detailed listing of study courses, see under Special Information (Students).

CULTURE PLUS

ARCHAEOLOGICAL SITES

(Details in the "Places" section)

The Etruscans (8th-2nd centuries BC): There are sites at Island of Elba, Volterra, Fiesole, Arezzo, Chiusi, Vetulonia, an archaeological museum in Florence and other museums in Volterra, Chiusi, Cortona, Asciano, Grosseto and Massa Marittima.

The Romans (8th century BC-5th century AD): Notable remains at Fiesole, Cosa, Roselle, Volterra and Arezzo.

ARCHITECTURE

Romanesque (11th-12th centuries): Churches and buildings of this period are found all over Italy, mostly with regional differences, such as the Pisan-Romanesque style. Main examples in Tuscany are at Pisa, Florence, Lucca, Siena, Pistoia, and Arezzo.

Gothic (12th-14th centuries): The most important buildings are in Florence, Siena, Pisa, Pistoia, and Arezzo.

Renaissance (14th-16th centuries): Tuscany abounds in religious and secular Renaissance buildings, Florence being the most important.

ART

The most outstanding art collections of the Renaissance in Tuscany are the **Uffizi Gallery**, **Pitti Palace Gallery** and **San Marco Museum** in Florence. Works of art during the Late Renaissance and Mannerist periods (16th-17th centuries), the Baroque (17th-18th centuries) and the Neo-classical and romantic (18th-19th centuries), and the 20th century are exhibited at most art galleries and museums in main cities.

AREZZO

Archaeological Museum, Via Margaritone 10. Tel: 20882. Open: 9 a.m.-2 p.m. Closed on Monday. Varied collection of Etruscan and Greek vases and sculpture.

Casa di Girogio Vasari, Via XX Settembre, 55. Tel: 20295. Open: Tuesday-Saturday 9 a.m.-2 p.m., Sunday 9 a.m.-1 p.m. Closed on Monday. The house of Giorgio Vasari (1511-1574), the painter, architect and writer, has vaulted, frescoed ceilings in small rooms. Display of paintings by Mannerist artists.

Museum of Medieval and Modern Art, Via S. Lorentino 8. Tel: 23868. Open: 9 a.m.-1 p.m.; Sunday and holidays 9 a.m.-12 p.m. Closed on Monday. Works by Vasari and Spinello Aretino, follower of Giotto. Important collections of ceramics, goldsmiths' work, ivories, seals and coins.

ASCIANO, Siena

Museum of Sacred Art, Piazza Sant'Agate. Tel: 718207. Open: 8 a.m.-noon, 3-7 p.m. Houses 14th and 15th century Sienese painting, including Lorenzetti and Valdambrino.

CAMALDOLI

Monastery, founded in 1012 by St. Romuald. Works by Vasari and Mina da Fiesole in the 16th-century church.

CAPRESE MICHELANGELO

The birthplace of Michelangelo Buonarroti, born in 1470. Well-restored little stone house. The oldest wing of the castle, restored in modern times, has become an exhibition hall for full-sized reproductions of Michelangelo's sculpture.

CARRARA

Civic Museum of Marble, Viale XX Settembre, Localita Stadio, Carrara. Tel: 0585- 840561. Open: 9.30 a.m.-12.30 p.m. and 3.30-6.30 p.m.. Closed on Saturday afternoon and Sunday. Entrance: free.

Marble Quarries/Marble caves: The marble quarries of Colonnata and Fantiscritti are open for visitors on week-day mornings. Souvenir shop are located on site. Tours can be organised by Carrara Tourist office or you can drive around the quarries independently.

Professional Institute of Marble Workers (Istituto Professionale del Marmo), Piazza Alberica.

CASTIGLION FIORENTINO

A medieval centre surrounded by walls and dominated by the Cassero fortress. The **Gothic Church of St. Francis**, the **Collegiate Church** and the **Gesu Church** are rich in art works. There is a library of paintings, tablets and priceless gold of the 12th to 15th centuries. A short distance beyond the walls is the octagonal **Church of the Consolation** (Renaissance).

CHIUSI

National Etruscan Museum, Piazza del Duomo. Tel: 20177. Open: Tuesday-Saturday 8.30 a.m.-2 p.m., Sunday 9 a.m.-1 p.m.. Closed on Monday. Fine collection of Etruscan remains in Chiusi. Etruscan tombs nearby.

CORTONA

Museum of the Etruscan Academy, Palazzo Pretorio. Tel: 63677. Closed on Monday. Etruscan and Egyptian art.

ELBA

Villa dei Mulini (Mill Villa), Portoferraio. Open: weekdays 9 a.m.-1 p.m. and 3-6 p.m.. The house Napoleon lived in. Library and small museum.

Villa Napoleone (Napoleon's villa) at San Martino. Open: weekdays 9 a.m.-1 p.m. and 3-6 p.m.. Has a museum.

EMPOLI

Museo della Collegiata, Piazza della Propositura. Tel: 72220. Closed on Monday. Good collection of Renaissance art and sculpture.

FLORENCE

A free monthly publication *Welcome to Florence* is published in Italian and English and lists current exhibitions and concerts and has informative articles about museums and places of interest.

The Friends of Florentine Museums Association (Via degli Alfani, 39) have 12,000 members. They arrange museum visits from 9-11 p.m. in the summer, with orchestral recitals, to allow Florentine workers to visit museums during the tourist season, and for tourists to get a further insight into Florentine culture.

Horne Museum (Museo Horne), Via de'Benci 6. Tel: 244-661. Open: daily 9 a.m.-1 p.m. Closed on Sunday.

Jewish Museum of Florence, Via Farini 4. Tel: 245-252. Open: May-September: Sunday, Monday, Wednesday, 9 a.m.-6 p.m.; Tuesday, Thursday, 9 a.m.-1 p.m.; from October-April: Sunday-Thursday, 9 a.m.-1 p.m.

Opera di S. Croce Museum, Piazza S. Croce 16. Tel: 244-619. Open: 9 a.m.-12.30 p.m. and 3-5 p.m. Closed on Wednesday.

Opera di Santa Maria del Fiore Museum, Piazza del Duomo 9. Tel: 213-229. Open: weekdays 9 a.m.-6 p.m.; holidays 9 a.m.-1 p.m.

Palazzo Medici Riccardi, Via Cavour 1. Tel: 2760. Open: 9 a.m.-12.30 p.m. and 3-5 p.m.; holidays 9 a.m.-12 p.m. Closed on Wednesday.

Stibbert Museum (Museo Stibbert), Via Stibbert 26. Tel: 475-520. Open: 9 a.m.-2 p.m.; holidays 9 a.m.-12.30 p.m. Closed on Thursday.

STATE MUSEUMS & GALLERIES

Archaeological Museum, Via della Colonna 36. Tel: 247-8641. Open: 9 a.m.-2 p.m.; holidays 9 a.m.-1 p.m. Closed on Monday.

Bargello Museum, Via Del Proconsolo 4. Tel: 210-801. Open: weekdays 9 a.m.-2 p.m.; Sunday and holidays 9 a.m.-1 p.m. Closed on Monday.

Collection Contini Bonacossi, Giardino di Boboli, Palazzina della Meridiana. Visits only by appointment at the ticket office of the Uffizi.

Gallery of the Academy (L'Academmia), 60 Via Ricasoli. Tel: 214-375. Open: weekdays 9 a.m.-2 p.m.; Sunday and holidays 9 a.m.-1 p.m. Closed on Monday. Michelangelo's "David" exhibited here (very crowded – go in February or November to have a clear view.)

Gallery of Plaster casts of the Institute of Art, P.le di Porta Romana, 9. Tel: 220-521. Open upon request, Monday-Saturday 8.30 a.m.-12 p.m.

Ghirlandaio Refectory, Ghirlandaio's Last Supper (Cenacolo del Ghirlandaio), Ognissanti, Piazza d'Ognissanti. Tel: 296-802. Open: daily 9 a.m.-12.45.

Historical Costume Gallery (Galleria del Costume), Giardino di Boboli, Palazzo Pitti, Piazza Pitti. Tel: 294-279. Open: 9 a.m.-2 p.m.; holidays 9 a.m.-1 p.m. Closed on Monday.

Historical Florentine House Museum, Palazzo Davanzati, Via Porta Rossa 13. Tel: 216-518. Open: 9 a.m.-1.15 p.m.; holidays 9 a.m.-12.15 p.m. Closed on Monday.

Medici Chapels (Cappelle Medicee), Piazza Madonna degli Aldobrandini. Tel: 213-206. Open: weekdays 9 a.m.-2 p.m.; Sunday and holidays 9 a.m.-1 p.m. Closed on Monday.

Modern Art Gallery (Galleria d'Arte Moderna), Palazzo Pitti, Piazza Pitti. Tel: 287-096. Open: weekdays 9 a.m.-2 p.m.;

Sunday and holidays 9 a.m.-1 p.m. Closed on Monday.

Monumental or Royal Apartments (Appartamenti Monumentali), Piazza Pitti, Palazzo Pitti. Tel: 210-323. Open: 9 a.m.-2 p.m.; holidays 9 a.m.-1 p.m. Closed on Monday. The ticket is also valid for the Palatine Gallery and the Silver Museum.

Museum of San Marco (Museo di San Marco), Piazza San Marco 1. Tel: 210-741. Open: weekdays 9 a.m.-2 p.m.; Sunday and holidays 9 a.m.-1 p.m. Closed on Monday.

Museum of semi-precious Stone Inlaid Work (Opificio delle Pietre Dure), Via Alfani 78. Tel: 210-102. Open: weekdays 9 a.m.-1 p.m. Closed on Sunday and holidays.

Palatine Gallery, Piazza Pitti. Tel: 216-673. Open: weekdays 9 a.m.-2 p.m.; Sunday and holidays 9 a.m.-1 p.m. Closed on Monday. (Entrance ticket can also be used for the Monumental Apartments and the Silver Museum.)

Perugino's Crucifixion (Crocifissione del Perugino), Borgo Pinti 58. Open: 9 a.m.-12 p.m. and 5-7 p.m..

Porcelain Museum (Museo delle Porcellane), Giardino di Boboli, Palazzina del Cavaliere. Tel: 287-976. Open: Tuesday, Thursday and Saturday 9 a.m.-2 p.m. Closed on holidays.

Refectory of Andrea del Sarto, Via S Salvi, 16. Tel: 677-570. Open: daily 9 a.m.-2 p.m. Closed on Monday.

Scalzo Cloister (Chiostro dello Scalzo), Via Cavour 69. Tel: 472-812. Open: 9 a.m.-2 p.m.; holidays 9 a.m.-1 p.m. Closed on Monday.

Silver Museum (Museo degli Argenti), Piazza Pitti, Palazzo Pitti. Tel: 212-557. Open: weekdays 9 a.m.-2 p.m.; Sunday and holidays 9 a.m.-1 p.m. Closed on Monday. (Ticket also valid for the Palatine Gallery and the Monumental Apartments.)

St. Apollonia's Last Supper (Cenacolo di S Apollonia), Via 27 April 1. Tel: 287-074. Open: 9 a.m.-2 p.m.; holidays 9 a.m.-1 p.m. Closed on Monday.

St. Salvi's Last Supper (Cenacolo di S. Salvi), Via Andrea del Sarto 16. Tel: 677-570. Open: 9 a.m.-2 p.m.; holidays 9 a.m.-1 p.m. Closed on Monday.

Uffizi Gallery, Loggiato degli Uffizi, 6. Tel: 218-341. Open: weekdays 9 a.m.-7 p.m.; Sunday and holidays 9 a.m.-1 p.m. Closed on Monday.

Vasari Corridor. Viewing by appointment only. Open: Tuesday to Saturday. To book, phone Florence 218-341.

CITY GALLERIES & MUSEUMS
(Gallerie e Musei Communali)

Bardini Museum and Corsi Gallery, Piazza de'Mozzi 1. Tel: 296-749. Open: 9 a.m.-2 p.m.; holidays 8 a.m.-1 p.m. Closed on Wednesday.

Historic Topographic Museum, "Florence as it was" and Garden of the Oblates, Via dell'Oriuolo 4. Tel: 217-305. Open: 9 a.m.-2 p.m.; holidays 8 a.m.-1 p.m. Closed on Thursday.

Hospital of the Innocents (Spedale degli Innocenti), Piazza SS Annunziata 12. Tel: 243-670. Open: 9 a.m.-2 p.m.; holidays 8 a.m.-1 p.m. Closed on Wednesday.

Museum and Cloisters of S. Maria Novella, Piazza S M Novella. Tel: 282-187. Open: weekdays 9 a.m.-2 p.m.; holidays 9 a.m.-1 p.m. Closed on Friday.

Museum of Antique Musical Instruments (Museo degli strumenti musicali antichi), Palazzo Vecchio. Visits by appointment at: Ufficio Belle Arti e Musei Comunali, Via S. Egidio 21 (Tel: 217-305).

Palazzo Vecchio, Piazza della Signoria. Tel: 27681. Open: 9 a.m.-7 p.m.; holidays 8 a.m.-1 p.m. Closed on Monday.

Refectory of Santo Spirito, Last Supper in S. Spirito (Cenacolo di S. Spirito), Piazza

S. Spirito 29. Tel: 287-043. Open: 9 a.m.-2 p.m.; holidays 8 a.m.-1 p.m. Closed on Monday.

Rinaldo Carnielo's Gallery (Galleria Rinaldo Carnielo), Piazza Savonarola 18. Open: Saturday 9 a.m.-2 p.m..

The A della Ragione Modern Art Collection (Raccolta d'Arte Moderna "A. della Ragione"), Piazza della Signoria 5. Tel: 283-078. Open: 9 a.m.-2 p.m.; holidays 8 a.m.-1 p.m. Closed on Tuesday.

SCIENTIFIC MUSEUMS
(Musei Scientifici)

Anthropology Museum (Museo di Antropologia), Via Proconsolo 12. Tel: 296-449. Open: on the 1st and 3rd Sunday of the month, 9 a.m.-1 p.m.

Botanical Gardens and Museum (Museo e Orto Botanico), Via Micheli 3. Tel: 284-696. Open: Monday, Wednesday and Friday, 9.30 a.m.-12.30 p.m.

Geological and Paleontological Museum (Museo di Geologia e Paleontologia), Via La Pira 4. Tel: 262-711. Open: Monday 2 p.m.-6 p.m.; Tuesday, Wednesday, Thursday and Saturday, 9 a.m.-1 p.m.; 1st Sunday of the month (excluding July, August, September), 9.30 a.m.-12.30 p.m. Closed on holidays.

History of Science Museum (Istituto e Museo di Storia della Scienza), Piazza dei Giudici 1. Tel: 293-493. Open: Monday, Wednesday, Friday, 9.30 a.m.-1 p.m. and 2-4 p.m.

La Specola Museum (Museo della Storia Naturale) Via Romana 17. Tel: 222-451. Open: Waxworks: Saturday, summer 3-6 p.m., winter 2-5 p.m.; Zoology: Tuesday 9 a.m.-12.30 p.m., Sunday 9 a.m.-12 p.m.

Museum of Mineralogy (Museo di Mineralogia), Via La Pira 4. Tel: 287-140. Open: weekdays 9 a.m.-1 p.m. and Wednesday 3 - 6 p.m.

Prehistoric Museum (Museo di Antropologia), Via Proconsolo 12. Tel: 296-449.

Open: 9.30 a.m.-12.30 p.m.; in June and July from 9 a.m.-1 p.m. Closed on Sunday.

Wood Museum (Museo del Legno), Piazzale Edicon. Can be visited on Fridays by appointment at Istituto per la Ricerca sul Legno, Tel: 570-210.

Suggested Itineraries for Florence

(inclusive of sights listed under Things To Do)

(1) Piazza del Duomo; Baptistry; Giotto's Bell Tower; Cathedral; Cathedral Museum; Palazzo Medici-Riccardi; San Lorenzo; Laurentian Library; Medici Chapels.

(2) Piazza del Duomo, Orsanmichele, Via Calzaioli – garden of the Monastery of San Michele, rebuilt as a church; Palazzo dell'Arte della Lana (Wool Guild Hall); Piazza della Signoria; Neptune Fountain by Bartolomeo Ammannati; Palazzo Vecchio; Uffizi Gallery.

(3) Piazza della Repubblica; Straw Market; Ponte Vecchio – the oldest bridge in Florence; Pitti Palace – The Palatine Gallery – The Monumental or Ex-Royal Apartments – The Gallery of Modern Art – The Silver Museum; Boboli Gardens; the Brunelleschi Church of Santo Spirito; Santa Maria del Carmine with its Brancacci Chapel.

(4) Piazza del Duomo; Via Tornabuoni; Strozzi Palace; Church of Santa Trinita with the famous frescoed cycle by Domenico Ghirlandaio in the Sassetti Chapel; Palazzo Davanzati, Via Porta Rossa; Santa Maria Novella.

(5) Piazza del Duomo; Church and Museum of San Marco; Gallery of the Academy with Michelangelo's "David"; Santissima Annunziata; Hospital of the Innocents; Archaeological Museum.

(6) Piazza San Firenze – Museum of Anthropology and Ethnology; House of Dante; Bargello Museum; Badia Fiorentina; Buonarroti House; Church and Museum of Santa Croce; Horne Museum; Bardini Museum.

Fort Belvedere: Important art shows and cultural events held at Fortezza Belvedere.

FIESOLE

Primo Conti Museum, Le Coste, Via Dupre 18, Fiesole. Tel: 597-095. Open: weekdays 10 a.m.-1 p.m. and 3-6 p.m. Closed on Sunday and holidays.

GROSSETO

Museum of Art and Archaeology of the Maremma, Piazza Baccarini, 3. Tel 27290. Closed on Wednesday. Archaeological discoveries from Roselle, Vetulonia, Populonia and Vulci. Also Sienese paintings.

LUCCA

Lucca Museum in the School of Music, Corte S. Lorenzo 9. Tel: 0583-584-028. Giacomo Puccini was born in Lucca and the Tourist Office have a planned tour of the places associated with him. His birthplace in Via di Poggio is now a museum in the School of Music. Open: 1 April-30 September 10 a.m.-6 p.m.; 1 October-31 March 10 a.m.-4 p.m. Closed on Monday.

Exhibits include his Steinway piano, original manucripts, records, photographs of costumes worn in performances. The guide – a volunteer music student – plays requested records of Puccini's music. Entrance: free.

Museo Nazionale di Villa Guinigi Via della Quarquonia, Tel 46033. Closed on Monday. A 14th-century villa with sculptures and Renaissance paintings.

Also visit the nearby **Torre del Lago Puccini**. Puccini Operas are performed in the open-air theatre in August.

LUCIGNANO

A town built on a circular plan with streets concentrically arranged inside the walls. The 13th- to 18th-century buildings are perfectly preserved. The Palazzo Comunale has frescoes of the Sienese and Aretine schools. A small museum holds a valuable collection of gold and furnishings, with a unique gold reliquary.

MONTERCHI

Note that the chapel just outside the town that contains the Madonna del Parto closes promptly at noon.

MONTALCINO

Museo Civico e Diocesano, Via di Ricasoli, 29. Tel: 848-235. Good collection of Sienese paintings.

MONTE OLIVETO

Monastero di Monte Oliveto Maggiore, 14th-century monastery with famous frescoes including the *Self Portrait* by Sodoma.

MONTICCHIELLO

Thirteenth-century **Cistercian Church** of the Saints Leonardo and Cristoforo with beautiful frescoes from the 14th and 15th centuries.

A **Fortress** or Wall was built at the same time, with 17 towers, though only a third now remain. The magnificent entrance door was blasted by the cannon fire of the army of Charles V. The elegant watch tower of Ugo Monaco, finished in 1260, was bombed by the Spanish but did not fall; it only inclined to one side.

The **Church of Monticchiello** is decorated with frescoes of the Sienese school of the 14th and 15th centuries. There is also a fine panel by Pietro Lorenzetti.

PISA

Museo dell'Opera del Duomo, Piazza Arcivescovado, Pisa. Tel: 050-560-547. Open: daily in Winter 9 a.m.-5 p.m.; Summer 9 a.m.-7 p.m. A display of works from the monumental structures of the Cathedral Square. Includes sculpture from the 11th-13th centuries; treasure and ancient robes; paintings from the 16th-18th centuries; wood marquetry, illuminated manuscripts, and textiles. Entrance: L.4,000.

Museo dell Sinopie (Museum of the Sinopie), Piazza del Duomo. Tel: 050-560-547. Open: Winter 9 a.m.-5 p.m.; Summer 9 a.m.-7 p.m. Entrance: L.2,000.

Museo Nazionale di San Matteo (National Museum of Saint Matthew), Piazza San Matteo in Soarta, Lungarno Mediceo, Pisa. Tel: 050-23750. Open: weekdays 9 a.m.-7 p.m.; holidays 9 a.m.-1.30 p.m. Closed on Monday. Entrance: L.3,500 (Italian citizens under 18 and over 60, free). On city bus route No. 7.

PISTOIA

Centro Marino Marini, Palazzo del Comune. Tel: 368-182. Closed on Monday. Paintings and sculptures by contemporary artist Marino Marini.

Museo Civico, Palazzo del Comune. Tel: 367-871. Closed on Monday. New museum in 14th-century palace with excellent collection of Pistoian paintings and altarpieces.

PONTREMOLI

Museo delle Statue Stele, Castello Piagnaro. Tel: 831-439. Collection of prehistoric menhirs.

PRATO

Museo dell'Opera del Duomo, Piazza del Duomo. Tel: 29339. Paintings, sculptures, and reliefs by Donatello.

Prato Museum of Contemporary Art, Viale della Repubblica 227. Open: 10 a.m.-7 p.m. Closed on Tuesday. Important new museum designed by architect Italo Gamberini, for exhibitions of contemporary work.

RADICOFANI

A hill-top castle town with gothic arches and 15th-century windows, though little remains of the medieval buildings because of many earthquakes. The parish **Church of St. Peter** survived and houses several works of art including Francesco di Valdambrino's (1375-1435) wooden statue, "Madonna del Castello"; two paintings by Andrea della Robbia (1437-1528) are in each side altar. Other works of art are in the near **Church of S. Agata**.

SAN GIMIGNANO

The Romanesque-Gothic **Church of Sant'Agostino** (1280-98) holds the bones of San Bartolo, the patron of the city, in an urn in a chapel dedicated to him. There is an altar by Nenedetto da Maiano (1494).

The 12th-century **Collegiate Church** (Romanesque Collegiata) has frescoes by Lippi Memmi, Domenica Ghirlandaio among others. Fine paintings by Italian masters. A fee of 100 and 200 lire will allow you to operate the lights for the frescoes.

Museum of Sacred Art, next to the Collegiate Church. Houses fragments from the 13th and 14th centuries, sculpture, chorals and sacred vestments.

Etruscan Museum, in the same building. Has a collection of oil and wine amphoras, urns of the 3rd and 2nd century BC, coins, bronze mirrors etc.

Palazzo del Popolo or **Palazzo Nuovo del Podesta** (1288-1323) with a fresco of the Maesta by Lippo Memmi (1317) and a collection of 16th- to 17th-century medicine bottles.

SIENA

To make the most of your time and budget, you may wish to plan your visit to Siena from the following guide. Opening hours and entrance fees may vary. There are special rates for students and groups. If no entrance fee is quoted, entry is free. The Tourist Office can provide a list of authorised guides.

L'Accademia dei Fisiocritici Natural History Museum, Piazza S. Agostino, 4. Open: Monday-Friday, 9 a.m.-1 p.m. and 3-6 p.m. (except Thursday afternoons). Geological, mineralogical and zoological museum.

Museo dell'Opera della Metropolitana (Museum of the Cathedral), Piazza dell Duomo. Open: 12 March-31 October, 9 a.m.-7.30 p.m.; 1 November-31 December, 9 a.m.-1.30 p.m. Entrance fee: L.4,000.

Pinacoteca National Picture Gallery, Palazzo Buonsignori, Via San Pietro, 29. Open: Tuesday-Saturday 8.30 a.m.-7 p.m.; Sunday 8.30 a.m.-1 p.m. Entrance fee: L.3,000.

VOLTERRA

Guarnacci Museo Etrusco e Biblioteca, Via Don Minzoni, 15. Tel: 86347. Open: all year except major holidays from 9.30 a.m.-1 p.m. and 2.30-6 p.m..

Museo Diocesano d'Arte Sacra (The Museum of Sacred Art), Via Roma 13. Tel: 86192. Free entrance. Visit by appointment.

The **Art Gallery** and **Civic Museum**, Palazzo Minucci Solaini, Via dei Sarti, 1. Tel: 87580.

MUSIC, OPERA & BALLET

Concerts: Concerts of popular and classical music are held regularly, often in churches or in the open-air, in all towns and cities. The ORT, Orchestra della Toscana (Tel: 055-242-767), and the Filarmonica di Firenze "Gioacchino Rossini" are two of Tuscany's orchestras.

FLORENCE

The *Maggio Musicale* music festival, held from mid-May to the end of June, is a big event with top names in concert, ballet and opera performing in various venues throughout the city. Tickets are available from the Teatro Comunale, Corso Italia 16 (Tel: 277-9236). Concerts, formal and informal, are held throughout the summer in cloisters, piazzas or the Boboli Gardens. The main concert hall and venue for opera and ballet is the Teatro Comunale. The opera season opens at the end of September or beginning of October. During the *Estate Fiesolina* – Fiesole's summer festival – concerts, opera, ballet and theatre are held in the Roman amphitheatre.

SIENA

The **Accademia Musicale Chigiana** (Chigiana Academy of Music), Via di Citta 89, 53100 Siena (Tel: 0577-46152) provides proficiency courses in July and August for young performers, both Italian and foreign.

Public performances of rare, unpublished and new music are held in August each year during the Sienese Music Week. They include opera, symphonic concerts and chamber orchestras plus international congresses of music studies.

A theoretical and practical course of Jazz music is held annually at the Seminari Nazionali Senesi, Via Vallerozzi 77, 53100 Siena (Tel: 0577-47552). This training centre is among the most well-known for Jazz music in Europe.

PISA

In May and June, concerts are held at various annual festivals and fairs, especially during the "Gioco del Ponte" on 26 June.

THEATRE

The main theatre is the **Teatro della Pergola**, Via della Pergola 18 (Tel: 247-9651). Most productions are in Italian.

MOVIES

The cinema is well attended by Italians. There are numerous foreign films, often in English or other foreign languages with Italian subtitles.

In the summer, open-air cinemas are set up in country towns and in quiet squares of cities, such as the one in Lucca.

The only English-language cinema in Florence is the **Astro**, Piazza Simone, near Santa Croce, which shows films every night except Monday. In summer, occasional English-language films are shown on outdoor screens at Fort Belvedere.

LIBRARIES

All main towns of Tuscany have reference libraries with very helpful, usually English speaking, staff. These are free and open to anyone, as are the libraries of religious centres, universities, schools and State offices. Lending libraries exist in some towns.

FLORENCE

Medici Laurenziana Library (Biblioteca Medici Laurenziana), Piazza San Lorenzo 9. Open: daily 10 a.m.-1 p.m. Closed Sundays. Tel: 210-760.

FOREIGN LIBRARIES

American Library, Via S. Gallo 10. Tel: 296-114. Open: 9 a.m.-12.30 p.m. Closed on Saturday.

British Institute Library, Lungarno Guicciardini, 9. Tel: 284-031. Open: 9.45 a.m.-12.45 p.m. and 3.15-7.15 p.m. Closed on Saturday.

Library of the French Institute, Piazza Ognissanti, 2. Tel: 298-902. Open: 10 a.m.-1 p.m. and 3-6 p.m.. Closed on Saturday.

Library of the Dutch University Institute, Via Torricelli, 5. Tel: 221-612. Open: 9 a.m.-1 p.m. and 2-6 p.m. Closed Saturday.

SAN GIMIGNANO

In the **Communal Library** are 18th-century manuscripts, civic documents etc. In the **Medical Library** are herbalists' and medical books of the 17th and 18th centuries.

SIENA

Libreria Piccolomini (Piccolomini Library), inside the Cripta delle Statue Duomo. Open: 1 April-31 October, 10 a.m.-1 p.m. and 2.30-6 p.m. Entrance fee: L.1,500.

DIARY OF EVENTS

AREZZO

First Sunday in September: Saracens' Joust (Giostra del Saraceno). Mounted knights representing the four districts of the city attack the wooden effigy of a Turk. A procession is held before the event.

An antique fair is held in the square on the first Sunday of every month.

CORTONA

15 August: Sagra della Bistecca (Feast of the Beefsteak).

July/August: The "Cortona Summer Festival" offers a full artistic programme.

September: An exhibition of antique furniture is held during this month.

FLORENCE

February/March: "Carnevale", the Lenten festival. Almost as dramatic as the Venice Carnival.

May and June: "Maggio Musicale Fiorentino" – performace of opera, ballet and concerts; much patronised by the Florentines themselves.

24 and 28 June: "Calcio in Costume" (Calcio Fiorentino) – football in medieval costume in Piazza della Signoria

"Lo Scoppio del Carro" (Easter Day): The burning of a "carriage" (float) and the emergence of a dove among the crowds. Fireworks display.

Ascension Day: Festival of the crickets in Cascine Park. Sale of crickets and sweets.

7 September: Night festival of the "Rificolone" (lanterns). A procession of carts, lanterns and singers.

LUCCA

September: Luminaria di Santa Croce, a religious procession.

LUCIGNANO

Last two Sundays in May: "Maggiolata Lucignanese", a Lucignano festival that takes place in May, includes a procession of carts decorated with allegorical scenes in flowers.

MASSA MARITTIMA

Sunday following May 20 and the second Sunday in August: Twice a year the "Balestro del Girifalco" (crossbow competition with mechanical falcon) and flag-wavers recall the ancient republic.

MONTICCHIELLO

Each year "Il Teatro Povero" (the Poor Theatre) presents, in the last 15 days of July, a drama written and acted by everyone about the local history and the culture of the farmer.

PIENZA

August/September: Each year, "A meeting with a Master of Art" takes place in the council chamber (1500) of the Civic Hall, Pienza. Many famous artists have displayed their work.

On the first Sunday of September, the Fiera del Cacio (Sheep Cheese Fair) is held, as Pienza is considered the supreme centre for sheep cheese production.

PISA

In May and June concerts are held at various annual festivals and fairs, but especially during the "Gioco del Ponte" on 26 June.

PISTOIA

25 July: A traditional festival – the Giostra dell'Orso or Joust of the Bear is held in Piazza del Duomo. The "bear" is made of wood and a mock battle takes place between the "bear" and 12 knights in costume.

SIENA

28-30 April: The Feast of St. Catherine.

July 2 and August 16: The Palio (traditional horse race) takes place. For tickets and hotel bookings, write to the tourist office six months in advance.

The Contrade: Visits may be made to the Museums of the 17 Contrade (districts) of Siena by giving at least one week's advance notice. (The Tourist Office will supply a list of museums.) Each district has its own Church and Museum and celebrates the festival of its Patron Saint.

Public performances of rare, unpublished and new music are held in August each year during the Sienese Music Week. They include opera, symphonic concerts and chamber orchestras plus international congresses of music studies.

VIAREGGIO

February: Carnevale.

VOLTERRA

July/August: Cross bow tournament (torneo di tiro con la balestra) in Piazza dei Priori.

Last Monday in September: Regional bird fair (fiera regionale degli uccelli).

September: National Festival of Choral Groups (festival nazionale dei gruppi corali).

NIGHTLIFE

Italians enjoy playing and listening to music: violin players stroll round restaurants, small orchestras and bands play at large gatherings in preference to taped music. Summer "discos" are set up in resorts, usually dancing takes place outside a restaurant or rustic bar. Increasingly popular are displays of traditional flag-waving ceremonies and peasant dancing.

All the cities have a wide variety of music and entertainment, but nightclubs often do not stay in business, so it is advisable to ask your hotel for the name of a recommended place to go.

These are the addresses of several more permanent places:

FLORENCE

Central Park, Via Fosso Macinante, 13, Parco Cascine. Tel: 356-723. Open: May-September.

River Club, Lungarno Corsini, 8. Tel: 282-465.

PIANO BARS/LIVE MUSIC

Piazza della Libert'. Opens every evening from 9.30 p.m. Beer, long drinks, cocktails, crepes. Live music: jazz, rock, classic, cabaret, performances, recitals. Entrance: free.

Be Bop, Via dei Servi 76c. Cocktail bar; live music: jazz, blues, country. Entrance: free.

Caffé Donatello, Piazza Donatello. Opens at 7 p.m. for cocktails, drinks, dinner; from 10 p.m. – live music, performances, poetry, cabaret, rock 'n roll.

Caffé, Piazza Pitti 9. Tel: 296-241.

Chapeau, Via Verdi, 57-59r. Tel: 298-738.

Jackie O', Via dell'Erta Canina, 42b. Tel: 216-146.

KGB, Borgo degli Albizi 9r. Bar opens at 10.30 p.m..

Tabasco (Gay), Piazza S. Cecilia, 3. Tel: 213-000.

DISCOS

Chalet Fontana, Via S. Leonardo, 8r. Tel: 221-187.

Full-up, Via della Vigna Vecchia, 21. Tel: 293-006.

Space Electronic, Via Palazzuolo, 37. Tel: 293-082. Has lasers and videos.

Tiffany, Lungarno Colombo, 23. Tel: 676-912.

SIENA

Jet Set, Via Paneaneto 13. Tel: 288-378.

Club Enoteca, Fortezza Medicea. Tel: 285-466.

Tom Cat, Via dei Termini. Tel: 280-152.

SHOPPING

WHAT TO BUY

The quality of goods in Italy is very high and prices reasonable.Some suggested purchases are:
Fashions: Dresses, hats, linen, shoes, gloves, silk ties and shirts.
Knitwear, boutique goods, lace, tablecloths, jewellery.
Leather goods: handbags, beauty-cases, boxes, luggage.
Cloth: silk, linen, wool, cotton.
Pottery and ceramics, gold and silver ware, alabaster and marble objects. Woodwork; straw and raffia goods; glass and crystal work; local handicrafts; art books and reproductions.
Wines and spirits, Liqueurs and aperitifs: Grappa, Strega, Campari, Cinzano, Martini, Carpano etc.

DUTY-FREE GOODS

DUTY-FREE ALLOWANCES FOR UK CITIZENS GOING TO OR RETURNING FROM ITALY:
(Travellers under seventeen are not entitled to tobacco and drinks allowances)

(1) **Goods obtained duty and tax paid within the EEC**: 300 cigarettes or 150 cigarillos or 75 cigars or 400 g of tobacco. Alcoholic drinks over 22 percent volume: 1½ litres; or alcohol not over 22 percent volume: 3 litres; or fortified or sparkling wine plus still table wine: 4 litres. Perfume: 75 g (3 fl oz or 90 cc) and toilet water 375 cc (13 fl oz). Other goods: £250 worth.

(b) **Goods obtained in a duty- and tax-free shop or duty and tax free on a ship or aircraft**: 200 cigarettes or 100 cigarillos or 50 cigars or 250 g of tobacco. Alcoholic drinks over 22 percent volume: 1 litre; or not over 22 percent volume: 2 litres; or fortified or sparkling wine plus still table wine: 2 litres. Perfume: 50 g (2 fl oz or 60 cc) and toilet water 250 cc (9 fl oz). Other goods: £32 worth.

CLOTHES/SHOES SIZES GUIDE

Women's Dresses and Suits
English 34, 36, 38, 40, 42, 44
Continental 40, 42, 44, 46, 48, 50

Women's Shoes
English 3, 4, 5, 6, 7, 8
Continental 35, 36, 37, 38, 39, 40

Men's Suits and Overcoats
English 36, 38, 40, 42, 44, 46
Continental 46, 48, 50, 52, 54, 56

Men's Shirts and Collars
English 14, 14½, 15, 15 1/2, 16, 16½, 17, 17½
Continental 36, 37, 38, 39, 40, 41, 42, 43,

Men's Shoes
English 1, 2, 3, 4, 5, 6, 7, 8, 9, 10, 11, 12
Continental 35, 36, 37, 38, 39, 40, 41, 42, 43, 44, 45, 46

SHOPPING AREAS

Chain stores such as La Rinascente, Upim and Standa can be found in most towns in Tuscany. Foreign languages are spoken in most shops in cities, large towns and tourist resorts.

Open-air markets are held usually once or twice a week in almost all tourist resorts.

Supermarkets are found in most of the tourist resorts and in all towns. Baby food can be bought everywhere at Chemists (*Farmacia*), supermarkets and grocers.

Tobacconists are licensed to sell postage stamps, salt and candles besides cigarettes and tobacco.

FLORENCE

MARKETS

Straw Market (Mercato del Porcellino): Hand embroidered work, florentine straw, leather goods, wooden objects, flowers.

Flea market (Mercato delle Pulci): Objects from the past.

San Ambrogi (Piazza Ghiberti): Vegetables, fruit, other foods, flowers.

San Lorenzo Market (Mercato S. Lorenzo): Vegetables, fruit, food.

Cascine Market (Mercato delle Cascine): Tuesdays only. Produce, household goods, clothing.

Sugar Blues, Via XXVII Aprile 46-48/r. Tel: 483666. The largest natural food store in Florence. All products guaranteed without added sugar.

SHOPS

Gimar, Via Vacchereccia 9 red. Florentine marble, bronze, clay, ceramics and china arts. All pieces are signed and come with a guarantee.

Redi di Anna Pistaccioni, Via Vacchereccia 14r. Sells **lingerie**.

LEATHER

Leather is the best buy in the city. Quality ranges from beautiful creations of local artisans to shoddy goods aimed at undiscerning tourists. For top quality (and prices), start with the designer boutiques in the Via Tornabuoni or shops in streets around the Piazza della Repubblica.

Raspini at Via Roma 25-29 has superb leather shops, bags and coats as well as high quality fashions. For more down to earth prices, head for the market of San Lorenzo northwest of the Duomo, where numerous street stalls sell shoes, bags, belts, wallets (as well as cheap woollen sweaters, silk ties and scarves).

Sbraci, Strawmarket square 20r has high fashion leather goods. Custom-made leather wear are ready in 48 hours.

BOUTIQUES

Florence is a highspot for fashion, and the centre is full of top designer boutiques. The most elegant street is the Via Tornabuoni where Gucci, Ferragamo, Valentino and other big names in fashion have their outlets. Other exclusive streets are the Via Calzaiuoli and Via Roma (both of which have some stunning leather goods), Via della Vigno Nouvo and Via del Parione.

Alex, Via della Vigna Nuova, 19. Tel: 214-952.

Emilio Pucci, Via de Pucci, 6. Tel: 283-061/2.

Enrico Coveri, Via Tornavuoni, 81. Tel: 211-263.

Ferragamo, Palazzo Feroni-Spini, Via Tornabuoni 2. Tel: 43951.

Gianni Versace, Via Tornabuoni, 13. Tel: 296-167.

Gucci, Via Tornabuoni 73. Tel: 287-251 or 213-175.

Lietta Cavalli, Via della Vigna Nuova, 45. Tel: 298-572.

Raspini, Via Roma 25-29. Tel: 213-077.

Zanobetti, Via Calimale, 22. Tel: 210-646.

FABRICS

Antico Setifico, Via della Vigna Nuova, 97. Tel: 282-700.

Casa dei Tessuti, Via de'Pecori, 20-24. Tel: 215-961.

BOOKSHOPS

The **Paperback Exchange**, Via Fiesolana 31r, in the Santa Croce district, is no ordinary bookshop. For a start, it stocks just about every book ever written on Florence currently in print, and many that are no longer published. In addition, it operates a system whereby you get a credit of 25 to 40 percent of the original price of any book you trade in which can be used to buy books from their vast stock of quality secondhand English and American paperbacks. The shop is run by enthusiasts who know everything there is to know about Florence and books.

SUPERMARKETS

Consorzio Agrario, Piazza S. Firenze 5r.
Standa, Via Pietrapiana 42/44.
Coop, Via Nazionale 32r.
Conrad, Via L Alamanni 2r.

PESCIA

Flower Market: The huge flower market is now housed in a new specially designed building. The market begins early, try to get there by 7 a.m. For details, contact the Pescia tourist office, Mercato dei Fiori, Via Amendola, 28 (Tel: 0572-476-897).

SIENA

Siena is known for its **confectionery**, particularly a type of bread, *panforte*, made from a sweet dough, flavoured with vanilla and candied citrus fruits, covered with almonds. The most famous maker of such specialities is Panforte Nannini at Piazza Matteotti 21, Piazza del Monte 95/99 and Bar Pasticceria Nannini at Banchi di Sopra 24.

"Pan co' Santi" is another Sienese cake made with raisins and nuts, traditionally eaten on All Saints' Day. "Cavallucci" are small biscuits with chopped nuts and "Copate" are biscuits made of soft nougat with wafers on each side.

Giogi Leonardo & Co. at Antica Siena, Piazza del Campo 28 (Tel: 46496) sells beautiful blue and yellow **porcelain**.

Local production of wrought **iron** and **copper**, ceramics, crystal and stained glass provide a wide choice for visitors.

The province of Siena produces a variety of good **wines** including Chianti, Brunello di Mantalcino, and Nobile di Montepulciano. The Permanent Italian Wine Exhibition in Fortezza Medicea (Tel: 288-497) was set up for the display and sale of regional wines. Visitors can discover and appreciate a wide variety of Italian wines. Wine traders may purchase and export their selections.

SHOPPING HOURS

Food, vegetable and general stores mostly open from 8.30 a.m. to 6 p.m., closing from 1-4 p.m. in the afternoon. Supermarkets, departmental stores and city shops open at about 9 a.m. until 1 p.m., then from 3.30 to 7.30 or 8 p.m.

Some shops are closed Monday morning or all day Monday, others on Saturday afternoon or all day Saturday. Everything closes on Sunday except tourist shops in resorts or tourist centres. Shops are also closed on Public Holidays and some Saints Days.

EXPORT

Items obtained in Italy, up to a maximum total value of 520,000 lire, can be exported duty-free. For goods exceeding this value, an application to export must be presented, through a Bank or Forwarding Agent, to the Customs Authorities.

For the exportation of antiques and modern art objects, an application must be presented to the Export Department of the Italian Ministry of Education. If the request is granted, a tax in accordance with the value of the items must be paid.

SPORTS

PARTICIPANT

It is possible to play any popular sport either at private clubs or at municipal centres under the National Olympic Committee (CONI). There are tennis courts at most resorts, and swimming, scuba diving, windsurfing and boating on the coast. In villages, bowls (*boccie*) and cards are popular. Gambling, often for high stakes, is widespread, though illegal except in approved casinos and betting shops.

GOLF

There are **golf** courses in Tuscany at:

Florence, 50015 Grassina. Tel: 055-205-1009. 18 holes.

Tirrenia 9, 56018 Tirrenia. Tel: 050-37518.

Punta Ala 18, 58040 Punta Ala. Tel: 0564-922-121.

Acquabona, Elba 9 57037 Portoferraio. Tel: 0565-940-066.

Argentario 18, 58015 Orbetello. Opening shortly.

FISHING

Sea sport fishing may be practiced both from the shore and from a boat. In some ports, a special permit is required from the Harbourmaster's Office. Only those over sixteen are allowed to use underwater guns and such equipment. When submerged, an underwater fisherman is required to indicate the fact with a float bearing a red flag with a yellow diagonal stripe, and must operate with a radius of 50 metres of the support barge or the float bearing the flag. Fishing is prohibited at under 500 metres from a beach used by bathers and 50 metres from fishing installations and ships at anchor.

The rocky shores of the Tuscan Tyrrenhian coast are ideal for fishing.

Freshwater Fishing: Fishing in rivers and lakes for trout, grayling, char and bleak, chub, carp, tench, pike, perch, roach etc. is generally satisfactory. Foreigners need a temporary membership of FIPS (Federazione Italiana della Pesca Sportiva) and a Government licence issued by the Provincial Administration. A licence for rod-fishing with or without a reel costs about £1.50 and is valid for one year. Every provincial town has an office to give advice and notice of restrictions on fishing-times and places.

WATERSPORTS

At all Tuscan sea resorts, it is possible to water-ski and row with hired boats. **Yacht chartering** facilities are available in Marina di Pisa and Tirrenia.

Warning: Sharks have occasionally been sighted off the Tuscan coast and a diver had been killed by a 20-foot shark...so beware!

SWIMMING

Most luxury hotels have swimming pools and there are communal pools in most towns.

Swimming pools in Florence

Piscina Costoli, Viale Paoli. Tel: 675-744.

Piscina Comunale Bellariva, Lungarno Colombo, 6. Tel: 677-521.

Piscina Le Pavoniere, Viale degli Olmi (Parco delle Cascine). Tel: 367-506.

SKIING

Tuscany has a major ski resort at Abetone in the Appenines, north of Pistoia.

Pegasus at 24a Earls Court Gardens, London SW5 (Tel: 01-370-6851) can provide inclusive packages or self catering holidays. The skiing area extends over four valleys and 30 km (19 miles) of trails. Tourist information on ski passes, pistes etc. from Azienda Autonoma Soggiorno e Turismo, Abetone. Tel: 0573-60231.

HUNTING & SHOOTING

Shooting birds and animals is a popular sport in Italy but not encouraged by the Tourist Boards. There are strict rules on the importation and use of firearms. Information may be obtained from the Federazione Italiana Caccia, Viale Tiziano 70, Roma (Tel: 394-871).

The Maremma and the Volterra surroundings are areas of wild boar hunting and there are several reserves for shooting pheasant.

HORSE RIDING

In Siena, the Club Ippico Senese, Loc Pian del Lago (Tel: 53277), has horse-riding. There are also over forty Centres of the National Association of Equestrian Tourism (ANTE) where it is possible to spend your holiday on horseback. For further information, write to: ANTE, Largo Messico, 13, Roma; or to the Federazione Italiana Sport Equestri, Viale Tiziano, 70, Roma (Tel: 390-228).

SPORTS CENTRES (Siena)

Circolo Tennis Siena, Loc Vico Alto. Tel: 44925 or 283-397.

Piscina Communale (swimming), Piazza G. Amendola. Tel: 47496.

Tiro a Segno Nazionale (target shooting), Viale Sclavo. Tel: 52417.

SPECTATOR

The main spectator sports in Tuscany are football, horse racing and speed cycling which culminates in the Grand Tour of Italy. All important events are watched avidly on television.

SPECIAL INFORMATION

DOING BUSINESS

Business transactions are unfortunately long-winded and bureaucratic. The Commune normally monitors anything requiring legislation; most paperwork is processed by a lawyer and is issued in triplicate, with official stamps (everything must be authorised). Most public sector offices are open only in the mornings. To conduct any sort of business, make the first approach in writing a long time ahead., If possible, acquire credentials and contacts who can act as referees. The *raccommendata* is all-powerful.

Be prepared to wait in endless queues, sign several documents and receipts, and lose much time. Even withdrawing cash on a credit card or sending a parcel is a lengthy process. In business transactions, be prepared for unorthodox methods of negotiation or settlement: payment may be required in goods or in foreign currency. If you can get anyone else to transact your business, do so – it is worth every extra lira!

DISABLED

Despite difficult cobbled streets and poor wheelchair access to many sights and hotels, many disabled people visit Florence and Tuscany. Unaccompanied visitors will experience difficulty so it is best to travel with a companion. Sources of further information are Radar, 25 Mortimer Street, London W1M 8AB (Tel: 01-637-5400), and the publication *Access* in Florence available from Mrs V. Saunders, 005A Office, Sherwood House, Sherwood Drive, Bletchley, Hilton Keynes HK3 6AN (Tel: 0908-71131).

LANGUAGE SCHOOLS

There are numerous language schools, mostly in Florence and Siena. These are a selection:

The **Institute of Italian Language** "Galileo Galilei" Via degli Alfani, 68, 50121 Firenze. Tel: 055-294-680.

Centro Pontevecchio, Piazza del Mercato Nuovo 1 (Loggia del Porcellino), Firenze. Tel: 294-511. (Small classes in Italian language and culture in Florence or in Chianti.)

Koin, Via Pandolfini 27, Firenze. Tel: 213-881.

Leonardo da Vinci, Via Brunelleschi 4, Firenze. Tel: 294-247.

Machiavelli, Piazza S Spirito 4, Firenze. Tel: 296-966.

As the "pure Italian language" is spoken in Siena, the **Italian Language and Culture School for Foreigners**, Piazzetta Grassi 46, Siena 53100 (Tel: 0577-280-695) runs courses for foreigners and Italians who are permanent residents abroad. It is a recognised Institute of Higher Education for Language and Culture, awarding a Diploma to successful students.

ART COURSES

At the **Universiti Internazionale dell'Arte**, Villa II Ventaglio, Via delle Forbici, 24/26, 50133 Florence (Tel: 055-570-216 or 571-503), various art appreciation courses are held with specialisation in museum collections, conservation and restoration, design and graphic design.

British Institute, Palazzo Lanfredini, Lungarno Guicciardini 9, Florence. Tel: 055-284-031. Conducts art and language courses.

FASHION INSTITUTES

Centro Moda, Via Faenza, 109. Tel: 219331/2/3.
Polimoda, Via Pisana, 71. Tel: 717173.

MUSIC

The **Accademia Musicale Chigiana** (Chigiana Academy of Music), Via di Citta 89, 53100 Siena (Tel: 0577-46152) provides proficiency courses in July and August for young performers, both Italian and foreign.

A theoretical and practical course of Jazz music is held annually at the **Seminari Nazionali Senesi**, Via Vallerozzi 77, 53100 Siena (Tel: 0577-47552). This training centre is among the most well-known for jazz music in Europe.

LAUNDRETTES

Lavanderia Biagioli, Via Palazzo del Diavoli 45r. Tel: 709-796.
Lavasecco Rapido Isa, Via Arctina 80r. Tel: 677-602.
Lavarex Duse, Viale Duse 15a. Tel: 690-400.
Lindoget, Via Rocca Tedalda 68r. Tel: 690-400.

LANGUAGE

Many Italians in tourist destinations will speak some English but attempts to speak Italian are always encouraged. In more remote places you will need to have some knowledge of Italian. A brief list of useful phrases is given below.

GENERAL VOCABULARY

Please	*Per favore* or *per piacere*
Thank you	*Grazie*
You're welcome/	*Prego*

Don't mention it	
Where is…	*Dov' è…*
…a chemist	*…una farmacia?*
…a post-office	*…un ufficio postale?*
…the Town Hall	*…il municipio* or
	la commune
How much?	*Quanto?*
My change?	*Il mio resto?*
Hotel/Inexpensive	*Albergo/Pensioni-*
hotel	*Soggiorno*
Help!	*Aiuto! (Ayootoh!)*
Day	*Il giorno*
Morning	*La mattina*
Afternoon	*Il pomeriggio*
Evening	*La sera*
Night	*La notte*

DAYS OF THE WEEK

Monday	*Lunedi*
Tuesday	*Martedi*
Wednesday	*Mercoledi*
Thursday	*Giovedi*
Friday	*Venerdi*
Saturday	*Sabato*
Sunday	*Domenica*

MONTHS

January	*Gennaio*
February	*Febbraio*
March	*Marzo*
April	*Aprile*
May	*Maggio*
June	*Giugno*
July	*Luglio*
August	*Agosto*
September	*Settembre*
October	*Ottobre*
November	*Novembre*
December	*Dicembre*

NUMBERS

0	*zero*
1	*uno*
2	*due*
3	*tre*
4	*quattro*
5	*cinque*
6	*sei*
7	*sette*
8	*otto*
9	*nove*
10	*dieci*

11	*undici*
12	*dodici*
13	*tredici*
14	*quattordici*
15	*quindici*
16	*sedici*
17	*diciassette*
18	*diciotto*
19	*diciannove*
20	*venti*
21	*ventuno*
30	*trenta*
40	*quaranta*
50	*cinquanta*
60	*sessanta*
70	*settanta*
80	*ottanta*
90	*novanta*
100	*ottanta*
200	*duecento*
1,000	*mille*
2,000	*duemila*
3,000	*tremila*
4,000	*quattromila*
5,000	*cinquemila*
1,000,000	*un milione*

FOR SIGHTSEEING

Abbey, monastery	*Abbazia, convento*
Frescoes	*Affreschi*
Tickets	*Biglietti*
Library	*Biblioteca*
Chapel	*Capella*
House	*Casa*
Castle	*Castella*
Church	*Chiesa*
Cloisters	*Chiostro*
Closed	*Chiuso*
City	*Citt'*
Courtyard	*Cortile*
Cathedral	*Duomo*
Fair, regatta etc.	*Fiera*
Garden	*Giardini*
Seashore promenade	*Lungomare*
(Bank of the River	*(Lungarn)*
Arno)	
Market	*Mercato*
Walls	*Mura*
Nave	*Navata*
Works	*Opere*
Panel, altarpiece	*Pala*
Palace, grand house	*Palazzo*
Walk, promenade	*Passeggiata*
Storey	*Piano*

Picture gallery	*Pinacoteca*
Picture	*Quadro*
Feudal castle	*Rocca*
ruderi Ruins	*Rovine,*
Sacristy, vestry	*Sagrestia*
Stairs, ladder	*Scala*
Excavations	*Scavi*
Beach	*Spiaggia*
Treasure	*Tesoro*
Tower	*Torre*

ROAD SIGNS

No Entry	*enso Vietato*
No entry for	*Vietato Ingresso*
vehicles	*Veicoli*
Parking permitted	*Sosta Autorizzata*
(times given)	
No parking	*Sosta Vietata*
Closed to	*Vietato Transito*
heavy vehicles	*Autocarri*
Level crossing	*Passaggio a Livello*
Slow down	*Rallentare*
Bend	*Svolta*
Crossroads	*Incrocio*
Exit or way out	*Uscita*
Entrance or way in	*Entrata*
Road works ahead	*Lavori in Corso*

FURTHER READING

The Italian State Tourist Office: *Italy Traveller's Handbook* (updated yearly).

Italian Touring Club Regional Guides and maps from McCarta Ltd., 122 King's Cross Road, London WC1 (Tel: 01-278-8278).

An excellent selection of books and maps on Italy is available from The Travel Bookshop, 13 Blenheim Crescent, London W11 2EE. Tel: 01-229-5260.

BACKGROUND READING

Barzini, Luigi. *The Italians*. Hamish Hamilton.

Berenson, Bernard. *The Italian Painters of the Renaissance*. Phaidon Press.

Burckhardt, Jacob. *The Civilization of the Renaissance in Italy*. Phaidon Press.

Cellini, Benvenuto. *Autobiography*. Penguin Classics.

Dickens, Charles. *Pictures from Italy*. Granville Publishing.

Forster, E. M. *A Room with a View*. Penguin.

James, Henry. *Italian Hours*. Century Hutchinson.

Keates, Jonathan. *The Love of Italy*. Octopus.

Lawrence, D.H. *D.H. Lawrence and Italy*. Penguin.

Lawrence, D.H. *Etruscan Places*. Olive Press.

McCarthy, Mary. *The Stones of Florence*. Penguin.

Michelin. *Guide to Italy*.

Murray, Peter. *The Architecture of the Italian Renaissance*. Thames and Hudson.

Newby, Eric. *Love and War in the Apennines*. Picador.

Norwich, John Julius. *The Italian World*. Thames and Hudson.

Origo, Iris. *The Merchant of Prato*. Penguin.

Vasari, Giorgio. *Lives of the Artists,* Vol. 1 & 2. Penguin Classics.

Willey, David. *Italians*. BBC Publications.

TUSCANY

Acton, Harold. *The Villas of Tuscany*. Thames and Hudson.

Bentley, James. *A Guide to Tuscany*. Penguin.

Hook, Judith. *Siena: A City and its History*. Hamish Hamilton.

Lyall, Archibald. *Companion Guide to Tuscany*. Collins.

Raison, Laura. *Tuscany, an Anthology*. Cadogan Books.

Scott, Rupert. *Florence Explored*. The Bodley Head.

Serpell, Christopher, and Jane Serpell. *Traveller's Guide to Elba*. Jonathan Cape.

Whelpton, Barbara. *Painter's Florence*. Johnson.

USEFUL ADDRESSES

TOURIST INFORMATION

General tourist information is available at the Ente Nazionale per il Turismo (ENIT) in each main town. Also, the Ente Provinciale per il Turismo (EPT) or the Azienda Autonoma di Soggiorno e Turismo have details of provincial towns. In small places, the Commune holds tourist information and some commercial banks and travel agencies also publish tourist guides. The Touring Club Italiano (TCI) in almost every town, provides free information about the local area.

AREZZO

Ente Provinciale per il Turismo, Piazza Risorgimento, 116. Tel: 0575-23952 or 20839. At Via Capucci, 2, Bibbiena (Arezzo). Tel: 0575-593-098.

CARRARA

Ente Provinciale per il Turismo, Piazza 2 Giugno 14, 54033 Carrara. Tel: 0585-70894.

Azienda Autonoma di Socciorno e Turismo, Piazza G Menconi 6/b 54036 Marina di Carrara. Tel: 0585-632-218.

Azienda Autonoma di Soggiorno e Turismo, Lungomare A Vespucci, 244, 54037 Marina di Massa. Tel: 0585-240-063. At Cinquale, Via delle Cateratte. Tel: 0585-309-317.

GROSSETO

Via Monterosa, 206. Tel: 0564-22534. Map in English, free on request, explaining the traditions and characteristics of the ancient villages, hermitages and convents.

FLORENCE

Assessorato Regionale Turismo, Via di Novoli 26, 50127 Firenze. Tel: 055-439311.

Ente Provinciale per il Turismo, Via Manzoni 16. Tel: 055-247-8141. Open: Monday-Friday 8.30 a.m.-1.30 p.m. and 4-6.30 p.m.; Saturday 8.30 a.m.-1 p.m.

Azienda Autonoma di Turismo, Via Tornabuoni, 15. Tel: 216-544. Open: Monday-Saturday, 9 a.m.-1 p.m. Situated between the station and the cathedral, this tourist office gives comprehensive guides, a free map and any assistance except hotel bookings.

LIVORNO

Piazza Cavour, 6. Tel: 33111. Open: Monday-Friday 9 a.m.-12.30 p.m.

Tourist Information Office, Central Railway Station. Tel: 0586-401-193. Also the Harbour Information Office, Tel: 0586-25320.

LUCCA

Piazza Guidiccioni, 2. Tel: 0583-41205.

Viareggio, Railway Station. Tel: 0584-46382. Open in summer only.

Bagni di Lucca, Lucca: Piazza J. Verraud 1. Tel: 0583-87245.

PISA

Ente Provinciale Per Il Turismo, Lungarno Mediceo, 42, Pisa. Tel: 050-20351/2.

Central Tourist Information Office, Piazza del Duomo, Pisa. Tel: 050-560-464.

Information Office, Piazza Stazione, Pisa. Tel: 050-42291.

Tourist Office, Via G. Turazza, Volterra. Tel: 0588-86150.

PISTOIA

Corso Gramsci, 110. Tel: 0573-21622 at Abetone (Pistoia), Piazza delle Piramidi. Tel: 0573-604-521.

SIENA

Ente Provinciale per il Turismo, Via dei Montanini 92, Siena. Tel: 0577-47051/2.

Azienda Autonoma di Turismo, Via di Citta, 43. Tel: 0577-42209.

Tourist Office, Piazza del Campo, 56. Tel: 0577-280-551. Open: Monday-Saturday, 9 a.m.-12.30 p.m.; July-September: Sunday, 3.30-7 p.m..

CONSULATES

American
Lungarno Vespucci 38, Florence. Tel: 298-276.

British
Palazzo Castelbarco, Lungarno Corsini 2, Florence. Tel: 284-133, 212-594, 287-449.

German
Borgo SS Apostoli 22, Florence. Tel: 294-722.

Netherlands
Via Cavour 81, Florence. Tel: 475-249.

USEFUL ADDRESSES IN LONDON

Italian Embassy
14 Three Kings Yard, London W1. Tel: 01-629-8200.

Italian Consulate
38 Eaton Place, London SW1. Tel: 01-235-9371.

Italian Institute
39 Belgrave Square, London SW1. Tel: 01-235-146.

Italian Trade Centre (ICE)
37 Sackville Street, London W1. Tel: 01-734-2412.

Italian Chamber of Commerce
Room 418-427 Walmar House, 296 Regent Street, London W1. Tel: 01-637-3153.

Italian State Railways
50 Conduit Street, London W1. Tel: 01-434-3844.

Italian State Tourist Office
1 Princes Street, London W1R 8AY. Tel: 01-408-1254.

Italian Airlines Alitalia
27 Piccadilly, London W1. Tel: 01-745-8200.

British Italian Society
172 Regent Street, 5th Floor, London W1. Tel: 01-437-9479.

CREDITS

INDEX

Q

S